P9-ARW-671

The Carter Administration's Quest
for Global Community

The Carter Administration's
Quest for Global Community:

Beliefs and Their Impact on Behavior

by Jerel A. Rosati

University of South Carolina Press

Copyright © UNIVERSITY OF SOUTH CAROLINA 1987

Published in Columbia, South Carolina, by the
University of South Carolina Press

FIRST EDITION

Manufactured in the United States of America

Library of Congress Cataloging-in-Publication Data

Rosati, Jerel A., 1953–
  The Carter administration's quest for global
community.

  Bibliography: p.
  Includes index.
  1. United States—Foreign relations—1977–1981—
Psychological aspects. 2. United States—Foreign
relations administration. I. Title.
E872.R67 1987   327.73   87-6006
ISBN 0-87249-508-6

To my wife,
Jo

Contents

Preface   3

1   The Controversy over the Carter Administration's Foreign Policy   7
      Conflicting Interpretations   7
      Addressing the Controversy: The Need for a Psychological
        Perspective   12

2   Beliefs and Their Impact on Behavior   15
      Images and Belief Systems   15
      Individual and Collective Images   17
      Image Consensus versus Image Dissensus   19
      Image Stability and Image Change   21
      The Link between Beliefs and Behavior   30
      Clarifying the Conflicting Interpretations   34

3   The Carter Administration's Images   39
      1977: Quest for Global Community in a Complex World   39
      1978: Emergence of Policymaker Differences in Images   58
      1979: A Divided Administration   69
      1980: In Search of Global Stability   81

4   Continuity and Change in the Administration's Image   96
      Key Issues and Actors   98
      Understanding Image Stability and Change   102

5   Foreign Policy Behavior   117
      The First Year   118
      The Second Year   125
      The Third Year   133
      The Fourth Year   142

CONTENTS

6   The Carter Years and Policymaker Beliefs in Perspective   **151**
      Understanding the Administration's Foreign Policy   **153**
      Historical Perspective   **154**
      Implications for the Study of Images   **158**

7   The Power of Beliefs   **164**
      Explanatory Power   **164**
      Predictive Power   **174**
      Policy Relevance   **176**

Appendix
  A The Administration's Foreign Policy Process   **181**
  B Research Method   **185**
  C Major Statements by Administration Officials   **200**
  D Major Foreign Policy Actions   **205**

Bibliography   **226**
Index   **249**

Figures

4.1   Evolution of the importance of major issues.   **99**
4.2   Evolution of the importance of major actors.   **101**
7.1   Summary of causal nexus approach.   **169**
7.2   Relationship between the psychological and objective environment.   **171**
7.3   Impact of beliefs on international behavior.   **173**
B.1   Summary of an actor's image of the international system.   **189**
B.2   Beliefs and their relationship for behavior   **191**

Tables

3.1   Issues Perceived, 1977   **44**
3.2   Actors Perceived, 1977   **50**
3.3   Actors Perceived for Each Major Issue, 1977   **51**
3.4   Image of the Soviet Union   **53**
3.5   Significance of the Soviet Union for Each Major Issue, 1977   **55**
3.6   Significance of the Soviet Union for Each Major Issue, 1978   **59**
3.7   Actor Importance for the Conflict in Africa   **60**
3.8   Issues Perceived, 1978   **67**

CONTENTS

3.9	Actors Perceived, 1978	**69**
3.10	Issues Perceived, 1979	**79**
3.11	Significance of the Soviet Union for Major Issues, 1979	**80**
3.12	Actors Perceived, 1979	**81**
3.13	Issues Perceived, 1980	**83**
3.14	Actors Perceived, 1980	**84**
3.15	Actors Perceived for Each Major Issue, 1980	**85**
3.16	Significance of the Soviet Union for Major Issues, 1980	**86**
4.1	Summary of the Carter Administration's Image of the International System	**97**
4.2	Evolution of Issue Importance	**100**
4.3	Evolution of Actor Importance	**103**
4.4	Summary of Relative Importance of the Soviet Union for Issues	**103**
5.1	Issues Acted Upon, 1977	**119**
5.2	Actors Acted Toward, 1977	**123**
5.3	Importance of the Soviet Union, 1977	**124**
5.4	Type of Action Toward the Soviet Union	**125**
5.5	Issues Acted Upon, 1978	**126**
5.6	Actors Acted Toward, 1978	**130**
5.7	Importance of the Soviet Union, 1978	**131**
5.8	Defense Spending	**133**
5.9	Issues Acted Upon, 1979	**135**
5.10	Actors Acted Toward, 1979	**139**
5.11	Importance of the Soviet Union, 1979	**140**
5.12	Issues Acted Upon, 1980	**143**
5.13	Actors Acted Toward, 1980	**147**
5.14	Importance of the Soviet Union, 1980	**148**
6.1	Summary of Major Findings and Relationships	**161**
B.1	Number of Major Statements by Officials	**193**
B.2	Thematic Statements by Officials	**194**

The Carter Administration's Quest
for Global Community

Preface

Wнiie living in Washington, D.C., during the late 1970s, I was often amazed at the speed with which political commentators and analysts moved to judge the Carter Administration. Throughout those years, the dust had barely settled on a Carter Administration policy when appraisals were rendered and echoed across the land. Even before Ronald Reagan officially assumed office in 1981, the Carter tenure was being characterized by many as a failure, an unsuccessful Democratic interlude between Republican administrations. Yet I could not help wondering how well we really knew or understood the Carter years. Outside of such political commentary and analyses, little has been written on the Carter Administration, especially its foreign policy (which is striking if one compares it to the onslaught of both popular and scholarly writings on foreign policy during the Nixon and Ford Administrations, when Henry Kissinger was National Security Council Advisor and Secretary of State). This paucity of information has only begun to change recently.

I was also interested in the Carter Administration because it was relevant to the research area I was currently investigating—psychological approaches to the study of foreign policy. The field of international relations and foreign policy analysis is interdisciplinary in nature in which knowledge from related disciplines is extremely useful when explaining international behavior. In my own work I have found it increasingly valuable to examine how the role of perceptions and beliefs improves our understanding of foreign policy behavior.

The Carter Administration seemed to be an excellent case study for applying some of the concepts of political psychology. Reports of policy

3

disagreements between high-level officials, especially Secretary of State Vance and National Security Council Advisor Brzezinski, dominated the political commentary of the time. Questions were constantly raised about how Carter Administration policy disputes affected a coherent and consistent presentation of foreign policy goals and means, as well as the actual conduct of foreign policy behavior. Such concerns over individual and group beliefs and their impact on behavior have been investigated for some time by people in psychology and social psychology. Consequently, I became motivated to analyze the foreign policy of the Carter Administration from a political psychology perspective in order to explore how the role of beliefs may be used to advance our understanding of American foreign policy. What follows is a brief discussion of the book's major areas of focus and its contributions.

First, the roles of individual and collective beliefs in foreign policy are examined. Most scholars who have systematically studied the foreign policy perceptions and beliefs of political leaders have focused on one key leader. In this book the beliefs of the Carter Administration's three most significant decisionmakers are analyzed—those of the President (James Earl Carter), the Secretary of State (first Cyrus Vance, then Edmund Muskie), and the National Security Advisor (Zbigniew Brzezinski). The collective beliefs of these political leaders as well as the unique beliefs of each individual are investigated.

Second, the level of stability and change in beliefs is analyzed over time. Most studies on perceptions and beliefs tend to be static and rarely integrate other factors that may affect the evolution of an image. I discuss the role of personality traits, external events, and domestic forces upon the beliefs of the individual decisionmakers in order to explain the stability or change of the Carter Administration's image over its four years in office. Therefore, this study considers the dynamic nature of both individual and collective beliefs, and the interplay between them.

Third, the relationship between beliefs and behavior is explored. Most work on perceptions and beliefs assumes that beliefs are important for shaping subsequent behavior. Unfortunately, this basic assumption has become so firmly accepted in the political psychology literature that the actual relationship between the two has rarely been tested. This study specifically addresses the relationship between beliefs and behavior over the tenure of the Carter Administration.

To satisfy the goals indicated above, four questions have guided my analysis of the Carter Administration: What was the Carter Administration's image of the international system throughout its four years in office? Was the image shared by major Carter Administration officials or did important differences in individual images exist? Did the images held by individuals remain

PREFACE

stable or did they change over time? Lastly, what was the relationship between the Carter Administration's image and its foreign policy behavior? Overall, this study found that the greater the consensus in beliefs among the individual decisionmakers, the greater the likelihood that collective beliefs will be cohesive and stable and, subsequently, the greater the likelihood that foreign policy behavior will be congruent with beliefs.

In addition to the political psychological focus, this book attempts to make up for the lack of systematic literature on the Carter Administration's foreign policy. What books have been written are limited primarily to memoirs (Carter, Jordan, Brzezinski, Vance) and contributions in textbooks (where usually one of the last chapters is devoted to the Carter years). Furthermore, those few analysts who have examined the topic have offered conflicting interpretations. This book seeks to address the controversy over the Carter Administration in order to understand its foreign policy throughout its four years in office.

Finally, an examination of the Carter Administration's policies abroad improves our more long-term understanding of American foreign policy. Most American scholars have concluded that U.S. foreign policy has been relatively stable since the end of World War II, devoted to preventing the spread of communism through a policy of containment. They argue that different administrations have not altered the fundamental thrust of this containment policy, but have only fine-tuned it to fit the peculiar styles and preferences of particular political leaders. This study, however, demonstrates that the Carter Administration represented a major break from this tradition, especially in its first two years. The Carter Administration was not preoccupied with maintaining global security but rather wanted to promote a global community based on an idealistic image of the international environment. Examining the Carter years in this way, then, sheds new light on the issue of continuity and change in American foreign policy.

While writing this book I had two audiences in mind. First, it is written for the social scientist, both the specialist in political psychology and the scholar who may have a more general interest in psychology and international relations. Second, the book is written for the policy analyst (both the scholar and the practitioner) primarily interested in American foreign policy. Writing the book for both audiences proved difficult since there is very little interaction between social scientists and policy analysts in the area of international relations and American foreign policy. It may be that in trying to communicate with both communities, I please neither. Nevertheless, I hope this work will help promote understanding and communication between the social scientist

PREFACE

and policy analyst. Those who are interested in psychology and international relations should read the entire book, including the appendixes. Those who are more interested in the substance of the Carter Administration's foreign policy may want to peruse the more theoretical and methodological sections, focusing instead on chapter 1, chapters 3–6, and appendix A.

Although the work and any deficiencies are mine, I am extremely indebted to a wide variety of individuals who have contributed to the thinking, research, and writing of the book. John Creed, Ken Menkhaus, Bobby Phillips, and Peter Schraeder read the entire manuscript and provided valuable comments. Rick Haeuber, Brant Keller, Baard Knudsen, Warren Lenhart, Larry Nowels, Nick Onuf, and Ray Moore provided important assistance. Charles Kegley and Don Puchala were kind enough to spend a considerable amount of time supporting and improving the product. I am also extremely grateful to all my friends and family for their refreshing interest and constant support of my activities.

Six people were critical in providing the conceptual and motivational foundation that eventually culminated into this book. Martin Weil and David Sears were very important in affecting my initial interest in the study of American foreign policy and political psychology. Steve Walker furthered my intellectual development, providing me with a firm foundation for future growth, as well as providing important guidance and support. Ted Couloumbis's insight, depth of knowledge, and friendship have been invaluable to my personal and academic growth. My active interest in political psychology solidified due to my interaction with Matt Bonham. He has been crucial in keeping me on the right scholarly path, always reasonable, friendly, and supportive. Finally, there is my wife, Jo, about whom I cannot say enough. She has acted as editor, consultant, motivator, and confidant, in addition to pursuing a professional career and becoming a mother. Very simply, without her there would be no book.

ONE | *The Controversy Over the Carter Administration's Foreign Policy*

T HE study of American foreign policy has always been characterized by disagreement and conflicting interpretations. It is not unusual to find the development of different schools of thought in describing and explaining United States foreign policy. Usually, one interpretation comes to dominate the initial analysis of an administration or series of events and becomes known as the orthodox school. With time, other new and varying interpretations— revisionist schools—emerge to challenge this orthodoxy. Given this penchant for evaluation and reevaluation, an understanding of the historiography and the different interpretations produced over time becomes important for a full understanding of American foreign policy.

Nevertheless, what has been written on the Carter Administration has resulted in conflicting interpretations—*no orthodoxy has arisen*. Though agreement has developed over the need to examine the foreign policy beliefs of Carter Administration officials in order to understand its foreign policy, there is nothing but disagreement concerning the content of the Carter Administration's foreign policy beliefs and its foreign policy. This book will utilize the insights of political psychology with an eye toward enhancing our understanding of American foreign policy during the Carter years.

Conflicting Interpretations

During the presidential campaign of 1976, Jimmy Carter (1976, p. 1528) argued that "this country must have a coherent foreign policy that matches words to deeds." Since the beginning of his term of office, however, major disagreement has arisen over whether the Carter Administration ever devel-

7

oped a cohesive worldview. Four divergent schools of thought have emerged concerning the foreign policy beliefs of the Carter Administration. Some individuals argue that the Carter Administration never developed a worldview; others claim that a worldview always existed; still others contend that the Carter Administration's worldview changed over time; and, finally, some conclude that the Carter Administration, although initially lacking a worldview, acquired one with time. Each orientation has important implications for understanding America's overseas behavior during the Carter years.

Lack of a Worldview

Those individuals who conclude that the Carter Administration never developed a worldview argue that the Administration's decisionmakers had no coherent and consistent image of the international environment. They argue, instead, that different officials represented and promoted different worldviews with the President gravitating from one set of beliefs to another. Each foreign policy issue was analyzed on its own unique merits, disregarding its links with other issues, and usually was resolved only after considerable internal disagreement. The overall result was foreign policy behavior that lacked a philosophical foundation and was consequently confusing and inconsistent.

According to John Lewis Gaddis (1982, p. 146), a prominent diplomatic historian, the Carter Administration had difficulty aligning itself "with any coherent and discernible conception of American interests in the world, potential threats to them, and feasible responses." The confusion resulted because a policy of limited containment of the Soviet Union continued to guide the Administration even though President Carter entered office intending to reverse America's preoccupation with such a policy. The difference between surface innovation and subsurface continuity, reinforced by the different perspectives of President Carter's advisors, produced overall policy incoherence.

Political scientists James Nathan and James Oliver (1981, p. 414) focus on the irreconcilable policy perspectives within the Carter Administration as the key reason its foreign policy was "frequently ambivalent; at worst, almost inexplicably incoherent and unpredictable." The ambivalence and indecision of the Carter years can be attributed to the differences between Secretary of State Vance and National Security Advisor Brzezinski, for they "represented subtly but consequentially different views of the world" (Nathan & Oliver, 1981, p. 419).

James Fallows (1979, p. 42), a journalist and former speechwriter to President Carter, maintains that the President never really knew what he wanted to do:

> I came to think that Carter believes fifty things, but no one thing. He holds explicit, thorough positions on every issue under the sun, but he has no large view of the relations between them, no line indicating which goals will take precedence over which when the goals conflict. Spelling out these choices makes the difference between a position and a philosophy, but it is an act foreign to Carter's mind.

Carter thought in lists, claims Fallows, not arguments. The President considered all the relevant items, but never organized them into some type of hierarchy. Therefore, although Carter attempted to set a steady course, he could not explain what he was attempting to accomplish. "He thinks he 'leads' by choosing the correct policy, but fails to project a vision larger than the problem he is tackling at the moment" (Fallows, 1979, pp. 42–43).

Arthur Schlesinger, Jr., likewise believes that the Carter Administration's foreign policy consisted of "tactical zig-zags" lacking any coherent philosophical foundation. "Carter has shown himself devoid of a consistent world view . . . and in consequence is buffeted hither and yon by emotional gusts of irritation, self-righteousness, and vainglory" (Schlesinger, 1980, p. 20). For Schlesinger, a well-known historian, too much effort was expended by the Administration in addressing detailed policy questions; an insufficient amount of time was devoted to developing a "central vision" for moving the country. Therefore, "lacking any central vision, Carter cannot impart consistency and coherence in his policies" (Schlesinger, 1980, p. 21).

A Complex Worldview

Other analysts argue that President Carter and his advisors did conduct American foreign policy according to a consistent and coherent worldview. Therefore, in order to understand the foreign policy of the Carter Administration it is imperative to understand the image it held of the international environment.

"It is not true," states Robert Tucker (1980, p. 23), "that the characteristic traits of the Carter foreign policy have reflected the absence of a world view in the President's mind, a view that can be and has been coherently articulated. Carter quite clearly has a world view." According to Tucker (1979, 1981), the dominant concern of the Carter Administration was with global change. The Administration believed that it was important to play a constructive role alongside developments taking place in the world—to get on the side of change rather than opposing it.

Tucker, a scholar in American foreign policy, believes that the Carter Administration had an image of a complex international system that was much more pluralistic than the images held by previous administrations. More issues were deemed important and more links between issues were recognized. One of the results of such a perception was that the international system was rarely susceptible to the use of force; in fact, Carter believed the use of force was more damaging to international stability than cooperative-oriented policies. Consequently, the great powers could no longer play their traditional roles. The East-West relationship was downplayed and an emphasis was placed on new, important relationships such as the North-South debate. Tucker concludes that the Carter Administration attempted to avoid traditional power politics in favor of world order politics.

In his review of American foreign policy since World War II, John Spanier describes the uniqueness of the Carter Administration's worldview. "Carter was, indeed, to be president of the only administration after 1945 that repudiated much of the traditional way of looking at international politics and to embrace a new vision of a more 'interdependent' world" (Spanier, 1983, p. 177). In Spanier's opinion the Carter Administration had broken with the past and operated from a new world order image of the international environment.

A Dynamic Worldview

Other analysts maintain that the Carter Administration always held a worldview but that it changed with time. Initially, the Carter Administration operated with an optimistic and complex view of the world, only to see it become pessimistic with time. There is little agreement, however, concerning when and why the change in image occurred.

As part of his general analysis of American foreign policy, Simon Serfaty (1978, 1984) believes that by early 1978 the Administration had moved toward a more pessimistic worldview—concerned primarily with containing Soviet expansionism through the use of political-military instruments. The key stimulus responsible for the alteration in worldview was Soviet behavior in Africa, especially Soviet activities in the Horn of Africa, "although it would take another eighteen months of bitter internal debates before the final transformation of the Carter foreign policy" (Serfaty, 1984, p. 342).

Robert McGeehan, a British analyst in international relations, believes that the Carter Administration's change in worldview did not occur until it was hit by the double blow of the taking of American hostages in Iran and the Soviet invasion of Afghanistan. In response, the Carter Administration "adopted a clear and determined position: the policy was containment and the strategy was to take every opportunity to deter further Soviet expansionism and to combat it militarily if deterrence failed" (McGeehan, 1980, p. 171).

CONFLICTING INTERPRETATIONS

From a sociological perspective, Jerry Sanders (1983, p. 263) agrees with the interpretation that "as he prepared for his final year in office, Jimmy Carter had come full circle—from an enthusiast of global interdependence who hoped to develop concrete structures of cooperation that would put detente on a firm and lasting basis, to the leadership of a doctrine of global confrontation." However, Sanders does not believe that the change in the Carter Administration's worldview was abrupt nor primarily a function of the events in Iran and Afghanistan. He instead argues that the change within the Carter Administration began as early as the first year in response to domestic politics and the rising challenge from the right. "For a time he [President Carter] attempted to walk the line between a North-South strategy of managerialism and East-West militarism," but by 1980 he had fully turned to a policy of containment militarism.

Political scientist Robert Osgood (1981) and diplomatic historian Gaddis Smith (1986) share the Sanders interpretation of the Carter Administration's evolution in image. "The history of the Carter administration's foreign policy was one of the steady abandonment, reversal, or muting of every component of this hopeful design for 'world-order politics' as the priority of familiar cold-war politics reasserted itself" (Osgood, 1981, p. 16). However, Osgood argues that international events forced the Carter Administration to constantly adjust its foreign policy, while Smith attributes the gradual change in worldview to the interplay of Brzezinski's hardline view, domestic politics, and international events.

Leslie Gelb, a *New York Times* correspondent and former Director of Political-Military Affairs in the Department of State in the Carter Administration, is less certain about whether a new worldview really evolved in the Carter Administration following the Iran hostage crisis and the Soviet invasion of Afghanistan. He posits that the new containment strategy was only a temporary political expedient and that the Administration would eventually return to its "center-left orientation" (Gelb, 1980a; see also Destler, Gelb & Lake, 1984).

A New Worldview

In addition to the three schools of thought just discussed, other foreign policy analysts argue that although the Carter Administration initially did not have a worldview, it eventually formed one. Seyom Brown, a scholar on American foreign policy, maintains that the lack of a coherent image was due to President Carter's ambivalent attempt to integrate three differing worldviews represented by Andrew Young, Zbigniew Brzezinski, and Cyrus Vance. This resulted in vacillation and ambivalence in American foreign policy throughout the first three years. Nevertheless, Brown (1983, p. 460) argues that the lack of worldview reflected the times and could not be blamed on President Carter.

> Carter was perhaps all too faithfully a man of the season—the season of confusion in U.S. foreign policy following the country's misadventure in Vietnam; . . . Neither Carter nor Brzezinski nor any other influential official had the genius to translate the mood of confusion and apprehension which brought Carter to the presidency into a coherent foreign policy.

But by 1980 Brown contends that a consensus perspective had developed among Carter Administration officials behind a policy of containment: "a semblance of coherence developed out of the perceived need to more effectively prosecute the rivalry with the USSR, especially after the Soviet invasion of Afghanistan" (Brown, 1983, pp. 461–462).[1]

Addressing the Controversy: The Need for a Psychological Perspective

From the previous discussion we are able to see that four schools of thought have developed regarding the Carter Administration's foreign policy.[2] There is no obvious explanation for the development of these four conflicting interpretations. Ideology does not seem to be a factor as analysts (like Osgood and Sanders) from different ideological backgrounds share the same position while analysts with a similar ideology (like Fallows and Gelb) have conflicting interpretations. Nor does the time of the analysis—whether written during the Administration or after its term of office—or the profession of the analyst seem to be significant. Therefore, it appears that different individuals simply have acquired different interpretations of the Carter Administration's foreign policy—that is, different perceptions of the same reality exist.

A number of problems exist with the literature reviewed that hinder a resolution of the debate over the Carter Administration's foreign policy. First, the concept of worldview is rarely defined. Second, it is usually unclear what officials comprise the "Carter Administration." Third, the interpretations are principally derived from limited historical research and intuitive analysis.[3] Finally, the impact of the Carter Administration's beliefs on its foreign policy behavior is rarely examined. Because the studies have not been systematic about their inquiry into the content and evolution of the Carter Administration's foreign policy beliefs, it is difficult to address the controversy over the

Administration's foreign policy. And because it is impossible to separate those beliefs that might be fruitful for understanding the Administration's foreign policy from those which are not helpful, it is necessary to go beyond the traditional foreign policy literature.

The field of political psychology has investigated perceptions and beliefs for some time and can provide a foundation for clarifying the four conflicting interpretations identified and can improve our understanding of the evolution of the Carter Administration's foreign policy. At the same time, an analysis of the Carter Administration over four years may result in a better understanding of the role of beliefs and their relationship to behavior. Specifically, four research questions guide this study:

1. What was the Carter Administration's image of the international system throughout its four years in office?
2. Was the image shared by Carter Administration officials or did important differences in individual images exist?
3. Did the images held by individuals remain stable or did they change?
4. What was the relationship between the Carter Administration's image and its foreign policy behavior?

The following chapters provide answers to these questions in order to resolve the disagreement over the Carter Administration's foreign policy.

A brief review of the political psychological literature on beliefs is presented in chapter 2 in order to provide a foundation for clarifying the basis of the conflicting interpretations about the Carter Administration's foreign policy. In chapter 3 the Carter Administration's image of the international system throughout its four years in office is described. Chapter 4 analyzes and attempts to explain the continuity and change that took place in the Carter Administration's image. In chapter 5 the relationship between the Carter Administration's foreign policy beliefs and behavior is examined. Chapter 6 discusses the implications of the analysis for the four conflicting interpretations of the Carter Administration's foreign policy and for the study of beliefs within political psychology. Chapter 7 concludes with an analysis of the power of beliefs in contributing to the explanation and prediction of international behavior.

Notes

1. See LaFeber (1984) for a similar interpretation.
2. These are actually the four most popular schools of thought. There exist two additional schools of thought represented by the radical left and the radical right. The radical left argues that

THE CONTROVERSY OVER FOREIGN POLICY

the Carter Administration is part of a power elite or ruling class that is driven by global capitalist expansion (see, e.g., Petras, 1980). The radical right argues that the Carter Administration is part of a conspiratorial power elite which is attempting to promote world socialism (see, e.g., Stang, 1980). Within both schools of thought the foreign policy beliefs of the Carter Administration are peripheral concerns. Ole R. Holsti (1974) provides an excellent analysis of the similarities and differences between the two perspectives.

3. In a few cases, there have been contradictory descriptions of the Carter Administration's foreign policy beliefs by the same analyst. For example, Kenneth Adelman (1978) and Eugene Rostow (1980) initially argue that the Carter Administration lacked a worldview, but by the end of their articles they both acknowledge that the Carter Administration did have a worldview after all. Richard Barnet (1977; 1985) and Stanley Hoffmann (1977–78; 1978a; 1978b; 1983) are both inconsistent and ambiguous throughout the course of their writings concerning this question.

TWO | *Beliefs and Their Impact on Behavior*

THIS chapter provides a conceptual foundation for addressing the controversy over the Carter Administration's foreign policy by examining the political psychological literature on beliefs. This literature not only provides a better understanding of the different interpretations by discussing the assumptions on which they are based, it also serves as a source of explanation for understanding the evolution of the Carter Administration's worldview and its foreign policy behavior.

Images and Belief Systems

The systematic study of attitudes and attitudinal change has been popular in psychology since the 1930s and has become even more prevalent since the 1960s. Within the field of social psychology, *attitudes*—the overarching concept representing values, beliefs, and opinions—are the focus of study. The most common definition breaks attitudes down into three major components: a "cognitive" component, referring to the information one has concerning an object; an "affective" component, referring to the feelings and emotions one has toward an object; and a "behavioral" component, which refers to the action-tendencies or intentions that one develops with regard to an object (Calder & Ross, 1973; Fishbein, 1967; Oskamp, 1977, pp. 7–14, 62–68).

Although this definition of attitudes has enjoyed considerable popularity, a number of social scientists have questioned its validity (Fishbein & Ajzen, 1972; McGuire, 1969; Rokeach, 1968). As described by Stuart Oskamp (1977, p. 10):

15

BELIEFS AND THEIR IMPACT ON BEHAVIOR

Honored as this tripartite division is in tradition, and clear as it seems conceptually, there is still an important question about its *empirical* validity and usefulness. It is conceivable that one or more of the components are really unimportant and do not have any relationship to events in the real world. Or, it is also possible that the three components are so closely interrelated as to be indistinguishable when we attempt to measure them carefully.

The result has been that though common agreement has emerged concerning the importance of attitudes for understanding individual behavior, there has "been little consensus between the definitions of 'attitudes' suggested by different social scientists" (Oskamp, 1977, p. 7).

A parallel development has occurred in the field of international relations, where the terms *beliefs* and *images* are commonly used when discussing attitudes (Brodin, 1972; Jervis, 1976; Kelman, 1965a). And as with the concept of attitudes in social psychology, there has been minimal agreement over the definitions of beliefs and images in international relations; more often than not the two concepts have been defined idiosyncratically. In this study, I define an *image*, as well as a *belief system* (they are used interchangeably), as a *set of ideas and thoughts concerning the environment that are held relatively constant*.[1] In other words, an image (or belief system) consists of a set of beliefs that are organized and are relatively constant over time—that is, the beliefs do not fluctuate abruptly from day to day.

The constant interaction of the individual with his environment allows for the possible formation of a multitude of images. The minds of individuals are filled with beliefs, values, and opinions; however, the key question is whether the beliefs that an individual holds are organized in a relatively stable fashion with regard to some aspect of the environment. If this is the case, then it can be said that the individual has developed a belief system concerning that aspect of the environment. Depending upon the particular environment to which one refers, an individual's belief system may range from the existence of a highly organized and coherent image to the lack of any image at all.

Given the developmental process by which an individual acquires his beliefs, it is likely that most people, most of the time, maintain a variety of images concerning the environment. This is the case for political leaders as well as the common individual. As described by Brecher, Steinberg, and Stein (1969, pp. 86–87) it is quite likely that foreign policy decision-makers develop images of the international environment:

Their images may be partial or general. They may be subconscious or may be consciously stated. They may be based on carefully thought-out assumptions about the world or they may flow from instinctive perceptions and judgements. In any event all decision-makers may be said to possess a set of images and to be conditioned by them in their behavior on foreign policy.

Determining the nature and content of an image of the international environment, however, is quite difficult and demanding. "Few practitioners of foreign policy have the time or the inclination to formulate and elaborate an integrated 'world view' " (Brecher, Steinberg & Stein, 1969, p. 87). This does not imply that policymakers rarely develop images of the international environment, only that the role of the scholar is critical in determining the existence and content of any belief system. "The fact that beliefs and premises are not articulated in a systematic fashion does not necessarily mean that they are nonexistent. But it does mean that considerable inferential leaps are necessary to bring them into the open" (Tweraser, 1974, p. 11).[2]

Obviously, the Carter Administration had a number of specific images about the international environment. However, the debate over the Carter Administration revolves around its general worldview—defined in this study as an image held of the "international system" (see appendix B for a complete discussion). Therefore, the key questions to be addressed are whether the Carter Administration had a cohesive image of the international system, whether the image was shared by major Carter Administration officials, whether the content of the Carter Administration's image changed throughout its four years in office, and whether the Carter Administration's image was related to its foreign policy behavior.

Individual and Collective Images

The concept of a *Carter Administration image* obviously simplifies reality somewhat. An administration does not have a belief system per se. Yet, when individuals are grouped so as to represent an administration, it can be argued that a collective belief system built out of the aggregation of individual beliefs does exist for the entire group. Therefore, a primary focus of this study is to determine the individual and collective images of the Carter Administration.

Discussion of a collective image has not received much attention. Most scholars in the area of foreign policy and international relations have focused on the beliefs of a key, single individual or leader. For example, Holsti (1967) has examined the beliefs of John Foster Dulles, and Starr (1984) and Walker (1977) have examined the beliefs of Henry Kissinger. Although analyzing an

BELIEFS AND THEIR IMPACT ON BEHAVIOR

individual leader minimizes the empirical problems for identifying the content of beliefs, it considerably simplifies the collective nature of most decision-making. Foreign policy decisions are rarely made by a single political leader.[3]

In order to examine the beliefs of a collective unit it is important to specify whose beliefs are to be addressed. However, the study of perceptions and beliefs has not been linked to various conceptualizations of foreign policy decision-making. As stated by Holsti (1977, p. 56), "it will not suffice to assume that foreign policy decisions merely reflect the beliefs of any given leader, or even group of leaders. Hence research on belief systems must be embedded in a broader context."[4]

Because this study focuses on the Carter Administration's general foreign policy throughout its four years in office, it is most appropriate to conceptualize the executive branch as an actor represented by the most important decisionmakers: the Head of State and his/her closest advisors. This is consistent with the decision-making literature that emphasizes the role of the Chief Executive and his key advisors as the most significant decisionmakers in foreign policy (Art, 1973; Krasner, 1978; Perlmutter, 1974; Rosati, 1981).[5]

The dominant participant in the decision-making process is the Chief Executive, either directly or indirectly through his closest advisors. According to Alexander George (1980, p. 98):

> All executives rely to some extent on a relatively small number of advisers and staff to ferret out information, make suggestions, develop and appraise policy options, and to monitor the implementation of decisions taken. The way in which advisers and staff perform these tasks is influenced by the expectations that develop regarding how they are to interact together for this purpose. These expectations, in turn, are shaped by the preferences of the executive or his surrogates.

From this one is able to see that the perspective of the chief executive acts as the principal force affecting the formulation and implementation of decisions. In other words, the collective image of an administration is dependent upon the images of those policymakers who have a disproportionate share of influence within the foreign policy process. As suggested by Snyder and Diesing (1977, p. 526), "the operative values and perceptions of the decision-making unit will depend on the balance of influence among its constituent members. . . . If one or two persons are in complete control, the operational 'interests' of the state will reflect their perspectives."

In the United States, the specific officials comprising the foreign policy-making core include, most importantly, the President, the Special Assistant for National Security Affairs (i.e., the National Security Advisor), and the

Secretary of State. These individuals have typically been the three major decisionmakers for U.S. foreign policy, particularly in the area of political-military affairs (see, e.g., Destler, 1972; Kegley & Wittkopf, 1979; Nathan & Oliver, 1983).[6] In fact, these were the three most important Carter Administration officials in the making of foreign policy (see appendix A for more in-depth analysis of the Carter Administration foreign policy process).

Therefore, the Carter Administration's collective image is based on the individual images of President Jimmy Carter, National Security Advisor Zbigniew Brzezinski, and Secretary of State Cyrus Vance, later replaced by Edmund Muskie. In order to analyze the content of the Carter Administration's collective image over time, the concepts of image consensus and image stability need to be addressed.

Image Consensus versus Image Dissensus

The collective image is the aggregation of the images of all the individuals who comprise the group. In this case the President, the National Security Advisor, and the Secretary of State comprised a collectivity for they shared a number of basic characteristics: they were the highest level officials primarily responsible for the conduct of American foreign policy within the Carter Administration. This definition of collectivity does not assume that the members of the group share the same beliefs about the international environment, however—they may or may not (Shaw, 1976). Therefore, it is important to determine the level of agreement or disagreement in the images among the key policymakers in order to understand the Carter Administration's collective image.

It is possible that the collective image may have a high level of consensus or a high level of dissensus among members of the group. On the one hand, different individuals are likely to perceive the environment differently, thereby contributing to dissensus. On the other hand, due to the process of socialization, it is also likely that individuals will always share a number of values that promote the adoption of similar images. In the final analysis, the relationship between shared images and individual differences in images is dependent upon the specific individuals examined within a collectivity and the particular context.

Within a specific administration, chances are there will be a relatively high degree of overlap in the belief systems of policy-making officials. This should be especially true when one is examining the highest-level policymakers. Because the President appoints the higher-level public officials and usually determines who is to advise and assist him in formulating decisions, a compatible viewpoint is generally a prerequisite in gaining access to the President (Cronin, 1975; James, 1974; Pious, 1979). Moreover, once entrenched in office, it is possible that differences in individuals' images may be minimized as a result of an administration's particular type of decision-making process. Janis (1982) has described how "groupthink" can occur in small groups that develop a high esprit de corp and are usually led by a domineering leader with the result being a high degree of individual conformity and group consensus in thought and image.

Nevertheless, particular differences in belief systems can also exist among the policymakers. "World view differences not only lie at the heart of interstate conflict and domestic debate on foreign policy, but are responsible for much of the difficulty in developing coherent policy intragovernmentally" (Cottam, 1977, p. 11). Because the literature on bureaucratic politics emphasizes differences in individual images, it focuses upon dissensus in image within the collectivity (Allison, 1971; Allison & Halperin, 1972; Halperin, 1974). This intragovernmental struggle over United States foreign policy has become a major preoccupation, especially by members of the media.

This was especially true for the Carter Administration where the concern with internal policy disagreement and its effect on foreign policy received considerable attention. Most of the focus at this time was on the policy controversies between the Secretary of State and the National Security Advisor (Burt, 1978; Drew, 1978; Gelb, 1980c; Schram, 1978). It was reported that Cyrus Vance and Zbigniew Brzezinski often disagreed on the conduct of U.S. foreign policy as a result of their divergent worldviews, especially with regard to their perception of the Soviet Union. The oversimplified but common argument is that Vance preferred a "softer line" toward the Soviet Union, while Brzezinski was more of a "hardliner." After Vance resigned in early 1980, Secretary of State Edmund Muskie also displayed many policy differences with Brzezinski since the new Secretary shared many of the same beliefs as Vance. Throughout the course of the policy debates between the Secretary of State and the National Security Advisor, President Carter was usually portrayed as indecisive and lacking a mind of his own, at times leaning toward Vance's position and at other times Brzezinski's, depending upon the context and the particular issue.

However, an often overlooked argument has been that President Carter did have an image of the international system and that it was somewhat different from those of his advisors. This was felt to be the case particularly during the early part of the Administration. According to Leslie Gelb (1980a, p. 26), "what fascinated me was the subtle struggle between the President on the one hand and almost all of his senior foreign policy advisors, including

Vance, on the other.'' President Carter attempted to implement a foreign policy in accordance with what he espoused as a candidate, which meant that, concerning defense spending, arms control, American troops in South Korea, and human rights, the senior advisors ''were, to varying degrees, to the right of Mr. Carter on most matters'' (Gelb, 1980b, p. 39).

In sum, in order to accurately describe the Carter Administration's collective image it is important to examine ''the range of core beliefs that are widely shared, as well as those on which there may be substantial variation'' (Holsti, 1977, p. 30). The collective image may vary from high consensus to high dissensus in individual images. The level of consensus or dissensus between policymaker images is important for determining whether or not the Carter Administration had a cohesive worldview. Although little work in political psychology has addressed the concept of collective images of political leaders, the literature reviewed suggests that both consensus and dissensus within the collective image are possible.

Image Stability and Image Change

Since the collective image is the aggregation of the individual images, a change in individual images over time is likely to produce changes in the collective image. Therefore, the concepts of stability and change in individual images are important for explaining the evolution of the Carter Administration's image.[7]

The debate over the stability of individual belief systems, once they have been formed, has been one of the most difficult and controversial issues addressed in the area of political attitudes (e.g., see Brim & Kagan, 1980). Originally, in the 1930s and 1940s, individual belief systems were considered to be highly open to manipulation and change. Later, in the 1950s and 1960s, it was common to describe belief systems in terms of their inherent stability and their resistance to change. Both positions are simplistic. Overall, while it appears that individual belief systems are resistant to change, change may still occur given the right conditions. As we shall see, this has direct implications for the evolution of the Carter Administration's image of the international system.

The Dominance of Image Stability

Once formed, belief systems are usually resistant to change. There are two major reasons for this. First, individuals usually strive to maintain cognitive consistency with the result being the formation of an image that is internally interdependent and, therefore, difficult to modify. Second, most of the communications that individuals receive reinforce preexisting beliefs.

Cognitive Consistency

The history of Western thought and practice has been based on the premise that individuals think in a highly "rational" manner (see, e.g., Allison, 1971, pp. 10–38; Steinbruner, 1974, pp.25–46). It is argued that in making any decision individuals have an open intellectual process: values are ordered, a search is made for all relevant information, a wide range of alternatives are considered, and a selection is made of the option that maximizes the benefits while minimizing the costs. Individuals who follow such a course are quite open to change in their belief system as information about the environment changes. While such rationality is indeed quite possible, other modes of thought less rational in nature are also possible and quite prevalent.

Most of the work on attitudes and attitudinal change is based upon theories of cognitive consistency, in which individuals rely on key beliefs and are closed to discrepant information. The main principle behind cognitive consistency is that individuals attempt to avoid the acquisition of beliefs that are inconsistent or incompatible with one another—especially in their relation to their most central beliefs (McGuire, 1985; Oskamp, 1977, pp. 191–221; Steinbruner, 1974).[8] In other words, "individuals do not merely subscribe to random collections of beliefs but rather they maintain coherent systems of beliefs which are internally consistent" (Bem, 1970, p. 13).[9] Cognitive consistency, therefore, promotes stability in the images that individuals acquire by promoting interdependence among beliefs. As Jervis (1976, p. 170) explains: "If a person's attitude structure is to be consistent, then incremental changes among interconnected elements cannot be made. Change will be inhibited, but once it occurs, it will come in large batches. Several elements will change almost simultaneously."

As a result of the research conducted during the late 1950s and early 1960s, it was commonly thought that political elites had more consistent belief systems than the mass public (Campbell, Converse, Miller, & Stokes, 1960; Converse, 1964).[10] This was supported by the fact that most members of American society shared very low levels of information in comparison to the most attentive public and opinion leaders (Erskine, 1962; Hyman & Sheatsley, 1947). However, a number of objections to the evidence in support of an elitist viewpoint have been raised. Many individuals have argued that the early differences found in attitude consistency between elites and masses were exaggerated (Bennett, 1975; Key, 1965; Lane, 1962; Wray, 1979) and that the belief systems of the American public have become more consistent and

IMAGE STABILITY AND CHANGE

sophisticated with time (Luttberg, 1968; Nie with Anderson, 1974; Nie, Verba & Petrocik, 1976). Hence, as Oskamp (1977, p. 117) concludes, "attitudes serve the same general functions for members of the mass public as for political elites," although political beliefs are likely to be less salient and central for the average citizen (see also Kinder & Sears, 1985).

Reinforcement through Communication
Once a belief system is formed, it usually becomes relatively stable and is highly resistant to change. Ironically, the early research on propaganda, especially during the 1930s and 1940s, assumed that communications could easily alter the "minds of men"—therefore the term *persuasive communications*. It was a time when societies seemed particularly susceptible to the rise of dynamic and charismatic political leaders, such as Adolf Hitler in Germany. "This early view, then, pictured political propaganda as having great persuasive impact, primarily because of wily 'tricks of the trade' performed upon gullible audiences who were entirely captive and unable to defend themselves" (Sears & Whitney, 1973, p. 2).

By the 1950s, however, it became apparent that most of the assumptions of the early research on persuasive communications were faulty (see Rossi, 1966). The literature that has developed on the persuasive appeal of both mass and personal communications quite clearly demonstrates that images and belief systems are not easily altered, but rather are more easily reinforced (McGuire, 1985; Sears & Whitney, 1973). The failure of most persuasive appeals can be found at two different but complementary stages of the communication process: reception and acceptance.

In order for image change to have a chance of occurring, a message must first be received and comprehended by an individual. However, major exposure problems that are difficult to overcome exist. Most individuals are indifferent to persuasive appeals, especially political propaganda, and when they are attuned they tend to be surrounded by people and communications with which they sympathize. "Even when a political communicator breaks the barriers of low absolute exposure and de facto selectivity, he runs into yet another and most formidable obstacle: resistance to change based on partisan evaluation of information" (Sears & Whitney, 1973, p. 8). In other words, incoming information typically gets interpreted in accordance with an individual's existing central beliefs and predispositions.

The prevalence of cognitive consistency and the reinforcement tendency of most communications produce images that maintain high levels of stability over time. The classic case of belief system stability is Newcomb's study of alumnae from Bennington College (Newcomb, Koenig, Flacks & Warwick,

1967). Newcomb found that once their political attitudes were formed as students during the 1930s, most of the same attitudes were retained twenty-five years later.

In the study of international relations, a similar emphasis on the stability of images has also been demonstrated. Ole Holsti (1962, 1967) found that Secretary of State John Foster Dulles's image of the Soviet Union was fundamentally constant over time. Starr (1980) reviewed the literature on Henry Kissinger's foreign policy beliefs and found that there was stability between his pre-office, official, and post-office beliefs. Bonham (1979) found no difference in the belief systems of American policy-makers before and after the 1973 Yom Kippur War. From this information one can conclude that beliefs tend to remain stable once they are formed.

The Occurrence of Change

Although images are stable over time, this does not imply that change does not or cannot occur, only that it is unlikely. As described by Milton Rokeach (1968, p. 3) "first, not all beliefs are equally important to the individual; beliefs vary along a central-peripheral dimension. Second, the more central a belief, the more it will resist change. Third, the more central the belief changed, the more widespread the repercussions in the rest of the belief system." A modification in image refers to either a change in the content of one or more central beliefs within the belief system or a change in the organization or structure of beliefs (Rokeach, 1966).

The images of political leaders may undergo change as a result of the interplay of three major factors: the importance of an individual's personality as a foundation for his beliefs, the impact of external events, and the role of domestic forces. Image change is most likely to occur when these factors combine in such a way that an individual's belief system is not dependent upon his personality characteristics, traumatic environmental events occur, and strong countervailing domestic forces are at work. The combination of these three sets of factors are likely to inhibit the maintenance of cognitive consistency and the reinforcement of most communications. Let us now examine each of these possibilities for image change more closely.

Individual Personality

Personality is important in the development of an individual's belief system and for any attitudinal change that may occur with time (Bennett, 1980, pp. 185–226). All beliefs are not equally resistant to change; those most central are usually the most intensely held by an individual and, therefore, the most stable (Lane & Sears, 1964, pp. 94–113).[11] According to David Sears and Richard Whitney (1973, pp. 8–9), "political attitudes to which the individual is highly committed, which we call 'enduring commitments,' should be difficult to change in any but a minor way, and high discrepancy appeals should be rejected out of hand."

The existence of enduring commitments—highly intense beliefs—is a function of the needs that the beliefs fulfill. This position was initially popularized by psychoanalytic theorists such as Freud (1930), Lasswell (1930), and Fromm (1941), culminating in *The Authoritarian Personality* (Adorno, Frenkel-Brunswik, Levinson, and Sanford, 1950), which argued that beliefs were dependent on ego-defensive needs. Developmental psychologists and other scholars such as Piaget (1932), Erikson (1950), and Maslow (1954) have emphasized that beliefs also fulfill more positive needs of individuals. "It can be said, then, that values form the blueprint which orders the individual's world and makes sense of it from a need-gratification point of view" (Sites, 1973, p. 15). When seen in this way, an individual's beliefs about the environment are heavily dependent on basic human needs. For Oskamp (1977, p. 175), this is "a valuable viewpoint which has important practical and theoretical consequences. However, functional approaches to attitude change have not been widely accepted nor frequently studied by researchers."[12]

The basic assumption of a functional approach, states Daniel Katz (1960, p. 167), "is that both attitude formation and attitude change must be understood in terms of the needs they serve and that as these motivational processes differ, so too will the conditions and techniques for attitude change" (see also Sarnoff & Katz, 1954; Smith, 1958). Beliefs that are based upon the inner needs of an individual—e.g., maintaining and enhancing one's self-identity, protecting against internal conflicts and external dangers—are the most resistant to change. Beliefs that help an individual to better understand and adapt to the environment—to obtain knowledge and to produce cognitive clarity—are more open to change.

> To the extent that object appraisal predominates, the person tends to react rationally, according to his lights and according to the information at his disposal. In terms of this function, his interests and values stand to be advanced by flexibility on his part in assimilating the implication of new facts. . . . To the extent that a person's attitudes serve to externalize inner problems, and are therefore imbedded in his defenses against obscure and unresolved tensions, we may expect them to be rigid and not particularly amenable either to reason and fact or to simple social manipulation. (Smith, Bruner, & White, 1956, pp. 277–278)

26

BELIEFS AND THEIR IMPACT ON BEHAVIOR

The implication is that different individuals have different propensities toward accepting changes in their images. The overall level of cognitive rationality is heavily dependent upon the psychological importance that an individual attaches to his belief system. As pointed out by Milton Rokeach (1960), individuals vary enormously along an "open-minded" and "closed-minded" continuum.

External Events

That an individual is relatively open to new information is not sufficient in itself to produce a change in image, however. Some type of stimulus from the environment is required to attract an individual's attention and to trigger the possibility for new information to be absorbed. Two general types of external events are particularly important in affecting the images that an individual has of the environment: spectacular events and cumulative events (i.e., lesser events that occur over a period of time; see Deutsch & Merritt, 1965).[13]

The importance of dramatic events for affecting images and behavior has long been recognized by international relations scholars. According to Kenneth Boulding (1969, pp. 428–429), "certain events—like the German invasion of Belgium in 1914, the Japanese attack on Pearl Harbor in 1941, the American use of the atom bomb at Hiroshima and Nagasaki, the merciless destruction of Dresden, and the Russian success of Sputnik I—have profound effects and possibly long-run effects on reorganizing the various national images." There is no guarantee that major events, such as crises, will necessarily alter an individual's image. Nevertheless, image changes are usually accompanied by the perception of an altered environment (Roskin, 1974; Thistlethwaite, 1974).

Beliefs about politics, and especially world politics, are formed and subsequently evolve as a result of events. As Jervis (1976) points out, events will greatly impact on individual beliefs if they are experienced firsthand, especially if they occur in early life or career, if it has important consequences for him or his nation, and if the extent of general relevant knowledge is low. Therefore, "since events with major consequences for a nation absorb so much of the citizen's time and attention, they both socialize the previously unconcerned and change the perceptual predispositions of many people with established views" (Jervis, 1976, p. 262).

International crises are particularly relevant when discussing how major events can stimulate image change. "Short of war, crises are the most salient and visible points of conflict between states. . . . Crises can therefore serve as the catalyst for the reorientation of a nation's foreign policies toward both its adversaries and allies'' (Lebow, 1981, p. 309). After reviewing twenty-six occurrences of international crises, Lebow (1981, p. 333) found that the ''trauma of crisis, brought about at least in part by behavior of the adversary that is at variance with the image the respondent has of him, may prompt or even force a revision of that image.''

The literature on persuasive communications based upon fear arousal supports the proposition that major events such as international crises are most likely to produce change in an individual's image. Strong fear appeals—e.g., smoking causes cancer accompanied by pictures showing decaying lungs— have been found to produce more attitude change than weak appeals (Higbee, 1969; McGuire, 1968). When individuals try to alleviate the fear-induced threat they often wind up changing their attitudes. Although there is minimal agreement on a definition of international crises, there is one fundamental element that can be found in all crises—a threat to an individual's values (Brecher, 1977; Hermann, 1972; Lebow, 1981; McCormick, 1978; Robinson, 1972; Snyder & Diesing, 1977).[14]

Moreover, it has been found that individuals are even more likely to experience attitudinal change during a time of high fear arousal when detailed and specific recommendations are made for allieviating that fear (Levanthal, 1970; McArdle, 1972). This suggests that during a crisis, individuals within a decision-making unit may be particularly susceptible to policy recommendations that are persuasively argued and presented. Therefore, not only is image change possible in a time of crisis, but certain individuals may be able to benefit from the situation and have their policy recommendations approved in an effort to address the crisis.

Domestic Forces

The third major factor that contributes to possible image change is the role of domestic forces. The interaction of public opinion, issues that become politicized, and democratic elections can create a domestic environment that policymakers are unlikely to ignore. In cases when these three factors coalesce and are perceived to be a strong force throughout society, they can be particularly potent in affecting belief systems.

Considerable disagreement exists concerning the exact role of domestic forces in American foreign policy. During the 1950s and 1960s, public opinion was considered relatively fickle and responsive to the political leadership (Almond, 1960; Rosenau, 1961).[15] During a time of crisis public opinion usually ''rallied around the flag'' in support of presidential policy (Lee, 1977; Mueller, 1973). The mass media most often reported and promoted governmental policy and were reluctant to critically investigate the news (Cohen,

BELIEFS AND THEIR IMPACT ON BEHAVIOR

1963; Hodgson, 1976, pp. 134–152). Thus, the public's input in the electoral connection was more often than not minimal relative to foreign policy (Page & Brody, 1972; Waltz, 1967).

The leeway enjoyed by policy-makers may be explained by the strong anticommunist "bipartisan consensus" that developed throughout much of American society after World War II and served as the bedrock of U.S. foreign policy (Hilsman, 1959; Hodgson, 1976, pp. 111–133). Though societal forces may not have directly influenced foreign policy, they still supplied an important indirect impact by setting parameters for legitimate action. During the cold war years, the anticommunist consensus reflected in public opinion certainly reinforced America's interventionist orientation overseas. For example, the fear of "losing" Vietnam to communism was fundamental in propelling U.S. military involvement in Southeast Asia (Gelb with Betts, 1979; Geyelin, 1966, Rosenberg, 1967).[16]

In fact, the public has demonstrated a marked tendency to tire of supporting presidential policy over time. Initial public support for U.S. military involvement in Korea and Vietnam fell ominously as time passed and the war continued (Elowitz & Spanier, 1974; Mueller, 1971). Furthermore, although foreign policy has rarely been a major issue in the minds of voters on election day, policy-makers are very attuned to public opinion. As reported by Morton Halperin (1974, p. 67), "compared with analysts, Presidents and potential Presidents themselves see a closer link between stands in foreign policy and the outcomes of presidential elections."[17]

The impact of the Vietnam War has dramatically altered the role of domestic politics in foreign policy. The foreign policy consensus was shattered by Vietnam and has been replaced by diversity of thought and disagreement over American foreign policy (Hodgson, 1976; Holsti and Rosenau, 1984; Rosati and Creed, 1987). This has resulted in public opinion having a much greater direct role in the making of foreign policy—presidents no longer enjoy an automatic majority who sympathize and support their general foreign policy orientation, as was the case during the cold war.

The role of the mass media has also changed. As it has grown in independence and increased in importance as an *agenda-setter* of issues (McCombs & Shaw, 1972; McLeod, Becker & Byrnes, 1974), it has become "stunningly successful in telling readers" and listeners "what to think about" (Cohen, 1963, p. 161). Most individuals are dependent on the media—especially television—for their information about the world, in particular with regard to the international environment. This is extremely important for the development of the public's opinion because media coverage may be far from objective, especially when reporting international crises or spectacular events (Braestrup, 1977; Epstein, 1973; Graber, 1984).

Kegley and Wittkopf (1979, p. 223), in their review of the role of public opinion, conclude that "public preferences in general, and during elections in particular, serve as a 'source' of American foreign policy . . . more by coloring the vocabulary of decision making than by determining the policy outcomes." This is of vital importance in affecting the legitimacy of political behavior and the general parameters of public policy. As issues have become more publicized and politicized, the impact of public opinion has grown more important to foreign policy-making (Bennett, 1980, pp. 227–247, 345–365; Harris, 1977). Ironically, the lack of a bipartisan consensus as a result of Vietnam's shattering impact allows for greater innovation in foreign policy, yet at the same time, the uncertainty of public support has forced policymakers to proceed cautiously.

When domestic forces are active and intense, especially during an election year, policy-makers are particularly susceptible to altering their images. This is supported by the social-psychological literature on conformity that demonstrates that individuals change their beliefs and behavior in order to adhere to widely accepted beliefs or standards (Bem, 1970, pp. 70–99; Rokeach, 1968, pp. 62–81). Social conformity is prevalent when an individual "accepts influence because he hopes to achieve a favorable reaction from another person or group" (Kelman, 1958, p. 53).[18] Kelman (1958) found that individual conformity was greatest especially under conditions of surveillance by authority, suggesting that the importance of domestic forces on public officials increases as election time draws near.[19]

The significance of conformity was first demonstrated in a series of famous experiments conducted by Solomon Asch (1951). In response to simple and straightforward perceptual problems, the subject often gave incorrect answers so as to conform with the dominant opinion of others (all of whom gave false answers knowingly). Baron and Byrne (1981, p. 241) conclude the following about the importance of conformity: "Together, reinforcement and social comparison set the stage for a high degree of conformity. Indeed, given the powerful and pervasive impact of these processes, it is far from surprising that conformity is our typical mode of behavior in a wide range of settings."

Although images may be resistant to change, a number of studies in international relations have demonstrated that the images of political leaders have occasionally undergone change. Ben-Zvi (1978) found that the images that American leaders held of Japan were dramatically altered following the attack on Pearl Harbor and the fighting of the war in the Pacific. In a particularly interesting study concerning Sweden's preferred role in world affairs, Thomas Hart (1976) found that of seventy Swedish elites interviewed, all heavily involved in national security policy, two-thirds reported that they had experienced "agonizing reappraisals" in which basic beliefs were fundamentally changed throughout the course of their careers. Similarly, Holsti and Rosenau (1979) found that the Vietnam War had a profound affect on the foreign policy views of American elites: almost 50 percent completely changed their beliefs concerning the war, and another 20 percent modified their position.[20]

To summarize the literature on image stability and change, most images that people acquire are resistant to change and, therefore, are highly stable over time. But while individuals strive to maintain consistency and the communication of information acts to reinforce one's belief system, images may still undergo change under certain conditions. Individuals with a minimal amount of emotional commitment invested in their beliefs are the most open-minded and receptive to new information. Major external events, such as international crises, may prompt individuals to modify their belief systems, and even the most closed-minded individuals may feel the necessity to reorient their images in response to a crisis when they need to adapt to the threatening environment. Finally, individuals are particularly prone to conform when they are in a minority position and they desire to gain what they deem to be important rewards. Political leaders are particularly attuned to strong domestic forces created by public opinion and politicized issues, especially as an election approaches. Together, the interaction of an individual's personality, external events, and domestic forces may cause a change in image. An analysis of the level of stability or change in individual images is important for understanding and explaining the evolution of the collective image of the Carter Administration.

The Link between Beliefs and Behavior

A considerable amount of research has been conducted in analyzing the significance of individual attitudes and beliefs: describing their content, discussing their origins, and determining their relative degree of stability over time. All of this work has been based on one fundamental assumption: that beliefs are major sources of behavior and, therefore, explain and predict human action. Unfortunately, this assumption is so integral in attitudinal research that the relationship between beliefs and behavior has rarely been tested and demonstrated. As described by Fishbein and Ajzen (1975, p. 355),

Despite the commitment of the social sciences to the study of human behavior, relatively little research in the attitude area has investigated overt behavior as such. Instead, most studies have used observable acts to infer beliefs, attitudes, or intentions. Until very recently, empirical investigations have rarely concerned themselves with the relation of these variables to overt behavior.

More recently, Barner-Barry and Rosenwein (1985, p. 58) point out that "there is a tendency—especially among political scientists—to 'assume away' the problematical nature of the relationship between attitudes and behavior."[21]

Though the relationship between individual beliefs and behavior has received some study in social and political psychology, the results have been inconsistent. While much of the earlier work lent little support for a linkage between beliefs and behavior, more recent studies have found that the relationship between individual beliefs and behavior is much more complex and varied.

One of the earliest studies by Richard LaPiere (1934) showed that the gap between beliefs and behavior may be a large one. In his classic experiment on the impact of racial beliefs on behavior, LaPiere traveled twice across the United States—extensively on the West Coast—accompanied by a young Chinese couple (husband and wife). Throughout the course of their travels, they were served at 184 eating places and obtained sleeping accommodations at 66 different establishments—they were refused service only once. Upon return, LaPiere sent out questionnaires to the same businesses and asked "will you accept members of the Chinese race as guests in your establishment?" Of the questionnaires returned, 92 percent responded that they would refuse to serve Chinese patrons—only one respondent gave a definite "yes" answer. Similar results demonstrating a discrepancy between beliefs and behavior have been found in studies of a similar nature (e.g., Kutner, Wilkins & Yarrow, 1952), and in a review of over 30 studies, Wicker (1969) found that there was little or no relationship between attitudes and overt behavior.

A number of critiques, however, have softened the impact of these earlier studies. For instance, pseudoinconsistency may have been operating between beliefs and behavior as a result of different "situational thresholds" (Campbell, 1963, Dillehay, 1973; see also Deutscher, 1973, chapter 10).[22] In his study on the subject, Minard (1952) found that while white miners were quite friendly toward black miners in the environment of the coal mine, once they returned to the local community white miners displayed racist behavior toward the same black people. Wicker (1969, p. 69), in fact, concludes that "the

BELIEFS AND THEIR IMPACT ON BEHAVIOR

more similar the situations in which verbal and overt behavioral responses are obtained, the stronger will be the attitude-behavior relationship.''

Although early work on this topic has been somewhat discouraging, more recent studies suggest that a link between beliefs and behavior does exist. Polls have shown an impressive propensity for predicting mass behavior (Crespi, 1971). The relationship between individual beliefs concerning presidential candidates and presidential voting has been demonstrated to be quite high (Fishbein & Combs, 1974). It has also been found that the behavior of subjects with respect to religion and social drinking was closely related to their beliefs about these issues (Kahle & Berman, 1979). As one person summed up the research over the years, ''though there is often a real inconsistency between attitudes and actions, the typical pattern is one of a moderate positive relationship'' (Oskamp, 1977, p. 245). Unfortunately, the conditions that affect the belief-behavior relationship have not been sufficiently specified or researched (see Calder & Ross, 1973; Wicker, 1969).

Despite this apparent link, three major problems exist with most of these studies that suggest caution when the findings are applied to the study of political leaders' beliefs. First, most of the psychological research has focused on only a few very specific attitudes and actions at one moment in time. The comment made by Milton Rokeach (1960,pp. 18–19) over two decades ago still applies today:

> Present-day theory and research are typically focused on the properties, the determinants, and the measurement of single beliefs and attitudes rather than on belief systems and attitude systems. . . . Much of man's social behavior can be better understood by relating such behavior to man's belief systems rather than to elements of such systems.

Additionally, problems arise because the attitudinal data have been based on a person's self-report of his own beliefs. When so few attitudes of a specific nature are being measured and analyzed, a dependence on the subjects as direct sources of their own attitudes maximizes the potential for inaccuracy or the reporting of ad hoc ''non-attitudes'' (Converse, 1970; Wahlke, 1979). The final shortcoming is that most of the studies on the significance of attitudes are conducted in the controlled environment of the laboratory. Recently, there has been growing awareness of the importance of field research. Nevertheless, ''despite the talk about field research, very little of it is yet being reported in the scientific literature'' (Oskamp, 1977, p. 235).

Given these problems, it is important when studying the impact of the beliefs of political leaders on international behavior to examine the role of more general beliefs and entire images, to incorporate the element of time, and to include complementary tools of research for validating the content of beliefs. Furthermore, it is essential to take into consideration the situation or context to insure that the beliefs and behavior that are derived and analyzed are compatible.

As with the attitudinal literature, most of the work on belief systems in international relations has been devoted to the description of images. A minimal amount of research has been directed toward determining the relationship between belief systems and international behavior. According to Holsti (1977, p. 60), the linkage between beliefs and behavior has rarely been tested: "It is not uncommon to find in the conclusion a statement to the effect that, 'the preceding analysis of X's belief system established its utility for understanding X's political behavior.' Less often do we find an explicit and compelling demonstration of why this is the case." As Michael Sullivan (1976, p. 60) suggests, "none of this is to say that belief systems do not relate to actual international behavior, but only that the empirical link has not been forged."

Some work conducted recently indicates that there is little relationship between beliefs and behavior. For example, Starr (1984) compared Henry Kissinger's images of the Soviet Union and China to actual American foreign policy output toward the two countries. He concluded that Kissinger's images are not congruent with American foreign policy behavior: "Although Kissinger was the dominant foreign-policy decision maker during the period under investigation, his words—and the evaluative assertions that they contained—did not simply and directly reflect American behavior toward the Soviet Union and China" (Starr, 1984, p. 142).

Other work conducted demonstrates that a close relationship between an actor's belief system and subsequent foreign policy behavior does exist. Loch Johnson (1977, p. 85) found that there was a strong correlation between Senator Frank Church's "beliefs and subsequent voting behavior which reinforces my impressions (as participant observer) of his belief-behavior consistency." Sullivan (1979) discovered that the symbolic commitments made by the United States concerning Vietnam were consistent with its escalation and de-escalation behavior under three presidents. And when Walker (1975, 1977) examined the relationship between the foreign policy beliefs of Henry Kissinger and his bargaining behavior toward the Soviet Union, the Arab-Israeli conflict, and the Vietnam War, he found (unlike Starr, 1984) that the "pattern of American behaviors in each case corresponded to the instrumental components of Kissinger's operational code, while the rationale for each policy was consistent with the philosophical principles of Kissinger's operational code" (1975, p. 53).

BELIEFS AND THEIR IMPACT ON BEHAVIOR

As with the study of attitudes in social psychology, the belief-behavior relationship in international relations is not straightforward. Although beliefs are often related to behavior, conditions need to be specified for explaining when and why the relationship is likely to hold. Nevertheless, it appears that an administration's foreign policy behavior generally cannot be explained or understood adequately without reference to its image of the international system. This is not to imply that there is a continuous, direct one-to-one link between individual beliefs and behavior. Rather, an individual's beliefs usually determine the parameters for possible action within which behavior occurs. As described by Alexander George (1980, p. 45) in his discussion of the operational code construct:

> Beliefs of this kind serve as a prism or filter that influences the actor's perception and diagnosis of political situations and that provides norms and standards to guide and channel his choices of action in specific situations. The function of an operational code belief system in decision-making, then, is to provide the actor with ''diagnostic propensities'' and ''choice propensities.'' Neither his diagnosis of situations nor his choice of action for dealing with them is rigidly prescribed and determined by these beliefs.

This makes it very difficult to use beliefs to explain specific international actions. This does not, however, lessen the significance of individual beliefs as causal forces of behavior. George (1980, p. 55) is quick to point out that ''sophisticated policymakers and academic scholars alike agree that relations among states are shaped by the way in which leaders view each other and, more generally, by their beliefs about the nature of conflict within the international system.'' Nevertheless, it remains unclear when and why foreign policy beliefs are related to international behavior. This is an open question that is directly addressed when analyzing the foreign policy of the Carter Administration.

Clarifying the Conflicting Interpretations

The literature on beliefs and images allows us to better understand the controversy over the Carter Administration's foreign policy. When examined in the context of this literature, the four schools of thought provide conflicting interpretations about the nature of the Carter Administration's belief system. Each school of thought describes the Carter Administration's collective image of the international system based on assumptions about the level of consensus between key policymakers and the level of stability of the individual images.

CLARIFYING CONFLICTING INTERPRETATIONS

The four schools of thought actually represent four positions about the content and evolution of a collectivity's beliefs:

Position 1a. According to the first school of thought, the Carter Administration *had no worldview*, due to a *dissensus* in individual images that remained *stable* over time.

Position 2a. According to the second school of thought, the Carter Administration *had a cohesive worldview*, due to a *consensus* in individual images that remained *stable* over time.

Position 3a. According to the third school of thought, the Carter Administration *developed two different worldviews*, based initially on a *consensus* in individual images that *changed* over time to a new consensus.

Position 4a. According to the fourth school of thought, the Carter Administration *eventually developed a worldview*, based initially on a *dissensus* in individual images that *changed* over time toward consensus.

Each school of thought also posits a relationship between the nature of the Carter Administration's foreign policy beliefs and its foreign policy behavior. The congruence between collective beliefs and collective behavior is based on the same assumptions about the level of consensus and stability among individual images. The four positions are as follows:

Position 1b. According to the first school of thought, the Carter Administration's beliefs and behavior were *incongruent* over time.

Position 2b. According to the second school of thought, the Carter Administration's beliefs and behavior were *congruent* over time.

Position 3b. According to the third school of thought, the Carter Administration's beliefs and behaviors were *congruent* over time.

Position 4b. According to the fourth school of thought, the Carter Administration's beliefs and behavior were *incongruent* until the final year when *congruency* was achieved.

All four positions concerning the Carter Administration's worldview and their relationship to foreign policy behavior are consistent with the belief system literature and, thus, all four interpretations are theoretically plausible. Nevertheless, it needs to be reinforced that the literature emphasizes the study of individual beliefs and behavior. Little conceptual or empirical work has been conducted in political psychology on the beliefs of multiple individuals who comprise a collectivity. This is what we turn to in order to address the conflicting interpretations about the Carter Administration's foreign policy.

Notes

1. A "belief" or "attitude" is the general concept that loosely refers to an empirical observation or a normative thought concerning the environment. "Values" are beliefs of a general and abstract nature that focus on desirable end-states and modes of conduct. "Opinions" refer to rather specific types of beliefs concerning the presence and/or favorability of an object and situation (see Rokeach, 1968, pp. 123–126).

2. Research strategies for determining the belief systems of individuals are discussed in appendix B.

3. There are some major exceptions to this common pattern. The early research on operational codes focused on collective beliefs (e.g., Leites, 1951, George, 1969). Bonham and Shapiro (1982) have adapted cognitive mapping to collective decision-making. Hermann (1985) focuses on the "prevailing view" of Soviet leaders to explain the motivations behind Soviet foreign policy. Larson's (1985) work examines the evolution of the Truman Administration's collective beliefs in order to contribute to the explanation of the origins of the cold war.

4. "The fact is we do not have an acceptable model of the manner in which the cumulative, interactive effects of individuals' attitudes aggregate to condition the structure of beliefs of the collectivity of which they are a part" (Kegley, 1986, p. 454). The study of groups in social psychology, surprisingly, has not addressed the concept of the beliefs of a group or collectivity. As explained by Jones (1985, p. 77):

> In a curious way, social psychology has always been ambivalent about the study of groups per se. Some of this ambivalence may be traced to the heated controversies of the 1920s over the conceptualization of group properties. McDougall's 1920 treatment of group processes was dramatically titled *The Group Mind*, even though he later vigorously denied consciousness as group property. The mystical idea that groups could be characterized by emergent anthropomorphis properties was mercilessly attacked by F. H. Allport and others in the mainstream of behaviorism, a fact that probably channeled subsequent psychological research toward the study of individual responses to group influences and away from the study of groups as groups.

5. Rosati (1981) originally discussed three types of decision-making units: Presidential Dominance, Bureaucratic Dominance, and Local Dominance. A decision unit of Presidential Dominance consists of the head of state and his/her closest advisors. Presidential Dominance has since been renamed Chief Executive Dominance in order to make the decision unit less American-centric.

6. This is occasionally acknowledged even by the proponents of bureaucratic politics:

> The center to which issues requiring strategic choice must come is the President. . . . In the American system of government, he—not Congress, or the Secretary of State, or any other official—stands at the center of the foreign policy process. (Allison, 1975, p. 34)

> The President stands at the center of the foreign policy process in the United States. His role and influence over decisions are qualitatively different from those of any other participant. In any foreign policy decision widely believed at the time to be important, the President will almost always be the principal figure determining the *general* direction of actions (Halperin, 1974, p. 17).

NOTES

7. As stated by Kegley (1986, p. 465), "If the meaning of Americans' foreign policy beliefs are to be adequately understood, the discovery and descriptive process will have to be grounded in a theoretical structure that can explain why and how mental or cognitive propensities are modified in response to changes in domestic and international circumstances. We must move from the observation of symptoms to analysis of causes. For that, a theory of *why* beliefs change or resist change must inform the analysis and the collection of data."

8. See Larson (1985), Markus and Zajonc (1985), and Nisbett and Ross (1980) for a discussion of the importance of "schemas" for beliefs and the processing of information.

9. Disagreement has ensued over the type of consistency for which individuals strive. As described by Rosenberg (1960, p. 45), "it is not assumed that total and perfect consistency need obtain in a stable attitude structure." Some people may think in terms of a *psycho-logic*, where belief systems are not based on pure deductive reasoning or logical rationality, but an imperfect form of consistency comprehensible to the individual (Abelson & Rosenberg, 1958; Jervis, 1976, pp. 117–142). Abelson (1968) has also argued that individual images are really based upon the existence of isolated *opinion molecules* (see Deutscher, 1973, for a discussion of compartmentalization). If such is the case, the argument for the stability of images is strengthened because opinion molecules "do not need to have logical interconnections between them, and they are notoriously invulnerable to argument because of their isolated, molecular character " (Bem, 1970, p. 39).

10. See Pomper (1978–79) for a discussion of the profound impact *The American Voter* had on political science and the study of political attitudes.

11. As stated by Rokeach (1968, p. 13), "while there is undoubtedly a positive correlation between centrality and intensity, the relationship is by no means a necessary one."

12. In a fascinating work, John Burton (1979) offers a new paradigm for understanding social control and evolution based upon the relationship between the larger society and the individual pursuit of human needs.

13. Sears and Whitney (1973) also suggest the importance of a turnover in objects, such as the rise of new actors and issues. However, this is likely to be more significant for attitude formation in young individuals—those who have not acquired many enduring commitments—and supports the notion of a generational effect for attitudinal differences within society (see Inglehart, 1971; Jervis, 1976).

14. It is important to point out that different individuals in different national cultures will have a different perception and understanding of international crises (see Bobrow, Chan, & Kringen, 1977, 1979).

15. The term *public opinion* is used in its broadest sense to include not only specific and immediate attitudes but also underlying values and ideological orientations. The concept refers to both "mass" opinion and "elite" opinion (the latter includes political leaders who are not officially associated with the administration; e.g., members of Congress).

16. A number of scholars discuss the importance of public opinion for policy: Francis Rourke (1970) describes the "latent power" of the public; Klingberg (1952, 1979), Roskin (1974), and Holmes (1985) investigate the significance of "public moods" as they affect the formulation of U.S. foreign policy; and Richard Neustadt (1960) documents the significance of "public prestige" and "professional reputation" in affecting presidential leadership.

17. According to Destler, Gelb, and Lake (1984, p. 38): "The conventional wisdom among academic analysts has been that foreign-policy issues are not voting issues, that public opinion does not constrain or impel Presidents in their decisions on such issues. Yet, since World War II most Presidential politicians and Presidents have acted otherwise." The importance of the domestic environment and elections on congressional behavior has been repeatedly demonstrated (see Fenno, 1978; Kingdon, 1973; Mayhew, 1974; Ripley, 1983).

BELIEFS AND THEIR IMPACT ON BEHAVIOR

18. This is consistent with the functional basis of attitudes. Smith (1958, p. 10) discusses the social adjustment function in which individual beliefs may be motivated by how other people perceive the object and situation in order to "affiliate or identify himself with them or to distinguish himself from or oppose them." In this case, the individual is acting similar to David Riesman's (1953) "other-directed" man. See also Ajzer and Fishbein (1980) for a discussion of the "subjective norm," i.e., the individual's perception of social norms for behavior.

19. This also has additional implications within the confines of a decision-making group. If policymakers make most of their input in a cohesive group that has strong concurrence-seeking tendencies, the overwhelming impact of the group on an individual member will likely be that: (a) if his image is already consistent with the dominant beliefs of the group, his image will become reinforced and more stable, (b) if his image is inconsistent with the dominant beliefs of the group, his image will either: (i) change in conformity with the group if the individual wants to remain a group participant, or (ii) his image will be maintained by voluntary opting out of the group or by being ostracized by the group (see Janis, 1982). Under "groupthink" the impact of external events and domestic forces will normally reinforce the group's image by fulfilling the needs of its dominant members to maintain their self-esteem, to gain approval, and, in a crisis situation, to reduce stress. This helps to explain why traumatic events are necessary, for only they are likely to shatter the cohesiveness and consistency of the group.

20. Holsti and Rosenau (1982) have subsequently found that the lessons political leaders had learned from the Vietnam War have been maintained and reinforced over the last four years (see also Holsti & Rosenau, 1984).

21. Barner-Barry and Rosenwein (1985, p. 58) emphasize the lack of research by political scientists in this area: "political behavior is less well researched than political attitudes and the relationship between the two is a subject causing considerable controversy among psychologists while being virtually ignored by political scientists" (see also Wahlke, 1979).

22. Rokeach (1968) argues that a person's behavior "must always be mediated by at least two types of attitudes—one activated by the object, the other activated by the situation" (p. 126).

| THREE | *The Carter Administration's Images* |

T HE term *worldview* in this study refers to an image of the international system. It is argued that policymakers choose policy and have their governments act with reference to the basic structures and processes that they believe exist in the international system. The determination of the Carter Administration's image is based on a content analysis of the public statements made over four years by the President, the Secretary of State, and the National Security Advisor (see appendix B for a discussion of the research method and appendix C for a list of major public statements made). What follows is a description of the Carter Administration's image of the international system revolving around the issues and actors perceived to be most important by the policymakers throughout their years in office. The public statements are quoted extensively in order to minimize distorting the beliefs of the Carter Administration.

1977: Quest for Global Community in a Complex World

At the beginning of the Carter Administration, policymakers shared an image of a complex international system. What made the system complex was the emergence of a variety of important issues and actors, all of which had to be addressed if the United States was to respond positively to the changes taking place throughout the globe. This image of complexity was based on

39

optimism about the future and provided the foundation of the Carter Administration's efforts to promote a cooperative, global community. As President
Carter declared to people throughout the world on assuming office on January
20:

> I want to assure you that the relations of the United States with the other
> countries and people of the world will be guided during my own adminis-
> tration by our desire to shape a world order that is more responsive to
> human aspirations. The United States will meet its obligation to help
> create a stable, just, and peaceful world order. (U.S., President Carter,
> 1983, p. 1)

Global change and an increasingly complex international system proved
to be the major themes of the new Administration in its first year. "In less than
a generation we have seen the world change dramatically," stated President
Carter in a major foreign policy address at the University of Notre Dame
(U.S., President Carter, 1977d, p. 621). The world was not perceived to be
principally bipolar in its global structure; rather, dramatic global changes were
ushering in a new international system containing a "new worldwide mosaic
of global, regional, and bilateral relations" (U.S., President Carter, 1977d, p.
625).

In this complex world envisioned by the Administration, interdependence
was a fact of life that could not be ignored.

> As Americans we cannot overlook the way that our fate is bound to that of
> other nations. This interdependence stretches from the health of our
> economy through war and peace, to the security of our own energy
> supplies. It's a new world in which we cannot afford to be narrow in our
> vision, limited in our foresight, or selfish in our purpose. (U.S., President
> Carter, 1977e, p. 193)

Beyond being highly interdependent, the international system was also viewed
as increasingly pluralistic, so that neither the United States nor the Soviet
Union could control the destiny of the planet. Therefore, the United States
"will not seek to dominate nor dictate to others. . . . We have, I believe,
acquired a more mature perspective on the problems of the world. It is a
perspective which recognizes the fact that we alone do not have all the answers
to the world's problems" (U.S., President Carter, 1977g, p. 547).

Although most issues previously revolved around the U.S.-Soviet relationship, today a variety of actors had become globally important:

1977: QUEST FOR GLOBAL COMMUNITY

Europe and Japan rose from the rubble of war to become great economic powers. Communist parties and governments have become more widespread and more varied, and I might say more independent from one another. Newly independent nations emerged into what has now become known as the "Third World." Their role in world affairs is becoming increasingly significant. (U.S., President Carter, 1977e, p. 194)

In fact, these changes were perceived to be the conclusion of a "long chapter in the history of the West, namely the West's predominance over the globe as a whole" (U.S., NSC Assistant Brzezinski, 1978a, p. 19).

Not only was it the end of Western and American dominance, the U.S.-Soviet rivalry was no longer the dominant issue throughout the globe. According to Brzezinski, "we have witnessed perhaps, the end of a phase in our own foreign policy, shaped largely since 1945, in which preoccupation particularly with the Cold War as a dominant [concern] of U.S. foreign policy, no longer seems warranted by the complex realities within which we operate" (U.S., NSC Assistant Brzezinski, 1978a, p. 19). The post-World War II era was believed to be at an end. As stated by President Carter, "our policy during this period was guided by two principles—a belief that Soviet expansion was almost inevitable, but it must be contained, and the corresponding belief in the importance of an almost exclusive alliance among non-Communist nations on both sides of the Atlantic. That system could not last forever unchanged" (U.S., President Carter, 1977d, p. 622).

Given the growing complexity of the international system, a focus on East-West issues and the U.S.-Soviet relationship was deemed to be anachronistic by members of the Carter Administration. In a world of greater interdependence and decentralization, new issues and actors had to be addressed.

Today, we do not have a realistic choice between an approach centered on the Soviet Union, or cooperation with our trilateral friends, or on North-South relations. Indeed, each set of issues must be approached on its own terms. A world where elements of cooperation prevail over competition entails the need to shape a wider and more cooperative global framework. We did not wish the world to be this complex; but we must deal with it in all of its complexity, even if it means having a foreign policy which cannot be reduced to a single and simplistic slogan. (U.S., NSC Assistant Brzezinski, 1977c, p. H11999).

The complexity of the international system made mutual cooperation a prerequisite to building a global community. President Carter expressed this belief in a speech before the United Nations:

We have already become a global community—but only in the sense that we face common problems and we share, for good or evil, a common future. In this community, power to solve the world's problems—particularly economic and political power—no longer lies in the hands of a few nations. Power is now widely shared among many nations with different cultures and different histories and different aspirations. The question is whether we will allow our differences to defeat us or whether we will work together to realize our common hopes for peace. (U.S., President Carter, 1977g, p. 547)

The Carter Administration attempted to promote a new system of world order based upon international stability, peace and justice. Mutual cooperation was believed to be necessary in order to address the important global issues and actors. The principal architect of this quest was Zbigniew Brzezinski, who believed that

a secure and economically cooperative community of the advanced industrial democracies is the necessary source of stability for a broad system of international cooperation. We are aware of the pitfalls of constructing a geometric world—whether bilateral or trilateral or pentagonal—that leaves out the majority of mankind who live in the developing countries. . . . At the same time, a wider and more cooperative world system has to include also that part of the world which is ruled by Communist governments. . . . We are therefore seeking to create a new political and international order that is truly more participatory and genuinely more responsive to the global desire for greater social justice, equity, and more opportunity for individual self-fulfillment. (U.S., NSC Assistant Brzezinski, 1977c, p. H12000)

In order to pursue a community among nations, the Carter Administration rejected the policy of containment as the basis of American foreign policy. According to President Carter:

Being confident of our own future, we are now free of that inordinate fear of communism which once led us to embrace any dictator who joined us in that fear. . . . For too many years, we have been willing to adopt the flawed and erroneous principles and tactics of our adversaries, sometimes abandoning our own values for theirs. We have fought fire with fire, never thinking that fire is better quenched with water. This approach failed, with Vietnam the best example of its intellectual and moral poverty. But through failure, we have now found our way back to our own principles and values, and we have regained our lost confidence. (U.S., President Carter, 1977d, pp. 621–622)

From this one can see that the Carter Administration emphasized the pursuit of positive goals instead of the traditional American postwar preoccupation with the advancement of negative goals, such as the containment of communism, which ended up being counterproductive in the long run. The Carter Administration intended to promote positive change throughout the international system. According to Brzezinski:

We have sensed that, for far too long, the United States had been seen— often correctly—as opposed to change, committed primarily to stability for the sake of stability, preoccupied with the balance of power for the sake of the preservation of privilege. We deliberately set out to identify the United States with the notion that change is a positive phenomenon; that we believe that change can be channeled in constructive directions; and that internationally change can be made compatible with our own underlying spiritual values. (U.S., NSC Assistant Brzezinski, 1977c, p. H11999)

Members of the Administration recognized that the effort to promote a more stable, peaceful and just international system would be difficult. President Carter realized that ''we can only improve this world if we are realistic about its complexities. The disagreements that we face are deeply rooted, and they often raise difficult philosophical as well as territorial issues. They will not be solved easily. They will not be solved quickly'' (U.S., President Carter, 1977b, p. 329). This was why the Carter Administration felt it was so important to work with others in resolving problems and building a global community. The United States could lead, but it could no longer command or control:

However wealthy and powerful the United States may be—however capable of leadership—this power is increasingly only relative, the leadership increasingly is in need of being shared. No nation has a monopoly of vision, of creativity, or of ideas. Bringing these together from many nations is our common responsibility and our common challenge. For only in these ways can the idea of a peaceful global community grow and prosper. (U.S., President Carter, 1977g, p. 552)

Though recognizing the difficulties, the Carter team felt America must rise to the challenge. President Carter was particularly optimistic about the future. ''It is a new world, but America should not fear it. It is a new world, and we should help to shape it. It is a new world that calls for a new American foreign policy—a policy based on constant decency in its values and on optimism in our historical vision" (U.S., President Carter, 1977d, p. 622).

A variety of international issues and actors were important to the Carter Administration in its effort to promote a global community. As Vance indicated, "when our Administration came into office, we decided that we were not merely going to react to situations, but that we were going to shape an agenda of items which we considered to be of the highest priority and would proceed to deal with those issues" (U.S., Secretary Vance, 1977d, p. 81). These included the promotion of human rights and democracy, normalization and the improvement of relations, arms control, the resolution of conflict in the Middle East, conflict resolution in Africa, Third World development, and the health of the global economy (see table 3.1).[1]

Human rights was the most important issue for the new administration, differentiating this administration from its predecessors. And because the goal of promoting human rights throughout the globe was widely shared by all three Administration officials, one cannot understand how the Carter Administration perceived the world and conducted foreign policy without taking into account its commitment to human freedom and democratic principles. This is clearly explained in an important passage by Brzezinski:

We believe that human rights is an idea whose historic time has come. Throughout the world, because of higher literacy, better communica-

Table 3.1

Issues Perceived, 1977

Issue	Beliefs (%)
Human Rights	16.9
Normalization	16.2
Arms Control	15.6
Middle East Conflict	14.4
African Conflict	13.1
Development	7.5
Economy	7.2
Other Conflict	5.2
Security + Defense	1.8
Energy	1.3
Southwest Asian Conflict	0.7
	N = 597

tions, and a closer sense of interdependence, people are demanding and asserting their basic rights.. This phenomenon manifests itself—though in different ways and with differing priorities—in the Far East and in Southern Africa; in Latin America and in Eastern Europe and the USSR; and it has asserted itself in recent years in our own society on the racial front and it is also making itself felt in other advanced industrial democracies. We do not make the acceptance of our view of human rights a precondition for specific bilateral relationships; nor do we wish to prescribe our specific norms for other societies. But we do believe that these two words "human rights" summarize mankind's social progress; and that neither the United States nor the West should be ashamed of our commitment to the advancement of human rights. (U.S., NSC Assistant Brzezinski, 1977c, p. H11999)

The concept of democracy was integrally linked to the promotion of human rights. President Carter was particularly willing to emphasize the positive pursuit of human rights and democracy over the traditional American pursuit of preventing changes to the status quo.

The basic thrust of human affairs points toward a more universal demand for fundamental human rights. The United States has a historical birthright to be associated with this process. . . . Ours is a commitment, and not just a political posture. I know perhaps as well as anyone that our own ideals in the area of human rights have not always been attained in the United States. But the American people have an abiding commitment to the full realization of these ideals. (U.S., President Carter, 1977b, p. 332)

For Carter, human rights and democracy were the essence of what America stood for and should be used as a beacon to attract people throughout the world. As suggested by Brzezinski, "if we do not stand for something beyond material consumption, and if we do not have a policy based on something more than anticommunism, then indeed we may confront the decline of the West" (U.S., NSC Assistant Brzezinski, 1978a, p. 25).

Secretary of State Vance specifically addressed the Carter Administration's policy toward human rights in a major speech at the University of Georgia School of Law. He indicated that there were three categories of human rights that would receive attention. First was freedom from governmental violation of the integrity of the person, including "torture; cruel, inhuman, or degrading treatment or punishment; and arbitrary arrest or imprisonment" (U.S., Secretary Vance, 1977c, p. 505). Second was the right to the "fulfillment of such vital needs as food, shelter, health care, and education." Third were civil and political liberties such as "freedom of thought, of religion, of assembly; freedom of speech; freedom of the press." Vance recognized that the implementation of a human rights policy would be difficult and that other factors needed to be taken into consideration on a case by case basis. "We must always keep in mind the limits of our power and of our wisdom. A sure formula for defeat of our goals would be a rigid, hubristic attempt to impose our values on others" (U.S., Secretary Vance, 1977c, p. 506). Nevertheless, American foreign policy should be firmly embedded in human rights:

> Our encouragement and inspiration to other nations and other peoples have never been limited to the power of our military or the bounty of our economy. They have been lifted up by the message of our Revolution, the message of individual human freedom. That message has been our great national asset in times past. So it should be again. (U.S., Secretary Vance, 1977c, p. 508)

Normalizing and generally improving global relations were also vital for dealing with change in a complex world. "It is now increasingly important to widen U.S. relationships of a cooperative type to include those new centers of power and those nations that have assumed newly important regional or international roles" (U.S., NSC Assistant Brzezinski, 1978a, p. 19). In addition to enhancing East-West and West-West relations, an improvement in North-South relations was very crucial for the Carter goal of promoting a global community. "We will cooperate more closely with the newly influential countries in Latin America, Africa, and Asia. We need their friendship in a common effort as the structure of world power changes" (U.S., President Carter, 1977d, p. 624).

Concluding the Panama Canal treaties would be an optimal way of improving relations with Latin America, as well as with all of the Third World. According to Secretary Vance:

> These treaties, in my judgement, will gain us respect among other nations of the world—both large and small—because of the responsible way they resolve complex and emotional issues which have been with us for most of this century. . . . They are, above all, a triumph for the principle of peaceful and constructive settlement of disputes between nations. That is a principle we seek to apply in all aspects of American foreign policy. (U.S., Secretary Vance, 1977f, p. 615)

It was also important to improve relations with former adversaries, such as Cuba, Vietnam, and the People's Republic of China. As explained by President Carter:

> We have a basic decision to make in our country in our foreign policy about how to deal with nations who in the past have not been our friends and who in some instances have been our enemies on the warfield. Should we write them off permanently as enemies and force them to be completely under the control and influence of Communist powers, or should we start the process of giving them an option to be both our friends and the friends of others, hoping that they will come to a more democratic free society and joining with us in making a better world? (U.S., President Carter, 1977f, p. 199)

No architecture for a more stable and just world order would be complete without normalizing relations with China. "We recognize not only that peace in East and Southeast Asia depends upon a constructive Sino-American relationship, but that China can help immensely in maintaining a global equilibrium as well" (U.S., NSC Assistant Brzezinski, 1977c, p. H12000).

Beyond promoting human rights and the normalization of relations, arms control was very important to the Carter Administration. The Strategic Arms Limitation Talks (SALT), the prevention of nuclear proliferation, and arms transfer limitations were at the top of its agenda. The continual military buildup by the United States and the Soviet Union was making the world, not safer, but a more dangerous place.

> The Soviet Union and the United States have accumulated thousands of nuclear weapons. Our two nations now have five times more missile warheads today than we had just eight years ago. But we are not five times more secure. On the contrary, the arms race has only increased the risk of conflict. (U.S., President Carter, 1977b, p. 329)

Arms control took the form of a moral issue for the President; the arms race was not only dangerous, but it was "morally deplorable. We must put an end to it" (U.S., President Carter, 1977d, p. 623). "By reducing the nuclear threat, not only will we make the world a safer place but we'll also free ourselves to concentrate on constructive action to give the world a better life" (U.S., President Carter, 1977e, p. 196).

The Administration hoped that its efforts to promote human rights, improve global relations and pursue arms control would help contribute to the resolution of regional conflicts such as in the Middle East and in Africa. These conflicts were particularly threatening in the eyes of Carter policymakers. The best way to resolve regional conflicts and preempt foreign intervention was to work closely with the parties directly involved in promoting constructive change.

Secretary Vance was the most heavily involved in Africa and the Middle East. He believed that the United States must support the independent efforts of Third World states and that the way to prevent local conflicts from turning into major global issues was through the use of *preventive diplomacy*. With respect to American foreign policy toward Africa:

> The history of the past 15 years suggests that efforts by outside powers to dominate African nations will fail. Our challenge is to find ways of being supportive without becoming interventionist or intrusive. We see no benefit if we interject ourselves into regional disputes. We hope that they can be resolved through the diplomatic efforts of the parties themselves in an African setting. (U.S., Secretary Vance, 1977e, p. 169)

For example, conflict resolution in southern Africa required a relatively peaceful transition to democracy and black majority rule in Rhodesia, Namibia, and South Africa. To achieve this the United States needed to "work with African nations, and with our European allies, in positive efforts to resolve such disputes. . . . *The most effective policies toward Africa are affirmative policies*. They should not be reactive to what other powers do, nor to crises as they arise" (U.S., Secretary Vance, 1977e, pp. 166, 169).

The need to take a preventive approach and resolve conflicts before they exploded into war and destruction was especially important when it came to the Arab-Israeli conflict.

> Of all the regional conflicts in the world, none holds more menace than the Middle East. War there has already carried the world to the edge of nuclear confrontation. It has already disrupted the world economy and imposed severe hardships on the people in the developed and the developing nations alike. So true peace—peace embodied in binding treaties—is essential. It will be in the interest of the Israelis and the Arabs. It is in the interest of the American people. It is in the interest of the entire world. (U.S., President Carter, 1977g, p. 551)

The Carter Administration believed that the key was to work toward a comprehensive settlement to the conflict in the Middle East.

The Carter Administration believed that efforts to foster Third World development and promote a healthy global economy would help insure international peace and cooperation. America could not ignore the complexity and interdependence of the international system.

American economic welfare does not exist, and cannot be nurtured, in a vacuum. The health of nations, in 1977, is measured in terms of economic cooperation among nations, for our fortunes are intertwined as never before. . . . In brief, the future of the world economy, including our own, rests on the steady expansion of a highly integrated international system of trade, finance, and investment. (U.S., Secretary Vance, 1977b, p. 284)

Throughout the Third World, "disadvantaged people in poor countries are rejecting the inevitability of their condition and look to their leaders to improve their lives." Therefore, as Vance explained, "equality of economic opportunity has become the paramount goal of diplomacy for more than 100 developing nations, just as it has through the years been the goal of disadvantaged citizens and regions in America" (U.S., Secretary Vance, 1977b, p. 284). In response to the complexities of the international political economy, the Carter Administration's goal was "not to encourage dissension or to redivide the world into opposing ideological camps but to expand the realm of independent, economically self-reliant nations—and to oppose attempts at new kinds of subjugation" (U.S., President Carter, 1977e, p. 196).

Addressing the problems of arms control, resolving regional conflicts in the Middle East and Africa, nurturing Third World development, and promoting a prosperous global economy would improve tremendously the fulfillment of basic human rights and local independence—all these issues were perceived as interrelated. According to Secretary Vance:

We cannot effectively promote multilateral diplomacy, control the proliferation of nuclear arms, fight international terrorism, reduce the levels of conventional weapons, or protect our interests in the oceans or space in a hungry, angry, embittered world. We are much more likely to achieve cooperation on these basically noneconomic issues if we can do our fair share in the long-term process of international development cooperation—if we are seen as furthering, not blocking, world aspirations. (U.S., Secretary Vance, 1977b, p. 285)

This perceived interrelationship among a variety of global issues, tied to the vision of developing a global community, signifies that the Administration did have a coherent image of the international system. Movement on one issue would help to promote movement on another issue, thereby promoting the ultimate goal of a global community.

Given the diversity of important issues perceived by the Carter Administration, no international actor or group of actors was considered predominant.

In fact, seven of the eight groupings of international actors were each addressed over 10 percent of the time—only Eastern European actors (discussed only .5 percent of the time) were consistently unimportant (see table 3.2).[2] A wide assortment of actors throughout the globe were considered important; their importance varied depending upon the issue being addressed (see table 3.3).

Actors in the Middle East (especially Israel, Egypt, the Arabs in general, and the Palestinians) received the most attention by the Carter administration and were perceived to be the key to resolving the Arab-Israeli conflict. Asian actors (especially China, Vietnam, and the Association for Southeast Asian Nations) were integral regarding the normalization of relations and the global economy. Western Europe, Canada, and Japan were important for human rights and democracy, the global economy, arms control (particularly Great Britain and France), and conflict in Africa (especially Western Europe in general and Great Britain). Africa, as a regional set of actors, was perceived to be critical for conflict resolution in Africa and the promotion of human rights (with an emphasis on South Africa and Zimbabwe), as well as Third World development. Actors throughout Latin America were significant for normalization (particularly Panama) and Third World development. Global actors were perceived to have an important role to play. For example, the United Nations was important for the issues of human rights and the conflict in Africa. Developing nations and U.N. financial institutions were looked to for promoting the global economy and Third World development. All in all, the Soviet Union was only one of many important actors in a world of complex interdependence.

Table 3.2

Actors Perceived, 1977

Actors	Beliefs (%)
Middle East	17.9
Soviet Union	16.6
China + Asia	16.4
Western Europe + Japan	14.3
Africa	12.5
Latin America	11.3
Global	10.5
Eastern Europe	0.5
	N = 391

Table 3.3

Actors Perceived for Each Major Issue, 1977

Issue	Middle East	Soviet Union	China + Asia	Western Europe + Japan	Africa	Latin America	Global	Eastern Europe	N
				Actor (%)					
Human Rights	7.5	5.7	5.7	24.5	17.0	13.2	24.5	1.9	53
Normalization	6.1	7.6	33.3	12.1	9.1	24.2	7.6	—	66
Arms Control	—	69.8	1.9	17.0	—	5.7	5.7	—	53
Middle East Conflict	86.3	6.8	—	5.5	—	—	1.4	—	73
African Conflict	—	4.4	—	13.3	60.0	6.7	15.5	—	44
Development	—	6.7	—	13.3	23.3	23.3	33.3	—	30
Economy	5.9	2.9	29.4	23.5	11.8	8.8	17.6	—	34

THE CARTER ADMINISTRATION'S IMAGES

Image of the Soviet Union

The Carter Administration's perception of the Soviet Union was fundamental in understanding the Administration's complex image of the international system and its quest for a global community. As suggested by general elite image studies or those utilizing an operational code approach (e.g., Holsti 1967; Starr, 1984), the image of the "opponent" or "adversary" serves as the foundation for understanding an actor's belief system about the larger international environment. The image of the Soviet Union held by Americans has played a key role in affecting U.S. foreign policy since World War II.

Basically, in 1977 the Soviet Union was not seen in a threatening light. Instead it was portrayed rather optimistically—having a limited capability to affect the environment, constrained by the complexity of the international system, and, although occasionally opportunistic, generally cooperative in its intentions. Vance and, especially, Carter were the most optimistic in this regard. Brzezinski was less optimistic about Soviet activity in a world of complexity.

Carter policymakers considered the United States to be much stronger economically, politically, morally, and militarily. President Carter, in fact, believed that the United States had an advantage in nuclear forces, although this was of little consequence for him. "At the present time, my judgement is that we have superior nuclear capability. The Soviet Union has more throw-weight, larger missiles, larger warheads. We have more missiles, a much higher degree of accuracy, and also we have three different mechanisms which are each independently adequate to deliver atomic weapons" (U.S., President Carter, 1977a, p. 158)." Based on this perception of limited Soviet capabilities, the Carter Administration believed the United States need not fear its longtime adversary.

The Carter Administration felt that the Soviet Union had limited national capabilities not only relative to the United States but also relative to the international environment. The international system was believed to be so interdependent, multifaceted, and pluralistic that no actor could dominate international behavior. The complexity of the system produced numerous constraints that limited the opportunities able to be exploited by the Soviet Union. "Both the United States and the Soviet Union have learned that our countries and our people, in spite of great resources, are not all-powerful. We've learned that this world, no matter how technology has shrunk distances, is nevertheless too large and too varied to come under the sway of either one or two superpowers" (U.S., President Carter, 1977e, p. 194).

1977: QUEST FOR GLOBAL COMMUNITY

It was also believed that the Soviet Union was relatively well-intentioned. Thus the Carter Administration perceived Soviet intentions to be primarily cooperative in nature—54.5 percent cooperative versus 9.1 percent opportunistic (see table 3.4). Carter officials understood that the Soviet Union had its own historical experience, goals, and national interests that occasionally brought them at cross-purposes with the United States—but this was to be expected. The Soviet-American relationship was based upon the interdependent nuclear threat of annihilation and this imposed upon the Soviet Union a concern with mutual security and cooperation. As stated by President Carter, "I remain fully aware that American-Soviet relations will continue to be highly competitive—but I believe that our competition must be balanced by cooperation in preserving peace and thus our mutual survival. I will seek such cooperation with the Soviet Union earnestly, constantly, and sincerely" (U.S., President Carter, 1977b, p. 330).

The Soviet Union was not only unlikely to be expansionist, but the Carter Administration believed it could contribute a cooperative hand in promoting a global community. In evaluating the Soviet intentions in the world, the Administration had a generally positive impression 71.4 percent of the time, as opposed to a negative evaluation 28.6 percent of the time (see table 3.4). According to President Carter, "we shape our own policies to accommodate a constantly changing world, and we hope the Soviets will do the same.

Table 3.4

Image of the Soviet Union

	Year			
Image	*1977*	*1978*	*1979*	*1980*
Soviet Intentions				
Expansionist, %	0.0	0.0	0.0	67.2
Opportunistic, %	9.1	22.2	−7.1	22.4
Coop + Comp, %	36.4	44.4	7.1	1.7
Cooperative, %	54.5	33.3	35.7	8.6
	N = 11	N = 18	N = 14	N = 58
Soviet Evaluation				
Negative, %	28.6	65.4	70.0	91.1
Positive, %	71.4	34.6	30.0	8.9
	N = 7	N = 26	N = 10	N = 45

Note: "Coop" refers to cooperative; "comp" refers to competitive. Given the limited number of cases, the frequency distributions should be used as a rough indicator.

Together we can give this change a positive direction'' (U.S., President Carter, 1977e, p. 196). Both Vance and Carter believed that the Soviet Union would play a constructive role and, therefore, should be involved in the effort to resolve the Arab-Israeli conflict.

President Carter was the most optimistic concerning the Soviet Union's peaceful intentions:

> Beyond all the disagreements between us—and beyond the cool calcula-tions of mutual self-interest that our two countries bring to the negotiating table—is the invisible human reality that must bring us closer together. I mean the yearning for peace, real peace, that is in the very bones of us all. . . . Mr. Brezhnev said something very interesting recently, and I quote from his speech: "It is our belief, our firm belief," he said, "that realism in politics and the will for detente and progress will ultimately triumph and mankind will be able to step into the 21st century in condi-tions of peace stable as never before." I see no hidden meanings in that. I credit its sincerity. And I express the same hope and belief that Mr. Brezhnev expressed. With all the difficulties, all the conflicts, I believe that our planet must finally obey the Biblical injunction to "follow after the things which make for peace." (U.S., President Carter, 1977e, p. 197)

Vance shared President Carter's general sense of optimism about United States-Soviet relations, but took a lower-key and more pragmatic approach:

> I think that detente does exist today, and I believe and hope that it will continue to exist. I think it is in the interests of both of our nations to search for common ground and to lessen the tensions which divide the nations. In this process I think it is necessary to try and work out a clear understanding of what the meaning of detente is as between the two nations. In a sense, it is the setting down or arriving at a set of ground rules which permit competition side by side with the resolution of out-standing questions. And it is not, again, a simple task. (U.S., Secretary Vance, 1977a, p. 280)

This optimistic vision of the Soviet Union explains why there was little attention toward it in 1977—it was rank-ordered second in importance and addressed only 16.6 percent of the time (see table 3.2 above). The Administra-tion did not believe it needed to concentrate on the Soviet-American relation-ship and East-West issues. The containment of Soviet expansionism as the foundation of American foreign policy was rejected. As described by Carter:

Our national security was often defined almost exclusively in terms of military competition with the Soviet Union. This competition is still critical, because it does involve issues which could lead to war. But however important this relationship of military balance, it cannot be our sole preoccupation, to the exclusion of other world issues which also concern us both. (U.S., President Carter, 1977e, pp. 193–194)

In fact, with respect to the seven major issues that were of principal concern throughout the first year, Carter policymakers believed that the Soviet Union had a major role to play only in arms control. The Soviet Union was discussed well under 10 percent of the time relative to the other six major issues: normalization of relations, the Arab-Israeli conflict, Third World development, human rights, the conflict in Africa, and the global economy (see table 3.5).

Although Carter Administration policymakers shared a similar image of the Soviet Union, minor differences in individual images could still be found. Despite Brzezinski's desire to promote a cooperative relationship with the Soviet Union, he was more skeptical than President Carter and Secretary Vance about the Soviets' peaceful intentions:

To be perfectly blunt . . . given the fact we still live in a world in which there is competition between the United States and the Soviet Union, given the fact that the Soviet Union has a different view of global change than we do in many significant respects, that the Soviet Union may be

Table 3.5

Significance of the Soviet Union for Each Major Issue, 1977

Issue	USSR (%)
Arms Control	69.8
Normalization	7.6
Middle East Conflict	6.8
Development	6.7
Human Rights	5.7
African Conflict	4.4
Economy	2.9
N = 391	N = 65

Note: Number of cases indicates the frequency relative to all the actors and to the Soviet Union.

tempted to adopt policies and to take actions which would exacerbate and fuel conflicts. (U.S., NSC Assistant Brzezinski, 1977d, p. 801)

This evaluation was largely derived from Brzezinski's appraisal that the Soviet Union was "still on the upswing of the historical cycle—of assertiveness, of expectations. I think it would like to be number one. I don't think it feels comfortable being number two militarily and a much lower number on many other areas—social, economic, and technological. So, I think they're driven by ambition, and they're assertive" (U.S., NSC Assistant Brzezinski, 1977d, p. 802). Thus, as long as the Soviet Union had high expectations and remained inferior, Brzezinski believed, it would have to be considered potentially dangerous.

Yet, at the same time, Brzezinski believed that "just as the United States has gone through an imperialist cycle, and then waned, so it is my hope that the Russians will increasingly move into the world in a more cooperative, less imperially assertive fashion and begin participating in what is gradually, truly emerging: namely, a global community" (U.S., NSC Assistant Brzezinski, 1977b, p. 29). Therefore, whereas Secretary Vance and, in particular, President Carter were basically *optimistic* concerning the Soviet Union's intentions to play a cooperative role, NSC Advisor Brzezinski was more ambivalent. On the one hand he was hopeful that a cooperative relationship could be promoted, on the other hand he was skeptical for it was likely that the Soviet Union would try to take advantage of trouble-spots and instability. This ambivalence is clearly revealed in the following statement:

We need to place the American-Soviet relationship in a wider context, in which it is part of a wider fabric of international cooperation, to the extent that we can engage the Soviet Union in such wider cooperation regionally or functionally or, specifically, on the strategic plane. At the same time, we need to remind ourselves and particularly our public that that relationship with the Soviet Union will be both cooperative and competitive for a very long time to come, with that competition imposing necessary limits on the scope of the cooperation. (U.S., NSC Assistant Brzezinski, 1978a, p. 21)

Brzsezinski was both *hopeful yet skeptical* concerning the future of Soviet behavior. He hoped that they would participate and cooperate in addressing the major global issues. Though he recognized the limited capabilities and international constraints imposed on the Soviet Union, he did not share Vance's and, in particular, Carter's optimism about Soviet intentions. Brzezinski saw a rockier road concerning the future of U.S.-Soviet relations and, consequently, the realization of a global community.

> I can say this: We are challenging the Soviets to co-operate with us or run the risk of becoming historically irrelevant to the great issues of our time. We're not being naive in the sense of expecting an instant accommodation. I think we're reasonably vigilant to the fact that the competition goes on and therefore we have to compete. But we are also very much aware of the fact that in this shrinking world the imperative of co-operation has become more urgent. (U.S., NSC Assistant Brzezinski, 1977a, p. 4)

For Brzezinski "the objective is thus to assimilate East-West relations into a broader framework of cooperation, rather than to concentrate on East-West relations as the decisive and dominant concern of our times." The United States needed to respond to global complexity and the changes taking place throughout the world.

> We must respond to a wider range of issues—some of which still involve the Cold War—issues stemming from a complex process of global change. A concentrated foreign policy must give way to a complex foreign policy, no longer focused on a single, dramatic task—such as the defense of the West. Instead, we must engage ourselves on the distant and difficult goal of giving shape to a world that has suddenly become politically awakened and socially restless. (U.S., NSC Assistant Brzezinski, 1977c, p. H12002)

Subtle differences in images of the international system did exist among the three policymakers during the first year, especially between President Carter's and Secretary Vance's optimistic image versus NSC Advisor Brzezinski's hopeful but skeptical image of the Soviet Union. President Carter was the most optimistic about the future of the international system. Yet even with these differences, the optimistic image of a complex international system and a quest for global community was widely shared within the Carter Administration. As summarized by President Carter:

> Our policy is based on a historical vision of America's role. Our policy is derived from a large view of global change. Our policy is rooted in our moral values, which never change. Our policy is reinforced by our material wealth and by our military power. Our policy is designed to serve mankind. (U.S., President Carter, 1977d, p. 625)

1978: Emergence of Policymaker Differences in Images

While the Carter Administration's image concerning a complex international system and global change continued into its second year in office, it was soon challenged by Soviet and Cuban intervention in Africa. With these events the Administration's shared image of the international system began to dissolve and differences in individual images clearly emerged. President Carter and Secretary of State Vance adhered to an image of global complexity and the pursuit of global community; however, National Security Advisor Brzezinski's image began to place greater emphasis on political-military issues and the need to contain the Soviet Union's foreign interventionism.

Foreign Interventionism in Africa

Conflict in the Horn of Africa became the most significant issue for the Carter Administration in 1978. The previous year, Somalia invaded Ethiopia in an effort to capture the Ogaden region—long claimed by Somalia. The Somali intrusion was successfully repulsed by Ethiopia, only after Ethiopia received a considerable amount of military assistance from the Soviet Union and Cuba, including the use of Cuban troops. During the early part of 1978 it appeared that Ethiopia might take advantage of its new-found strength and threaten the territorial integrity of Somalia and the surrounding region. Around the same time, Zaire's Katanga province, which contained valuable copper mines, was invaded by a force of uncertain origin from neighboring Angola.

These events prompted Carter Administration officials to question their optimistic image of the Soviet Union. What emerged as the dominant pattern in image was no longer a perception of Soviet intentions as primarily cooperative, but mixed—both cooperative and competitive (see table 3.4 above). Likewise, the Carter Administration's positive evaluation of the Soviet role in the world was replaced by a much more skeptical and negative perception (65.4 percent negative evaluation of the Soviet Union in 1978 versus 71.4 percent positive evaluation in 1977).

Along with this change in perception of Soviet intentions came a shift in thinking about the Soviet Union's importance in the globe. Whereas in 1977 the Soviet Union was perceived to be of major global significance only for the issue of arms control, now in 1978 it was considered to be important relative to five of the seven major issues: arms control, Western security and defense, the normalization of relations, the conflict in Africa, and human rights (see table 3.6). In Africa, the Carter Administration turned much of its attention toward the Soviet Union and Cuba, which administration policymakers believed acted as a surrogate for Soviet foreign policy. The events in Africa lifted them from minor players in the region to two of the area's most important actors in the eyes of the Carter Administration. (see table 3.7).[3]

This reassessment of the Soviet Union's global role affected the Administration's general image of the international system. Although President Carter and Secretary Vance became more skeptical of the Soviet Union, they retained their generally optimistic image of the international system. NSC Advisor Brzezinski was greatly affected by Soviet and Cuban interventionism in Africa. His image became pessimistic about the future of the international system—what hope he had about the future of Soviet behavior was lost. Thus we can see that the originally optimistic collective image of a complex international system was modified by the emergence of policymaker differences in images.

Continuity in Carter's and Vance's Image

The Soviet's activity in Africa was judged a serious breach of good faith in President Carter's mind:

To the Soviet Union, detente seems to mean a continuing aggressive struggle for political advantage and increased influence in a variety of ways. The Soviet Union apparently sees military power and military assistance as the best means of expanding its influence abroad. Obviously areas of instability in the world produce a tempting target for this effort

Table 3.6

Significance of the Soviet Union for Each Major Issue, 1978

Issue	USSR (%)
Arms Control	78.2
Western Security	53.3
Normalization	19.7
African Conflict	18.8
Human Rights	16.3
Economy	7.6
Middle East Conflict	1.9
N = 554	N = 153

Note: Number of cases indicates the frequency relative to all the actors and to the Soviet Union

Table 3.7

Actor Importance for the Conflict in Africa

	Year	
Actor	1977	1978
Soviet Union, %	4.4	18.8
Black Africa, %	22.2	13.5
South Africa, %	20.0	13.5
Cuba, %	6.7	10.5
Western Europe, %	13.4	8.3
United Nations, %	15.6	6.8
Nigeria, %	0.0	4.5
Angola, %	0.0	3.8
Ethiopia, %	2.2	3.0
Organization of African Unity, %	2.2	2.2
Somalia, %	0.0	2.2
Rhodesia, %	6.7	1.5
Others, %	6.6	11.4
	N = 45	N = 133

Note: Number of cases indicates the frequency relative to all the actors.

and all too often they seem ready to exploit any such opportunities. (U.S., President Carter, 1978d, p. 15)

Vance shared this concern:

The continued presence of large quantities of Soviet arms and thousands of Cuban troops in certain parts of Africa raises serious concerns. The size and duration of their military presence jeopardizes the independence of African status. It creates concern on the part of African nations that outside weapons and troops will be used to determine the outcome of any conflict on the continent. And it renders more difficult the efforts of Africans to resolve these disputes through peaceful means. (U.S., Secretary Vance, 1978d, p. 10)

It was in this context that President Carter in his Annapolis address on June 7 challenged the Soviet Union to "choose either confrontation or cooperation. The United States is adequately prepared to meet either choice" (U.S., President Carter, 1978d, p. 16).

Though the Soviet Union's foreign interventionism in Africa made President Carter and Secretary Vance more skeptical concerning their perception of

Soviet intentions, their optimism was not seriously shaken. Immediately after his challenge to the Soviet Union in the Annapolis speech, Carter acknowledged that he would like to avoid confrontation and stated:

> We would prefer cooperation through a detente that increasingly involves similar restraints for both sides, similar readiness to resolve disputes by negotiations and not by violence, similar willingness to compete peacefully and not militarily. Anything less than that is likely to undermine detente. . . . A competition without restraint and without shared rules will escalate into graver tensions, and our relationship will suffer. I do not wish this to happen, and I do not believe that Mr. Brezhnev desires it. (U.S., President Carter, 1978d, p. 16)

Carter and Vance believed that there was no need for the United States to overreact to the events in Africa. As conveyed by Secretary Vance:

> It will not be our policy to mirror Soviet and Cuban activities in Africa because such a course would not be effective in the long run and would only escalate military conflict with great human suffering. Our best course is to help resolve the problems which create the excuse for external intervention and to help strengthen the ability of Africans to defend themselves. (U.S., Secretary Vance, 1978d, p. 10)

In fact, the United States would continue to "welcome Soviet help—which we regret we have not had—in achieving a peaceful transition to majority rule in Rhodesia, Namibia, and elsewhere in Africa" (U.S., Secretary Vance, 1978c, p. 16).

Carter and Vance maintained that United States foreign policy needed to continue to pursue the goal of a global community in a complex environment. A reliance on military instruments of foreign policy would be counterproductive to this quest in the long run. During the crisis in the Horn of Africa, Carter reaffirmed his reluctance to use military force unless there was a direct threat to U.S. security. The lessons of Vietnam were clear.

> We don't have any inclination to be involved in the internal affairs of another country unless our security should be directly threatened, and that's a philosophy that I have espoused ever since I've been in the national political realm. I just think we've learned our lessons the hard way in Vietnam and in other instances. (U.S., President Carter, 1978g, p. 15)

As for preferred methods, Carter and Vance adhered to a preventive approach that directed the United States to take action as early as possible in order to resolve key global problems rather than wait for issues to reach the crisis stage. This approach attempted to address the fundamental causes (rather than treat the symptoms) through the employment of a variety of policy instruments—political, military, economic, and cultural. The use of diplomacy was particularly important for promoting peace in areas like Africa and the Middle East. Such an approach would hopefully defuse potentially explosive issues and avoid the tendency for American overreaction. A preventive approach "combines efforts to avoid East-West confrontation and positive regional policies that respond to local realities" (U.S., Secretary Vance, 1978d, p. 12).

Ultimately, Carter and Vance believed that the Soviets' opportunistic adventures would fail. They regarded the international system as too diverse and decentralized for foreign intervention to make much of an impact. While the Soviets might enjoy success temporarily, it was only a matter of time before the African states would reject them and turn to the West. "We come in later with economic aid, with trade, with friendship, with the commitment to democracy and human rights, and I believe in the long run our system will prevail" (U.S., President Carter, 1978c, p. 21).

Carter and Vance, though challenged by the Soviet Union's interventionist role in Africa, did not see it as part of a larger pattern of Soviet behavior. The U.S.-Soviet relationship, according to Vance,

> is not a relationship with a single dimension but with many; that even as we have sharp differences, as we inevitably will, there are many other areas in which we continue to cooperate and to seek useful agreement; and that to view U.S.-Soviet relations from the perspective of a single dimension is to run the risk of failing to identify our interests carefully and to act accordingly. (U.S., Secretary Vance, 1978c, p. 14)

Carter believed that there were two basic goals that motivated the Soviet Union's foreign policy. "First of all, they want peace and security for their own people, and they undoubtedly exaggerate any apparent threat to themselves . . . At the same time, as is the case with us, they would like to expand their influence among other people in the world, believing that their system of government, their philosophy, is the best" (U.S., President Carter, 1978g, p. 14). Given the mixed motives and complexity of the relationship, America's "long-term objectives must be to convince the Soviet Union of the advantages of cooperation and of the costs of disruptive behavior" (U.S., President Carter, 1978d, p. 14).

Continuing to see the United States as a more powerful and attractive force throughout the world, power, for Carter and Vance, meant much more than military capability:

> We in our country are in a much more favorable position. Our industrial base and our productivity are unmatched; our scientific and technological capability is superior to all others; our alliances with other free nations are strong and growing stronger; and our military capability is now and will be second to none. (U.S., President Carter, 1978d, p. 15)

The United States was surrounded by friends, the Soviet Union surrounded by enemies. Furthermore, America's commitment to the goals of justice, equity, human rights, and freedom "are the wave of the future. We should not fight this wave. We should ride it, be part of it, encourage it, let it nurture a better life for those who yearn and for those of us who already enjoy" (U.S., President Carter, 1978f, p. 13).

For Carter and Vance, the purpose behind American foreign policy in 1978 remained largely intact from that of 1977—the positive promotion of change, international cooperation, and global community. They continued to believe that mankind and the international system could be reformed and improved. As Vance stated early in January 1978, "in the past year, President Carter has led us to make hard decisions that have shown again that our country has not lost its faith in man's perfectability" (U.S., Secretary Vance, 1978a, p. 26).

Brzezinski's Change in Image

If Carter and Vance's image remained largely unaffected by events in 1978, Brzezinski's image of the international system was significantly transformed and seems to have been deeply influenced by Soviet interventionism in Africa. The pursuit of global community through international cooperation was no longer emphasized in his statements. Brzezinski lost his "hope" and became increasingly skeptical concerning Soviet cooperation and the positive benefits of a complex international system.

Brzezinski tended to see a larger pattern behind Soviet activities in Africa than either Carter or Vance:

> I am troubled by the fact that the Soviet Union has been engaged in a sustained and massive effort to build up its conventional forces, particularly in Europe, to strengthen the concentration of its forces on the frontiers of China, to maintain a vitriolic worldwide propaganda campaign against the United States, to encircle and penetrate the Middle East,

to stir up racial difficulties in Africa, and to make more difficult a moderate solution of these difficulties. (U.S., NSC Assistant Brzezinski, 1978c, p. 27)

In his opinion, the "debate about the Horn is really about the more fundamental question of what is the nature of detente. . . . It's about one's view of the world: should there be rules, or is the relationship an end in itself?" (Drew, 1978, p. 118). Brzezinski believed that Soviet behavior, for example in Africa, was incompatible with detente.

Detente really is a process of trying to contain some of the competitive aspects in the relationship, competitive aspects which I believe still are predominant, and to widen the cooperative aspects. . . . I would say that today the competitive aspects have somewhat surfaced and I would say categorically that this is due to the shortsighted Soviet conduct in the course of the last 2 or so years. (U.S., NSC Assistant Brzezinski, 1978c, p. 27)

At first Brzezinski suggested that the problem was that the international system was inherently unstable because of its complexity—that a turbulent and conflictual world was as likely a possibility as a cooperative world. It wasn't that the Soviet Union would or could expand throughout the globe. "I really don't believe that the Soviet Union, for example, can ever outbid us militarily, certainly not economically, certainly not ideologically. I therefore don't see the problem for the future that some hostile power will establish its supremacy over us, and thereby also gain world domination" (U.S., NSC Assistant Brzezinski, 1978b, p. 21). The principal danger was that the international system was undergoing changes that provided the Soviets numerous opportunities to exploit.

Two global changes had come together to make the world a much more complex place. "First, the world's population is experiencing a political awakening on a scale without precedent in its history; and second, the global system is undergoing a significant redistribution of political and economic power" (U.S., NSC Assistant Brzezinski, 1978d, p. 1). These changes provided the opportunity for greater global cooperation, but also had the possibility for producing greater turbulence and global conflict.

We are therefore confronted with the task of either developing broader, more diversified forms of cooperation worldwide, new institutions, new processes, or, alternatively, face the prospect of increasing turbulence, conflict, its exploitation by our adversaries, as, for example, we see right now in Africa, but eventually more and more chaos. (U.S., NSC Assistant Brzezinski, 1978b, p. 21).

This is why Brzezinski was extremely concerned about Soviet interventionist activities in the Horn of Africa; he was "fearful that the Soviets might be tempted to exploit this in a shortsighted fashion" (U.S., NSC Assistant Brzezinski, 1979e, p. 59).

Later in the year Brzezinski's concern with the Soviet threat heightened, and he emphasized a new theme—the *arc of crisis*. The international system was not only unstable and susceptible to adventurism, but the Soviet Union was growing in power and more willing to project this power globally. These two trends, "the increase in Soviet power and the disintegration of political fabric in some regions of the world," produced an arc of crisis—in the Persian Gulf, in Iran, all the way down to southern Africa (U.S., Brzezinski, 1979e, p. 71). In his view, if the international system continued to deteriorate "the resulting political chaos could well be filled by elements hostile to our values and sympathetic to our adversaries. This could face the West as a whole with a challenge of significant proportions" (U.S., NSC Assistant Brzezinski, 1978d, p. 6).

Brzezinski continued to discuss the importance of the United States leading global change and promoting a cooperative world order. "We seek to manage change skillfully, in ways that meet the legitimate hopes of people for peace, prosperity, justice, and liberty. At the same time, we recognize the fragility of the human institutions conceived to protect these values" (U.S., NSC Assistant Brzezinski, 1978d, p. 1). However, it became clear that by the end of the year Brzezinski lost his hope for Soviet cooperation and the positive benefits of a complex international system. Believing that the international system was becoming increasingly fragile and unstable, greater attention had to be spent on containing the Soviet Union and maintaining the security and defense of the West.

> We are committed to the shaping of a more cooperative and just world. But this does not mean ignoring concrete national security concerns, such as those mentioned above. The renovation of the international system through wider participation and more cooperation is the proper response to global political awakening, as is the maintenance of allied power and western will. (U.S., NSC Assistant Brzezinski, 1978d, p. 6).

The Collective Image

Thus, during 1978 the Carter Administration's collective image of the international system began to change. Individual differences in image surfaced and began to widen as Brzezinski's image of the Soviet Union became much more pessimistic. However, this was countered by the overlap between

Carter's and Vance's optimistic images and resulted in the Administration's continuing effort to promote a global community in a complex world.

Vance and particularly Carter did acknowledge they would have to be a bit more concerned with defense and security questions. The Soviet Union's military buildup and its foreign interventionism caused concern. The United States needed to be militarily prepared in case the global situation deteriorated. In Carter's view, "we can readily afford the necessary costs of our military forces, as well as an increased level, if needed, to prevent any adversary from destabilizing the peace of the world. . . . This investment purchases our freedom to fulfill the worthy goals of our nation" (U.S., President Carter, 1978b, p. 19).

Many other issues, however, also had to be addressed in "a changing and pluralistic international system, with over 150 independent nations and emerging new power centers. No single nation, or group of nations, can dictate solutions to these complex problems. They are truly international in their origins and in the necessary scope of their solutions" (U.S. Secretary Vance, 1979a, p. 13). President Carter clearly described the changes that had taken place in the last few decades:

> Before World War II, 80% of the world's land mass and 75% of its people were under Western authority, but today there are more than 100 new nations, each with insistent needs and insistent demands. A few years ago, the West made virtually all the decisions about the global economy, but now important resources are also under the control of the developing countries—as the energy crisis has made very clear. (U.S., President Carter, 1978d, p. 14)

In fact, the same issues that were of greatest importance to the Carter Administration in 1977 continued to be important in 1978 because of the overlap in Carter's and Vance's optimistic image. The promotion of arms control and the negotiation of a SALT II treaty, a flourishing global economy, the spread of human rights, the normalization of relations especially with China and through the Panama Canal treaties, and the peaceful resolution of the Arab-Israeli conflict, were all high priority items for the Carter Administration (see table 3.8).

It needs to be recognized that although Carter, Vance, and Brzezinski no longer shared a similar image of the international system, they did not differ over all the major issues. For those issues involving or affecting the Soviet Union, such as arms control and the conflicts in Africa involving the Horn and Zaire, the differences in image were severe. However, for other issues in which the Soviet Union was perceived to be peripheral, such as human rights,

1978: EMERGENCE OF DIFFERENCES

Table 3.8

Issues Perceived, 1978

Issue	Beliefs (%)
African Conflict	21.0
Arms Control	16.0
Economy	12.4
Security + Defense	11.9
Human Rights	11.6
Normalization	8.9
Middle East Conflict	7.4
Development	5.1
Other Conflict	2.7
Energy	2.0
Southwest Asian Conflict	0.9
	N = 886

the global economy, and the Arab-Israeli conflict, the Carter officials thought much alike.

For example, the promotion of human rights remained the cornerstone of the Carter Administration's foreign policy. All three policymakers believed it was important to identify the United States with the promotion of human rights and democracy. "I want to stress again," stated President Carter,

> that human rights are not peripheral to the foreign policy of the United States. Our human rights policy is not a decoration. It is not something we've adopted to polish up our image abroad or to put a fresh coat of moral paint on the discredited policies of the past. Our pursuit of human rights is part of a broad effort to use our great power and our tremendous influence in the service of creating a better world. (U.S., President Carter, 1979a, p. 2)

Brzezinski described how human rights was the unique province of the United States:

> If there's anything unique about America, it is that it's a nation that came together on behalf of certain ideals. We're not a nation that grew up organically out of shared experience, shared language. We're a nation that came together because there were certain compelling ideas that united us. That's why we're united more by the future than by our past.

> And our fundamental ideas involve some basic concepts relating to the nature of man, his relationship to government and to society, or what is currently called human rights. (U.S., NSC Assistant Brzezinski, 1978b, p. 26)

The promotion of human rights and democracy was the basis from which Vance attempted to resolve the conflict in southern Africa over Rhodesia, Namibia, and even South Africa.

> Some have argued that apartheid in South Africa should be ignored for the time being in order to concentrate on achieving progress on Rhodesia and Namibia. Such a policy would be wrong and would not work. It would be blind to the reality that the beginning of progress must be made soon within South Africa if there is to be a possibility of peaceful solutions in the longer run. It could mislead the South Africans about our real concerns. It would prejudice our relations with our African friends. It would do a disservice to our own beliefs. And it would discourage those of all races who are working for peaceful progress within South Africa. (U.S., Secretary Vance, 1978a, pp. 24–25)

Although the Soviet Union was the most important actor in 1978, it did not preoccupy the Carter Administration (see table 3.9). Western Europe and Japan, African actors, global actors, and Middle Eastern actors all maintained prominent places on the Carter agenda. As in 1977, a different set of actors were important for addressing each issue. The activities of Third World countries were particularly vital in explaining the Administration's reluctance to focus on Soviet interventionism and its continued optimistic image of the international system. "This diversity and the irrepressible thirst for national freedom among the Third World nations are the surest barriers to foreign domination. We can best promote our own interests in these areas of the world by welcoming this diversity and respecting this spirit" (U.S., Secretary Vance, 1979a, p. 16).

Though foreign interventionism made Carter and Vance more skeptical concerning their perception of Soviet intentions, their optimism was not seriously shaken. The international system was observed to be too diverse and decentralized for foreign intervention to make much of an impact. International cooperation with the Soviet Union continued to remain a primary goal. "I have a deep belief that the underlying relationship between ourselves and the Soviets is stable," stated the President, "and that Mr. Brezhnev, along with myself, wants peace and wants to have a better friendship" (U.S., President Carter, 1978e, p. 8). While more skeptical than before and beset by

Table 3.9

Actors Perceived, 1978

Actors	Beliefs (%)
Soviet Union	27.6
Western Europe + Japan	20.4
Africa	19.9
Global	11.9
Middle East	10.3
Latin America	4.9
China + Asia	3.1
Eastern Europe	2.0
	N = 554

internal differences, the Carter Administration remained committed to building a global community in a complex world.

1979: A Divided Administration

In 1979 the differences in individual images of the Carter Administration regarding the international system sharpened. Although Secretary Vance continued to adhere to an image of a complex international system and remained optimistic concerning a new world order, National Security Advisor Brzezinski perceived an increasingly fragmented and unstable international system open to Soviet interventionism. President Carter at times shared Vance's optimistic image of a complex international system but also displayed pessimism more in line with Brzezinski's view. Consequently, two competing images existed in 1979.

Vance's Optimistic Image

Secretary Vance continued to perceive a very complex, diverse and pluralistic international system in which "the simple notion of a bipolar world has become obsolete. Increasingly there is a profusion of different systems and allegiances and a diffusion of political and military power" (U.S., Secretary Vance, 1979f, p. 1). The present was a time of global interdependence where problems could only be solved through international cooperation. An interdependent age meant that "each nation can surmount its own difficulties only if it understands and helps resolve the difficulties of others as well" (U.S., Secretary Vance, 1979c, p. 35).

Vance remained optimistic about the prospects of a global community and the constructive role the United States could play. The changes that were occurring throughout this complex world meant that it was more important than ever for the United States to take the lead.

> We would imperil our future if we lost confidence in ourselves and in our strength and retreated from energetic leadership in the world. And we would imperil our future, as well, if we reacted in frustration and used our power to resist change in the world or employed our military power when it would do more harm than good. . . . If we appreciate the extraordinary strengths we have, if we understand the nature of the changes taking place in the world, and if we act effectively to use our different kinds of power to shape different kinds of change, we have every reason to be confident about our future. (U.S., Secretary Vance, 1979d, p. 16)

In fact, Vance believed that "we have a capacity for leadership—and an ability to thrive in a world of change—that is unsurpassed" (U.S., Secretary Vance, 1979d, p. 16).

While the United States could no longer dominate such a complex world, Vance believed that America could exercise leadership for the purpose of promoting positive change and a more cooperative world order.

> A world where many must participate in designing the future rather than a few, where progress often requires cooperative effort, demands more— not less—American leadership. It requires us to exercise that leadership creatively, to inspire others to work with us toward goals we share but cannot achieve separately. It calls for a new kind of diplomacy. (U.S., Secretary Vance, 1979d, p. 18).

Thus, the United States had to work with others to foster a global community. "Such multilateral efforts are time consuming and complex. But they can often be more productive than working alone" (U.S., Secretary Vance, 1979d, p. 18).

Vance insisted that the United States emphasize positive and peaceful change.

> We cannot let ourselves be diverted by the myth that if we encourage change or deal with the forces of change, we only encourage radicalism. The fact is that we can no more stop change than Canute could still the waters. Our strengths and our principles can help us promote peaceful change and orderly reform that strengthen the ties between government and people. For once such ties are broken, and a government has lost its

legitimacy in the eyes of its people, no amount of outside intervention can secure its long-term survival. It is profoundly in our national interest, therefore, that we support constructive change before such ties erode and the alternatives of radicalism or repression drive out moderate solutions. (U.S., Secretary Vance, 1979e, p. 8)

Support for constructive changes meant the United States must practice preventive diplomacy and promote the welfare of the Third World. "Peace and prosperity for ourselves, now and for the future, is directly related to the strength of our relations with the developing nations and the political and economic paths they choose to pursue" (U.S., Secretary Vance, 1979e, p. 7).

Vance took an active interest in attempting to resolve regional conflicts throughout the world. He realized that, if these conflicts were allowed to fester, they could stifle America's efforts at building a more cooperative and better world order. "As more nations acquire more sophisticated arms, regional conflicts become more dangerous. They pose a constant threat of wider confrontation. As a result, the United States must be more active in working to help settle these disputes peacefully" (U.S., Secretary Vance, 1979d, p. 17).

The key was to understand and respond to the local causes of the conflict, not to treat the regional conflict as part of the East-West competition. Vance was aware that "there are areas where the Soviets have gained influence in recent years. But there are as many, if not more, areas where their influence has waned" (U.S., Secretary Vance, 1979e, p. 8). Therefore, "it should not and will not be our policy to mirror Soviet tactics in developing nations" (U.S., Secretary Vance, 1979b, p. 22). The United States, instead, should emphasize a preventive policy of becoming involved before the situation deteriorated, promoting constructive change in order to help the Third World "develop their own institutions, strengthen their own economies, and foster ties between government and people" (U.S., Secretary Vance, 1979d, p. 18).

This strategy of affirmative involvement and support for the independence and the diversity of developing nations serves us well. It capitalizes on the West's inherent strengths. And it improves our ties to developing countries in a context which does not force them to make an explicit choice between East and West. (U.S., Secretary Vance, 1979d, p. 18).

The one thing the United States could not afford to do was to rely on the use of military force to resolve regional conflicts. In Vance's mind, utilizing military means to resolve internal conflicts would prove counterproductive in the short as well as the long run. Force was to be used only when the vital interests of the United States were directly threatened.

> Let me state first that the use of military force is not, and should not be, a desirable American policy response to the internal politics of other nations. We believe we have the right to shape our destiny; we must respect that right in others. We must clearly understand the distinction between our readiness to act forcefully when the vital interests of our nation, our allies, and our friends are threatened and our recognition that our military forces cannot provide a satisfactory answer to the purely *internal* problems of other nations. (U.S., Secretary Vance, 1979d, p. 18)

In responding to regional conflicts and other issues it would be counterproductive to become preoccupied with the Soviet Union. This is why, for example, it was crucial for the United States to take an "evenhanded" approach in relations with China and the Soviet Union. "It is U.S. policy that we will treat the People's Republic of China and the Soviet Union in a balanced way. Our policy toward them will be balanced and there will be no tilt one way or the other, and this is an absolutely fundamental principle" (U.S., Secretary Vance, 1979b, p. 21).

Given the complexity of the international environment, Secretary Vance believed that the United States should, and could, successfully respond to the global changes taking place. He believed that if the United States made a positive commitment in global leadership it was possible to promote a more stable, cooperative, and just world order.

> Most Americans now recognize that we alone cannot dictate events. This recognition is not a sign of America's decline; it is a sign of growing American maturity in a complex world. . . . There can be no going back to a time when we thought there could be American solutions to every problem. We must go forward into a new era of mature American leadership—based on strength, not belligerence; on steadiness, not impulse; on confidence, not fear" (U.S., Secretary Vance, 1979d, p. 19).

Brzezinski's Pessimistic Image

By 1979, Brzezinski's image of the international system was decidedly at odds with the vision held by Vance. For Brzezinski, the principal concern had become the growing arc of crisis and the Soviet willingness to exploit situations of instability. He was now very pessimistic about the prospects for global change. "Shaping a framework for global change while disregarding the realities of power would contribute to a fundamental instability in world affairs; it would transform global change from a potentially positive process into a condition of increasing fragmentation and eventual anarchy'' (U.S., NSC Assistant Brzezinski, 1979c, p. 1). Therefore, the United States needed to promote a strong national defense and emphasize the security of the West.

One still heard about the importance of promoting international cooperation and pursuing a global community, but these themes were overshadowed by Brzezinski's perception of an increasingly fragmented and unstable international system.

> This is why we have to be concerned about the arc of crisis that stretches across southern Asia to southern Africa. Within the area are countries whose internal difficulties make them vulnerable to external exploitation. We must not make the mistake of assuming that change and turbulence, by themselves, are evidence of external mischief. On the contrary, they are usually products of the particular historical dynamic of a particular country. But we must not make the equally serious mistake of ignoring the possibility of exploitation by outside forces that could create negative consequences for international stability. (U.S., NSC Assistant Brzezinski, 1979a, p. 4)

Priority was now given to the need to maintain global stability, although the United States would continue to promote a cooperative world order. ''Our collective security requires that the United States successfully maintain a global power equilibrium while helping to shape a framework for global change. These two imperatives—a power equilibrium and a framework for change—are not slogans. Each represents a difficult and vital process, critical to our national security'' (U.S., NSC Assistant Brzezinski, 1979c, p. 1).

The world was undergoing dramatic changes that were increasingly difficult to control. ''We are living through an era of the most *ex*tensive and *in*tensive political change in human history. Never before at one time have so many nations and peoples been subjected to so many political upheavals, to so many competing political ideologies, to so much rapid growth in mass political awareness'' (U.S., NSC Assistant, Brzezinski, 1979b, p. 1). The increase in political awakening and the redistribution of economic and political power were making the international system unstable and open to exploitation.

> This is creating enormous strains on the social fabric of some countries— and these strains become unmanageable when they are exploited by outside forces. The duty this imposes upon us is to engage other like-minded states in wider patterns of regional and international security and

development, so that a framework is created that cushions change and provides regional stability. (U.S., NSC Assistant, Brzezinski, 1979a, p. 4)

Brzezinski believed that the Soviets were the immediate cause behind growing global instability. Not only was the Soviet Union becoming stronger with time as a result of its military buildup, but it was not exercising restraint, thereby exacerbating regional conflicts and global tensions.

My concern for the future is not that some day the Soviet Union will achieve the kind of global predominance that we once had in the fifties. There will be no pax Sovietica to replace pax Americana. But if the Soviet Union is shortsighted and tries to exploit global turbulence in South Asia, in Africa, the Caribbean or elsewhere, it will contribute to a very unstable world which it will not be able to control, but which it will make it very incongenial for them and for us, and this is why we have to oppose these efforts. (U.S., NSC Assistant Brzezinski, 1979d, p. 38)

Brzezinski believed that the United States needed to strengthen its defense forces so as to deter Soviet aggression and promote Western security. "The military power of the United States is clearly a very important factor in such a world. For we must maintain adequate military power if we are to help steer change in positive directions. Military weakness on the part of the United States can create openings and temptations for our ideological opponents to exploit turbulence for their own selfish ends" (U.S., NSC Assistant Brzezinski, 1979b, p. 3). Hence, it was imperative that the United States emphasize the role of military power in order to respond to regional conflict and global instability.

American military power must be capable of protecting our key interests abroad, including the three vital strategic zones beyond our hemisphere: Western Europe, the Middle East, and the Far East. This means we must assure that we have the reach and the means to project our power where it is needed, and to do so in the appropriate form and level of intensity. (U.S., NSC Assistant Brzezinski, 1979b, p. 4)

Moreover, Brzezinski hoped that by making the necessary commitment to build up American power, this would lead to an end of the nation's "Vietnamese complex" (U.S., NSC Assistant Brzezinski, 1980a, p. 19).

Where once Brzezinski had hoped for a world made up of a community of nations, he now increasingly feared global fragmentation and chaos. Global changes were making the world a more dangerous place. The foundation of

American foreign policy, thus, should be to deter the threat of foreign expansionism in order to insure global stability and security, especially in Europe, the Far East and throughout the arc of crisis.

> Since 1945 the United States has been the pivotal element in the maintenance of global stability. Initially our primary focus was on the defense of Western Europe. Today, Western Europe, the Far East, and the Middle East represent three interrelated strategic zones of central importance to the survival of the West as a whole and to global economic stability. This is an important strategic reality, and it has political as well as military implications. The United States must work with the countries in all three zones to protect the independence of these regions. (U.S., NSC Assistant, Brzezinski, 1979c, p. 1).

Carter's Inconsistent Image

President Carter's image wavered between Vance's optimism and Brzezinski's pessimism. On the one hand, he was hopeful about the possibility of working with change and building a cooperative global community. On the other hand, he displayed skepticism concerning Soviet activities and the possibility of attaining a new world order. Statements that once described a peaceful transition to a global community now contained elements of worry and doubt about a world of turbulence.

Carter continued to adhere to many of the basic principles and preconceptions that had guided him through the first two years. At the beginning of the year President Carter attempted to coin a new phrase to represent his foreign policy—a *new foundation*. As he asserted in his State of the Union address, "we are building a new foundation for a peaceful and prosperous world" (U.S., President Carter, 1979c, p. 1).

Carter saw a world of great complexity, which the United States was no longer able to dominate.

> The problems we face today are different in nature from those that confronted earlier generations of Americans. They are more subtle, more complex, more interrelated. . . . Abroad, few of them can be solved by the United States alone. . . . We cannot resort to simplistic or extreme solutions which substitute myths for common sense. (U.S., President Carter, 1979c, p. 1)

Though the world had become interdependent and pluralistic, the United States continued "to be the most powerful nation on Earth—militarily, economically, and politically" (U.S., President Carter, 1979f, p. 4). Therefore, the United States actually had little to fear and could be confident about the future by providing leadership for a more cooperative world order. "We have no desire to be the world's policemen," stated President Carter, yet, "America does want to be the world's peacemaker" (U.S., President Carter, 1979c, p. 1).

Although the President continued to express hope for a cooperative and just global future, he also began to see the negative side of global complexity and change.

> We do not oppose change. Many of the political currents sweeping the world express a desire that we share—the desire for a world in which the legitimate aspirations of nations and individuals have a greater chance for fulfillment. The United States cannot control events within other nations. A few years ago, we tried this and we failed. But we recognized as inevitable that the uncertainty and the turmoil that come with change can have its darker side as well. (U.S., President Carter, 1979e, p. 21)

As Carter admitted, "one thing has not changed as much as I had hoped. It is still a world of danger, a world in which democracy and freedom are still challenged, a world in which peace must be rewon day by day" (U.S., President Carter, 1979e, p. 21). The choice was not between which super-power or way of life would dominate. "None can and will. The choice instead is between a world of anarchy and destruction, or a world of cooperation and peace" (U.S., President Carter, 1979c, p. 1).

Carter's ambivalence between his hope for the future versus fear of increasing turbulence was most clearly displayed relative to the problem of regional conflicts. A number of new events attracted the attention of the Carter Administration including the Iranian revolution, the Vietnamese invasion of Cambodia and China's attack on Vietnam, the crisis in Yemen, the Soviet brigade in Cuba, and the turmoil in Central America, and all raised doubts in Carter's mind about the possibility for a more peaceful world order. At times he seemed to acknowledge that something resembling Brzezinski's arc of crisis existed. "At this moment there is turmoil or change in various countries from one end of the Indian Ocean to the other" (U.S., President Carter, 1979f, p. 4). This situation could be very disruptive in a world of turbulence if exploited by foreign interventionism.

Carter thus became more concerned with the need to strengthen defense forces and protect the security of the West in order to promote global stability.

> In a world of accelerating change, fraught with potential danger and uncertainty, and marked by a continuing Soviet military buildup, we

must have, together with our allies, unsurpassed military capability to deter attack or attempts at political coercion. Moreover, we must have the military force to mount an effective defense at any level of hostilities where our vital interests are jeopardized. (U.S., President Carter, 1979d, p. 26)

He specifically proclaimed at the Georgia Institute of Technology that, "in the Middle East, in Southeast Asia, and elsewhere in the world, we will stand by our friends, we will honor our commitments, and we will protect the vital interests of the United States, and you can depend on it" (U.S., President Carter, 1979e, p. 23).

Although President Carter became more concerned about foreign interventionism and stability in a turbulent world, he was reluctant to use force or directly intervene in response to regional conflicts. He believed that the United States did not need to overreact to events around the world. "As the world becomes more complex, it's more important than ever before that we do not oversimplify events abroad. Bad analysis inevitably leads to bad policy" (U.S., President Carter, 1979f, p. 4).

Carter's image straddled the line between both Vance's optimistic and Brzezinski's pessimistic image. With respect to the Iranian revolution, Carter was hopeful that the situation would be peacefully resolved. He downplayed the need for a strong American response, recognizing the constraints on American power. "Certainly we have no desire nor ability to intrude massive forces into Iran or any other country to determine the outcome of domestic political issues. This is something that we have no intention of ever doing in another country. We've tried this once in Vietnam. It didn't work well, as you well know" (U.S., President Carter, 1979b, p. 3). At the same time, because Carter was also concerned that the situation could deteriorate and be exploited by foreign interventionism, he threatened possible American reprisal. "But just as we respect Iran's independence and integrity, other nations must do so as well. If others interfere, directly or indirectly, they are on notice that this will have serious consequences and will affect our broader relationships with them" (U.S., President Carter, 1979e, p. 22). Therefore, though Carter was reluctant to use force, he became more willing to do so. "We've learned the mistake of military intervention in the internal affairs of another country when our own American security was not directly involved. But we must understand that not every instance of the firm application of the United States is a potential Vietnam" (U.S., President Carter, 1980a, p. 58).

Carter saw two possible futures and was increasingly unsure which one would prevail: a future of positive change and movement toward a cooperative, peaceful world order or a future of negative change in which the world would become more turbulent and chaotic. "We need to resist two temptations: to see all change as inevitably against the interests of the United States, as kind of a loss for us or a victory for them; or to imagine that what happens in a country like Iran will not have consequences for us and for other regions as well" (U.S., President Carter, 1979f, p. 4). Wanting to protect America's security, yet not wanting to overreact, he was unsure how to respond.

> Our concern is twofold. We must work to dampen conflict, to maintain peace, and we must make clear that it's dangerous for outside powers to try to exploit for their own selfish benefits this inevitable turmoil. That kind of exploitation can damage not only the integrity and independence of the nations that happen to be in a transition phase but also can damage the effort to build a more secure and a more peaceful world for us all. (U.S., President Carter, 1979f, p. 4).

Much of Carter's uncertainty about the present and the possibilities for the future were a function of his image of the Soviet Union. The President had grown more skeptical about the Soviet Union's military buildup and its willingness to intervene in unstable situations abroad. He appeared to be increasingly torn between the cooperative and competitive aspects of the U.S.-Soviet relationship.

> As I have often said, our relationship with the Soviet Union is a mixture of cooperation and competition. And as President of the United States, I have no more difficult and delicate task than to balance these two. I cannot and I will not let the pressures of inevitable competition overwhelm the possibilities for cooperation any more than I will let cooperation blind us to the realities of competition, which we are fully prepared to meet. (U.S., President Carter, 1979e, p. 23)

Two Competing Images

Clearly, major differences in individual images of the international system intensified within the Carter Administration during 1979. Two divergent worldviews coexisted uneasily. Secretary Vance saw a complex international system that offered an opportunity to promote positive global change and the creation of a global community. Brzezinski observed a disintegrating international system that the Soviet Union was ready to exploit. President Carter attempted to fuse both optimistic and pessimistic visions, which resulted in an inconsistent image where he sometimes leaned toward Vance, other times toward Brzezinski.

1979: A DIVIDED ADMINISTRATION

The inconsistency and incoherence in the collective image is revealed when the major issues perceived by the Carter Administration are examined (see table 3.10). There was little consensus within the Carter Administration over the importance of the relative issues or how they should be addressed. The increased concern with the security and defense of the West and other regional conflict reflected a more pessimistic image of the international system. The other important issues focused on by the Administration reflected a more optimistic image of the international system: the Arab-Israeli conflict, the promotion of human rights, Third World development, arms control, normalization of relations, the global economy, and conflict resolution in Africa. But disagreement over the importance of the issues and America's role and purpose in addressing each issue was the norm.

Wherever the Soviet Union was perceived to be involved, dissensus and disagreement predominated. The Soviet Union was perceived to be important for those issues that directly affected the political-military situation of the United States, such as arms control, Western security and defense, and other regional conflicts (see table 3.11). These issues created the greatest amount of internal dissent within the Carter Administration, such as over the concept of linkage, the necessity for a military buildup, and the appropriate response to foreign interventionism. The Soviet Union remained relatively unimportant for the other major issues that the Carter Administration addressed. But even over these issues a lack of consensus was manifest: with disagreement

Table 3.10

Issues Perceived, 1979

Issue	Beliefs (%)
Middle East Conflict	15.0
Security + Defense	11.4
Human Rights	11.2
Development	10.8
Arms Control	10.0
Normalizaton	9.7
Economy	8.7
African Conflict	8.4
Other Conflict	8.1
Energy	4.4
Southwest Asian Conflict	2.2
	N = 712

existing, for example, over the pace, intensity, and purpose in normalizing relations with China and in resolving the conflict in southern Africa.

The development of this incoherent collective image of the international system stemmed from the two differing perceptions of the Soviet Union in 1979. One vision, represented by Vance, was relatively optimistic, regarded the Soviet Union in more cooperative terms, deemphasizing the conflictual side of the relationship. The other vision, represented by Brzezinski, perceived an opportunistic Soviet Union and was relatively pessimistic, deemphasizing the cooperative aspects of the U.S.-Soviet relationship (See table 3.4 above). Carter, as already discussed, attempted to straddle these two divergent images of the Soviet Union.

Overall in 1979, the Soviet Union continued to be only one of many important international actors that concerned the United States (see table 3.12). The Soviets were discussed 15.5 percent of the time, and were rank-ordered third in importance behind general global actors and Middle East actors (this reflected a drop of 12.1 percentage points from the previous high in 1978 when the Soviet Union received 27.6 percent of the attention). For those issues in which the Soviet Union was important, few other actors were perceived to be relevant. However, for those issues in which the Soviet Union remained unimportant, the Carter Administration perceived a variety of actors to be significant.

Table 3.11

Significance of the Soviet Union for Major Issues, 1979

Issue	USSR (%)
Arms Control	77.8
Western Security	61.1
Other Conflict	12.1
Normalization	6.3
African Conflict	3.2
Economy	3.0
Middle East Conflict	0.0
Development	0.0
Human Rights	0.0
N = 420	N = 65

Note: Number of cases indicates the frequence relative to all the actors and to the Soviet Union.

In summary, two divergent images, represented by Vance and Brzezinski, competed for ascendence within the Carter Administration. With Carter unable to fully adhere to either of the two competing images nor able to reconcile the differences between them, it was an incoherent image that survived as a divided Administration entered its fourth year.

1980: In Search of Global Stability

The fourth year witnessed the termination of the Carter Administration's search for a global community in a complex yet hopeful environment. In its place, the Administration developed a new image: a quest for global stability in an increasingly turbulent world. Global change was no longer seen as positive. The predominant focus became the containment of Soviet expansionism and maintenance of the West's security in Europe, the Far East and, of immediate concern, in Southwest Asia. President Carter and National Security Advisor Brzezinski were the major proponents of this new image of the international system.

Carter Administration officials still perceived a complex international system, but they were no longer optimistic concerning global change. "It's important that we take a hard, clear look together not at some simple world, either of universal goodwill or of universal hostility, but the complex, changing, and sometimes dangerous world that really exists" (U.S., President Carter, 1980d, p. 3). Unlike the earlier years, when the emphasis was on positive change and an effort to create a new world order, the international

Table 3.12

Actors Perceived, 1979

Actors	Beliefs (%)
Global	25.9
Middle East	21.9
Soviet Union	15.5
Western Europe + Japan	13.1
Latin America	11.2
China + Asia	9.3
Africa	3.1
Eastern Europe	0.2
	N = 420

system was now increasingly seen as turbulent and unstable. "The 1980s have been born in turmoil, strife, and change. This is a time of challenge to our interests and our values, and it's a time that tests our wisdom and our skills" (U.S., President Carter, 1980c, p. A).

Three simultaneous developments were believed to be challenging the United States and the West: the efforts for change occurring in many areas of the developing world resulting in the redistribution of global power; the overwhelming dependence of the industrialized democracies on oil from the Middle East; and the steady growth and global projection of Soviet military power (U.S., President Carter, 1980c, p. A). The arc of crisis had become the dominant feature of the international system with the result that "we are seeing the appearance of a new global process that has yet to take full shape, that has yet to acquire a stable framework, that is still in the process of significantly challenging the distribution of economic and political power" (U.S., NSC Assistant Brzezinski, 1980d, p. 1).

Two events in particular overwhelmed the thinking of Administration officials, especially Carter: the taking of American hostages in revolutionary Iran and the Soviet military intervention in Afghanistan.[4] According to President Carter, "these two acts—one of international terrorism and one of military aggression—present a serious challenge to the United States of America and indeed to all the nations of the world" (U.S., President Carter, 1980c, p. A). The Soviet invasion of Afghanistan was particularly upsetting because it represented the "first direct intrusion of Soviet Armed Forces beyond the borders of the Warsaw Pact nations since the Second World War" (U.S., President Carter, 1980d, p. 4). Accordingly, the Administration in 1980 focused primarily on the instability and turmoil emanating from the Persian Gulf and Southwest Asian region, and on the Soviet threat to the Western security.

It was argued that two goals were now the foundation of American foreign policy. "The first is to fashion and sustain a historically relevant relationship between the United States and the world, that for the first time in its history has become genuinely politically awakened. The second is to preserve and improve the geostrategic position of the United States in a world that remains very dangerous" (U.S., NSC Assistant Brzezinski, 1980c, p. 2). In other words, United States foreign policy goals were to promote global community and maintain global stability.[5] The need to respond to Soviet intervention and global instability, however, took precedence.

Issues integral to the earlier optimistic image of the international system receded in importance. Carter and Brzezinski still referred to the importance of other issues:

1980: IN SEARCH OF GLOBAL STABILITY

We will continue to work as we have for peace in the Middle East and southern Africa. We will continue to build our ties with developing nations, respecting and helping to strengthen their national independence, which they have struggled so hard to achieve. And we will continue to support the growth of democracy and the protection of human rights. (U.S., President Carter, 1980c, p. C).

But in comparison to the conflict in Southwest Asia and the promotion of Western security, conflict resolution in the Middle East, human rights, the normalization of relations, and arms control received much less attention. Other issues that in the past had been important to the Carter Administration were put on the back burner and forgotten: the conflict in Africa, the global economy, and Third World development (see table 3.13). As explained by Brzezinski: "We can not only help history along by positive deeds and by good intentions; we also have to play a stabilizing role, helping to provide a framework for orderly change, a framework of peace and stability" (U.S., NSC Assistant Brzezinski, 1980c, p. 4).

No longer was the world viewed as being increasingly pluralistic. Rather, the Soviet Union was now the dominant international actor, receiving 39.1 percent of the attention in 1980. Actors in the Middle East and Western Europe and Japan were also important, but other actors received much less attention

Table 3.13

Issues Perceived, 1980

Issue	Beliefs (%)
Southwest Asian Conflict	22.6
Security + Defense	18.0
Middle East Conflict	12.0
Human Rights	9.7
Normalization	9.6
Other Conflict	7.4
Arms Control	7.3
Energy	4.5
African Conflict	3.5
Economy	2.8
Development	2.6
	N = 1099

THE CARTER ADMINISTRATION'S IMAGES

(see table 3.14). Countries in the Middle East and Western Europe were seen as especially important for their roles in assisting America's drive to stop Soviet expansionism in Southwest Asia and the Soviet threat to Western security (see table 3.15). Only for the issues of human rights and normalization did the Carter Administration continue to see a variety of important actors.

Accordingly, U.S. foreign policy concentrated overwhelmingly on the Soviet Union. The Soviet Union received a disproportionate amount of attention for the two most important issues confronting the Carter Administration: the conflict in Southwest Asia and Western security and defense. It also was perceived to be the most important actor for other regional conflict and arms control. Where the Soviet Union was perceived to be important for only one of seven major issues (arms control) addressed in 1977, the Soviet Union was now perceived to be significant for five of the seven major issues addressed during a time of global turbulence (table 3.16).

Unlike the previous years, the Carter Administration viewed the Soviet Union very pessimistically. The Soviets were not only opportunistic, but primarily expansionistic in intentions and outlook. "The reality of the world today is that Moscow exploits unrest—not to address the discontent that underlies that unrest, not to overcome the inequalities that give rise to unrest, but to expand its own dominion and to satisfy its imperial objectives" (U.S., President Carter, 1980d, p. 4). The administration's evaluation of the Soviet Union's actions in global affairs was overwhelmingly negative in 1980 (see table 3.4).

The Soviet Union was considered the major destabilizing force in the world and a threat to the West. Soviet intervention in Afghanistan was associ-

Table 3.14

Actors Perceived, 1980

Actors	Beliefs (%)
Soviet Union	39.1
Middle East	20.8
Western Europe + Japan	15.1
Global	8.9
China + Asia	6.2
Latin America	5.3
Africa	3.6
Eastern Europe	1.1
	N = 663

Table 3.15

Actors Perceived for Each Major Issue, 1980

Issue	Soviet Union	Middle East	Western Europe + Japan	Actor (%) Global	China + Asia	Latin America	Africa	Eastern Europe	N
Southwest Asian Conflict	56.3	24.1	8.0	8.6	2.9	—	—	—	174
Security + Defense	63.9	—	32.0	—	2.0	—	—	2.0	97
Middle East Conflict	7.1	86.9	5.1	1.0	—	—	—	—	99
Human Rights	5.2	5.2	17.2	10.3	—	34.5	27.6	—	58
Normalization	17.5	2.5	22.5	13.7	27.5	8.7	3.7	3.7	80
Other Conflict	36.2	6.4	2.1	17.0	25.5	12.8	—	—	47
Arms Control	89.8	2.0	4.1	2.0	—	—	—	2.0	45

Table 3.16

Significance of the Soviet Union for Major
Issues, 1980

Issue	USSR (%)
Arms Control	89.8
Security + Defense	63.9
Southwest Asia Conflict	56.3
Other Conflict	36.2
Normalization	17.5
Middle East Conflict	7.1
Human Rights	5.2
N = 663	N = 253

Note: Number of cases indicates the frequency relative to all the actors and to the Soviet Union.

ated with aggression conducted by Hitler at Munich and during the war. ''The Soviet Union has taken a radical and an aggressive new step. It's using its great military power against a relatively defenseless nation. The implications of the Soviet invasion of Afghanistan could pose the most serious threat to peace since the Second World War'' (U.S., President Carter, 1980c, p. A).

Carter Administration officials did not believe that the Soviet Union could successfully achieve global hegemony, but it could instigate global chaos with shortsighted action, thereby indirectly threatening the United States.

> The Soviet Union is neither strong enough politically nor militarily to replace us in the role that we played in the '50s, when there was, for a brief historical lifespan, a pax Americana. But the Soviet Union has the capacity to contribute to some of the negative tendencies in these processes of change, exacerbating the elements of tension and conflict, and thus increasing the probability that instead of community we will have anarchy. (U.S., NSC Assistant Brzezinski, 1980c, p. 4)

Soviet interventionism in Afghanistan had major strategic consequences for global peace and stability. As described by Brzezinski,

> It has eliminated a buffer between the Soviet Union and Pakistan and Iran, has brought the Soviet Union within striking distance of the Indian Ocean and even the Gulf of Hormuz and it places Soviet power on the

very edge of two highly exposed and in some respects vulnerable countries, Iran and Pakistan. These countries are now likely to be the targets of
Soviet political intimidation. This is a more likely prospect than direct
invasion. . . . The threat in many respects is reminiscent of the threat in
1947 posed by the Soviet Union to Greece and Turkey. (U.S., NSC
Assistant Brzezinski, 1980b, p. 2)

In Brzezinski's view, the Soviet Union was attempting to expand its
influence throughout the arc of crisis by directly challenging the *third central
strategic zone* vital to the United States and the West. Following World War
II, global peace and security depended upon American commitment to two
central strategic zones: first Western Europe and then the Far East. ''In part to
overcome and to outflank these two strategic zones, the Soviet Union under
Khrushchev and later under Brezhnev launched a series of maneuvers, primarily in the Third World.'' Soviet interventionism in Africa, with the assistance
of Cuba, was the most blatant example of this strategy. Nevertheless, ''Soviet
gains were largely peripheral, occasionally reversed, and never sufficient to
threaten either of the two central strategic zones'' (U.S., NSC Assistant
Brzezinski, 1980e, p. 2).

With time a third central strategic zone developed in Southwest Asia—
including the Middle East and the Persian Gulf—as a result of the West's
dependence on this region for its economic well-being. Until the late 1970s,
the Soviets were successfully repelled from this region. But the Iranian revolution and the Soviet invasion of Afghanistan completely altered the situation.
''We are, if you will, in the third phase of the great architectural response that
the United States launched in the wake of World War II in order to compensate
for the devastation and ruin to the global security system that World War II
produced'' (U.S., NSC Assistant Brzezinski, 1980c, p. 5).

The Soviet Union was able to exploit unrest and expand its influence
because of its great increase in military power. Carter Administration officials
now emphasized the decline, not the strength, of U.S. power. Unlike earlier
years, power was now narrowly defined in terms of military capability.
Brzezinski believed that,

Over the last 15 years or so there has been a gradual decline in the relative
power of the United States, because of our engagement in the Vietnamese
war, because of the efforts made, particularly by the Soviet Union, to
erase the advantages that we had enjoyed until the '60s. These trends, by
the mid-'70s, reached certain dangerous levels, pointing to the possibility
that if not reversed somewhere in the '80s we could be faced with a very

THE CARTER ADMINISTRATION'S IMAGES

adverse geostrategic situation. (U.S., NSC Assistant Brzezinski, 1980c, p. 4)

Carter and Brzezinski insisted that the United States had to respond firmly and steadily. "In this ever more interdependent world, to assume aggression need be met only when it occurs at one's own doorstep is to tempt new adventures and to risk new and very serious miscalculations. Our course is clear. By responding very firmly, we intend to halt aggression where it takes place and to deter it elsewhere" (U.S., President Carter, 1980d, pp. 4–5).

Ultimately, President Carter's response was to reinstall the containment strategy to the forefront of American foreign policy. Following the invasion of Afghanistan, the *Carter Doctrine* was proclaimed:

Let our position be absolutely clear: An attempt by any outside force to gain control of the Persion Gulf region will be regarded as an assault on the vital interests of the United States of America, and such an assault will be repelled by any means necessary, including military force. (U.S., President Carter, 1980c, p. B)

Thus, containment was directly applied to Southwest Asia and the Persian Gulf region—the third central strategic zone within the arc of crisis. The significance of the Carter Doctrine was described by Brzezinski:

The net result of this statement was a new and historically important commitment of the United States, one which has long-term implications for the decade of 1980. *It reflects the recognition that the central challenge of this decade is likely to be as massive and enduring as that confronted by American leadership in the first post-World War II decades.* (U.S., NSC Assistant Brzezinski, 1980e, p. 3)

The Carter Administration now emphasized continuity with past American foreign policy. "Since the end of the Second World War, America has led other nations in meeting the challenge of mounting Soviet power" (U.S., President Carter, 1980c, p. A). As the challenge was met in the past, so it would be met today.

As part of this effort to contain the Soviets and insure the security of the West and the world, Carter officials held that it was mandatory for the United States and its Western allies to increase their defense forces and military capabilities. "We must pay whatever price is required to remain the strongest nation in the world. That price has increased as the military power of our major adversary has grown and its readiness to use that power been made all too evident in Afghanistan" (U.S., President Carter, 1980b, p. H). The projection

1980: IN SEARCH OF GLOBAL STABILITY

of U.S. military power became so central in the minds of Administration policymakers that it was argued that "the United States is engaged in the most far-reaching military modernization since the early sixties" (U.S., Secretary Muskie, 1980f, p. A). Other policy instruments were also deemed important, but military power was considered fundamental for promoting global stability.

Given the threat of instability and of Soviet expansionism, it was essential for the United States to be able to project its military power in the Middle East and Southwest Asia. Carter officials believed it was important to create a regional security framework in the region. "The trend is towards increased American military presence in the region, towards greater utilization of available facilities, towards a regional security framework including also the U.S." (U.S., NSC Assistant Brzezinski, 1980b, p. 1). Widespread support was necessary in order to successfully promote the security and stability of the region.

It demands collective efforts to meet this new threat to security in the Persian Gulf and in southwest Asia. It demands the participation of all those who rely on oil from the Middle East and who are concerned with global peace and stability. And it demands consultation and close cooperation with countries in the area which might be threatened. (U.S., President Carter, 1980c, p. B).

The purpose of U.S. policy to contain Soviet expansion in the third central strategic zone and throughout the world was to contribute to the stability of the international system. Once stability was achieved, this would allow the United States to pursue more cooperative efforts, including efforts with the Soviet Union.

By moving as we have to contain a possible Soviet push into Southwest Asia, we also position ourselves to work for a more constructive and positive relationship with the Soviet Union. It was Western, and especially American, resolve in Europe and in the Far East which built the basis for which detente began. Similarly, our ability to deter Soviet pressure against this third area of vital Western interest provides us, as well, with the foundation for a stable dialogue with Moscow. We do not seek to rekindle the Cold War by moving the contest to a new region. We seek a genuine relaxation of tension based on reciprocity and mutual restraint. (U.S., NSC Assistant Brzezinski, 1980e, p. 5)

But it was important to recognize that if the United States was successful in containing the Soviet Union or if Soviet actions were based on "reciprocity" and "mutual restraint," the U.S.-Soviet relationship would continue to be a very competitive one for a very long time to come. This would have to be taken into consideration when it comes to other relationships. For example, with respect to the normalization of relations with China, it would be foolish to maintain an "even-handed" policy between China and the Soviet Union.

> The President has very deliberately used the word "balanced." In balancing the two we have to take into account also the differences between them. The Soviet Union does pose a strategic challenge to the United States. China does not. The Soviet Union does impose regional and strategic strains upon us through its assertive behavior, directly or through proxies. China does not. . . . We therefore cannot pursue an identical policy towards both of these two major countries. (U.S., NSC Assistant Brzezinski, 1980b, p. 3)

Therefore, it would be in America's interests to use the new Chinese relationship to help promote a global equilibrium.

The Carter Administration's image had clearly changed by 1980. Where once the goal was to produce global community, the Administration was now committed to promote global stability in order to contain Soviet expansionism in a turbulent and dangerous world. As stated by President Carter: "our mission is to promote order, not to enforce our will; our mission is to protect our citizens and our national honor, not to harm nor to dishonor others; to compel restraint, not to provoke confrontation; to support the weak, not to dominate them; to assure that the foundations of our new world are laid upon a stable superpower balance, not built on sand" (U.S., President Carter, 1980d, p. 6).

Remnants of a Complex Global Community

Not all members of the foreign-policy-making triad shared the same image of an unstable, fragmented environment threatened by the Soviet Union. President Carter and NSC Advisor Brzezinski were the most committed to the pursuit of global stability, yet Secretary of State Vance was never completely comfortable with the new Administration image. Although he recognized that Soviet military intervention in Afghanistan was a threat to the area, Vance retained many of the beliefs that were central to the Carter Administration's initial worldview.

Vance, although unsure about the fundamental motivations behind the invasion, agreed that the United States needed to take strong action against the Soviet Union. "The Soviets' precise motives in attacking Afghanistan may remain unclear. But there is not lack of clarity about the fact of their aggression. The Soviet action requires an American response that is firm, sustained,

1980: IN SEARCH OF GLOBAL STABILITY

and effective'' (U.S., Secretary Vance, 1980a, p. 35). In response to Afghanistan, it was important for America to emphasize the defense and security of the West. Nevertheless, not only was it necessary to demonstrate resolve to the Soviet Union, other important issues and actors also demanded attention.

> The Soviet invasion of Afghanistan has had a definite impact on our foreign policy—on U.S.-Soviet relations and the common agenda with our allies. But it should not—it will not—turn us away from the fundamental goals our nation has been pursuing in the world. They remain deeply in our national interest. (U.S., Secretary Vance, 1980b, p. 14)

Vance maintained that the United States had to remain committed to the pursuit of a global community in the face of diversity. The Soviet invasion of Afghanistan did not fundamentally alter the complex nature of the international system or America's need to promote a more cooperative world order. "Even as we address these current challenges, we must constantly place our response within our broader strategy. Our present actions must not only meet immediate crises; they must advance our long-term interests as well'' (U.S., Secretary Vance, 1980c, p. 16). He steadfastly continued to believe in the importance of promoting positive global change. "We are well aware that seething frustrations can explode into radicalism and violence which imperil America's interests. But it remains true that more often today, change is taking place peacefully, and it is leading toward human freedom'' (U.S., Secretary Vance, 1980b, p. 14). The United States could not oppose change; this was the trend of the future that the United States had to promote.

> Some would say that in seeking peaceful change toward human justice in every area of the world, we encourage radicalism. I say that the world is changing, that human beings everywhere will demand a better life. The United States must offer its own vision of a better future, or the future will belong to others. (U.S., Secretary Vance, 1980c, p. 25)

A preventive approach remained the optimal way to resolve most regional conflicts and "the best way to thwart Soviet interference in the Third World'' (U.S., Secretary Vance, 1980b, p. 14). Vance advocated the use of military force only as a last resort and only when U.S. vital interests were directly threatened. He believed that the United States retained the ability to lead the world in a more positive and cooperative direction. It is a "reality that our strengths—military, economic, and political—give us an unmatched capacity for world leadership'' (U.S. Secretary Vance, 1980c, p. 25).

Although Vance realized that the events in Southwest Asia damaged U.S.-Soviet relations, he did not believe that the relationship would or should deteriorate to the point of open hostility. He remained hopeful that the United States and the Soviet Union would find areas of cooperation in the future.

> The Soviet invasion of Afghanistan and their adventurism in Africa and Asia have done real damage to this relationship and to the immediate prospects for a more peaceful world. We are prepared to impose costs on aggression for as long as necessary. We will promote America's interests and values in all of our dealings. But we seek no cold war, no indiscriminate confrontation. It is not in our interest, even during a period of heightened tensions, to dismantle the framework of East-West relations constructed over more than a generation. . . . Progress has been suspended, but when Soviet behavior allows, the door to a more stable and mutually beneficial relationship—a competition bounded by restraint and a regard for each other's interests—will be open.(U.S., Secretary Vance, 1980c, p. 20)

Although faced with an immediate challenge, he remained optimistic about the future of the world. "While we have known the world is a dangerous place, requiring our strength and our vigilance, we have also known that it need not be a hostile one. As the human condition is improved, as people everywhere find better and more secure lives, the world becomes a safer place for America" (U.S., Secretary Vance, 1980b, p. 14). But Vance's perspective during 1980 was a minority position in the Administration. Carter's and Brzezinski's images overlapped considerably, and together they dominated the making of American foreign policy. Though Vance attempted to promote policies in accord with his optimistic image, these were rarely followed. Vance resigned in protest after President Carter decided to go ahead with a military rescue attempt of the American hostages in Iran.

Vance was replaced by Edmund Muskie as Secretary of State in April 1980. He was more in agreement with President Carter and Brzezinski on the need to promote global stability.

> This whole broad region of the globe—the Middle East and Southwest Asia—is a strategic crossroads at which the interests of many nations are vitally engaged. The future of the United States and of our key friends and allies around the globe is now bound up with its fate. With turmoil in Iran and Soviet aggression in Afghanistan, the strategic concerns of the United States and its allies in that region are more seriously threatened than ever before. If hostile forces should gain control of the Persian Gulf region or if it should lapse into anarchy, the entire world economy would

be undermined, and the world strategic balance would be dangerously altered. (U.S., Secretary Muskie, 1980a, p. 3)

Nevertheless, Muskie also believed that the United States had to deal with other actors and issues beside the Soviet Union and the Soviet threat to the West. He espoused many beliefs that were seldom heard from Carter and Brzezinski during 1980 including: the promotion of human rights, the need for global economic growth and Third World development, the improvement of bilateral relations, and the importance of arms control.

Muskie hoped that the United States could maintain its concern with stability while at the same time foster a better international system. "We must not succumb to the voices which say we should now turn back. These voices are pessimistic about the possibilities of freedom in the world. They see change abroad, for the most part, as dangerous for America. They are hostile to it. We see change not only as threats to be met but opportunities to be seized" (U.S., Secretary Muskie, 1980d, p. C). He did not shrink from concern for security and defense, but the threat of Soviet expansionism and global instability was not to be exaggerated.

> Certainly we live in a tumultuous world, characterized by the unremitting nationalism and surging human aspirations of more than 100 new nations. But if such an environment is unsettling to us, it will prove to be even more perilous for nations seeking to dominate others and dictate their systems. Such imperial concepts are the wave of the past. (U.S., Secretary Muskie, 1980e, p. 27)

Therefore, Muskie was hopeful that a more positive U.S.-Soviet relationship could be restored, recognizing that it would be based on both cooperation and competition.

> We are prepared to accept the Soviet Union as a great world power with its own legitimate interests. We have no interest in an implacable cold-war approach which holds the Soviet Union responsible for all the world's instabilities; we know the world is too complicated for such simple-minded notions. But we will insist that Moscow respect the legitimate interests of other nations, and that it not pursue its own advantage in ways that threaten the fabric of peace. (U.S., Secretary Muskie, 1980c, p. 23)

The United States needed to emphasize more than just military force. "There is no doubt that in a dangerous world, the first requirement is military strength. . . . But too many voices would have us believe that military power

THE CARTER ADMINISTRATION'S IMAGES

in itself can protect our interests and bring order to an unruly world. So much more is needed' '' (U.S., Secretary Muskie, 1980g, p. 35). United States foreign policy should take an affirmative approach in responding to international change. "Our wisest course is to work to resolve crises before they erupt—through patient and persistent diplomacy and through support for human progress" (U.S., Secretary Muskie, 1980g, p. 36). "The point is this: Those most concerned about Soviet and Cuban activism in the world should be the strongest supporters of our efforts to support the moderate transition from repressive tyranny to democratic development. For by failing to support the alternatives to radicalism, we help radicalism to breed" (U.S., Secretary Muskie, 1980b, p. 29).

America had to stand for faith in a better future, not just for military strength. This is why it was so important for America to promote human rights. "For if America is not the companion of human progress in the world, if we do not work to shape events in progressive directions, the world will pass us by. If we do not promote freedom in the world, there will be less freedom in the future for Americans" (U.S., Secretary Muskie, 1980d, p. A). Muskie believed that America needed to be the beacon of a more peaceful and just world order.

> We must seek security not only in arms but also in a diplomacy that is generous, that is willing to cope with inevitable change, that is faithful to decent human values. If we do that, we can be in the 1980s not only as strong as steel but as resilient and enduring. We can be not only a fortress of arms but a fortress of hope and freedom as well. (U.S., Secretary Muskie, 1980d, p. C)

In sum, Secretary Muskie hoped that once the Soviet Union was contained and global stability insured, the United States could then continue to build a cooperative world order. However, Carter and Brzezinski were pessimistic and believed that it would take a considerable amount of time and effort before this future goal could take precedence. In the meantime, the United States had to respond to an increasingly fragmented and dangerous international system. The Administration's primary goal was to contain the Soviet threat to Western security in Southwest Asia in order to promote global stability. Zbigniew Brzezinski summed up the Carter Administration's foreign policy for 1980:

> Our larger purpose . . . is to create a stable framework of deterrence, so that peace can not only be preserved but can be transformed into active cooperation between the major powers of the world. Within that frame-

work, we can accommodate the changes that are inevitable. We can help guide the process of global changes toward institutional arrangements we can now only dimly perceive and only imperfectly imagine. We can use the balance of power to help rectify the imbalances—of wealth, of technology, of literacy, of health—which will otherwise threaten our way of life and our survival. But we can only move constructively on that set of challenges if we move resolutely and effectively to address the challenge in Southwest Asia. Should we fail there, the balance of power from which we must build stability could be irretrievably lost. (U.S., NSC Assistant Brzezinski, 1980e, p. 6)

Notes

1. An issue had to be addressed at least 7% of the time to be considered a major issue.

2. An actor had to be addressed at least 10% of the time to be considered a major actor.

3. As quickly as the conflict in Africa increased in importance for the Carter Administration in 1978, in 1979 it receded in importance (from 13.1% in 1977, to 21.0% in 1978, to 13.4% in 1979). The role of the Soviet Union (and Cuba) in Africa also increased and then diminished considerably from 4.4% in 1977 to 18.8% in 1978 to 4.2% in 1979 (from 11.1% to 29.3% to 8.4%). This supports the interpretation that the conflict in Africa, especially in the Horn, was perceived to be a major event by Carter Administration officials in 1978.

4. These two major events actually began in late November and December of the previous year.

5. Brzezinski argued that "there is no conflict between the first and the second objective, making America more relevant to a world of change, and seeking to enhance and maintain our geostrategic position. The two are consistent and complementary, and we as a country have to learn not to think in dichotoic terms about world affairs. Being historically relevent and being militarily present and powerful, are mutually reinforcing. The former encourages positive change. The latter creates a framework of stability that can absorb it" (U.S., NSC Assistant Brzezinski, 1980d, p. 7).

FOUR | *Continuity and Change in the Administration's Image*

ORIGINALLY, the Carter Administration perceived the existence of a complex and diverse international system. A variety of issues were deemed to be of global significance and, therefore, had to be addressed. The world was portrayed as highly interdependent and pluralistic—no actor, including the United States or the Soviet Union, was considered willing or able to dominate international behavior. As a result of this "global complexity," the Carter Administration was primarily concerned with ushering in an era of peace, justice and growth—a quest for "global community."

This early image was basically shared by the three major policymakers within the Carter Administration. However during 1978, individual differences began to emerge. While President Carter and Secretary of State Vance adhered to an image of global complexity and global community, National Security Advisor Brzezinski began to place greater emphasis on political-military issues and the need to respond to Soviet foreign interventionism, especially in Africa. Therefore, the original image of a complex international system and a quest for global community was slightly modified.

Although the concern with foreign intervention in Africa receded during 1979, differences in individual images continued to sharpen. Vance stuck to a vision of a complex international system and remained optimistic about a new world order. Brzezinski perceived an increasingly fragmented and unstable international system open to foreign interventionism. Carter wavered between Vance's optimism and Brzezinski's pessimism. Thus, in 1979, two images of the international system competed for ascendancy.

By the beginning of 1980, however, the Administration's conception of the international system had changed completely. As a result of the Iranian hostage crisis and in particular the Soviet military intervention in Afghanistan, a new consensus in worldview emerged. Global change was no longer looked upon positively—the complex world was too turbulent, unstable, and dangerous. Global turbulence was now the dominant trend. Political-military issues rose to the top of the Administration's agenda, and the Soviet Union received a disproportionate amount of attention. With the Soviet Union expanding into the third strategic zone within the arc of crisis, the Carter Administration emphasized the containment of Soviet expansionism and the promotion of "global stability" (table 4.1 provides a summary).

This new image was advanced primarily by President Carter and NSC Advisor Brzezinski. Secretary Vance never fully subscribed to the view and eventually resigned following the Iran hostage rescue attempt. Vance's replacement, Secretary of State Muskie, was more supportive of the new image, but also tried to retain some of the beliefs that were central to the original notion of a complex global community.

Table 4.1

Summary of the Carter Administration's
Image of the International System

International System	1977	1980
Current	Complex	Turbulent
Major Issues	Human Rights	Southwest Asian Conflict
	Normalization	Security + Defense
	Arms Control	Middle East Conflict
	Middle East Conflict	
	African Conflict	
	Economy	
	Development	
Major Actors	Middle East	USSR
	USSR	Middle East
	China + Asia	Western Europe + Japan
	Western Europe + Japan	
	Africa	
	Latin America	
	Global	
Image of Soviets	Optimistic	Pessimistic
Future	Community	Stability
View of Change	Positive	Negative

Key Issues and Actors

The evolution of the Carter Administration's image of the international system may be depicted more clearly by examining the changes that occurred in its view of the most important issues and actors. Although a number of diverse issues were perceived to be important during 1977 reflecting a more optimistic image, by 1980 the Carter Administration concentrated overwhelmingly on a much smaller set of issues, primarily of a political-military nature, reflecting a more pessimistic image.

Figure 4.1 depicts the changes that occurred for the most important issues. Three major patterns emerge over time. First, attention to two of the issues—Western security and the Southwest Asia conflict—increased dramatically. The rise in the importance of the Southwest Asian conflict was the most dramatic—it went from an insignificant concern to the most important issue for the Carter Administration in 1980. Second, three of the issues—the Arab-Israeli conflict, normalization, and human rights—remained important throughout the four years. The result was a net decline in the level of their significance by the last year relative to the rise of Western security and the Southwest Asian conflict. Finally, four of the issues—arms control, the global economy, Third World development, and the conflict in Africa (although of great importance in 1978)—also decreased in importance over time.[1]

Table 4.2 also reveals the evolution of the importance of the issues for the Carter Administration from 1977 to 1980. A large number of issues—at least seven—were consistently addressed throughout the four years. However, an additional pattern is also apparent: most of the significant issues were perceived to be of roughly similar importance in 1977 and 1979, unlike 1978 and 1980, when they were more clearly prioritized. During the first year, human rights, normalization, arms control, and the Middle East conflict were the most important issues, but none of them received a great deal of attention apart from the other issues—representing a time when the Carter Administration perceived a complex and pluralistic international system. In 1978 this image was altered as a result of the attention foreign interventionism received over the conflict in Africa. In 1979, nine issues were important, more than any other year, and all received a similar amount of attention (the Middle East conflict received the most attention). The incredible variety of issues addressed was an indication of a lack of focus and consensus within the Administration due to the coexistence of two competing worldviews. By 1980 the issues were hierarchically ordered in terms of their importance, with a concentration on the Southwest Asian conflict as well as the threat to Western

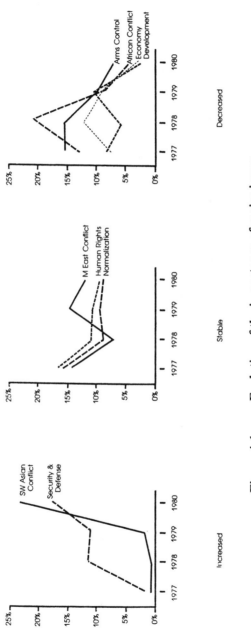

Figure 4.1   Evolution of the importance of major issues.

security and defense—a reflection of concern with global turbulence and instability.

The change in the Carter Administration's image is reinforced by changes that occurred in the substantive nature of the issues that were addressed. Very simply, political-military issues grew in importance with time. In 1977 only three of the seven most important issues (42.9%) involved political-military matters. In 1978 the importance of political-military issues increased (four of seven or 57.1%) and remained steady through 1979 (five of nine or 55.6%). In 1980 the overwhelming orientation was on political-military issues (five out of seven or 71.4%). Clearly, the Carter Administration perceived political-military issues as more and more important, which indicated the growth of pessimism within the collectivity.

The overall pattern of concentrating on key political-military issues over time is repeated and reinforced by the Carter Administration's perception of the most important actors. Figure 4.2 depicts the changes in how the Carter Administration perceived the relative importance of various groupings of international actors. As with issues, three patterns developed. First, one actor—the Soviet Union—increased in importance over time, especially in 1978 and most dramatically in 1980. Second, three groups of actors—those in the Middle East, Western Europe, and throughout the entire globe—remained important in attention received, but declined over time relative to the growing importance of the Soviet Union. Finally, three groups of actors—China and Asia, Latin America, and Africa—became significantly less important as the years progressed.[2]

Table 4.2

Evolution of Issue Importance

Level of Issue Importance	Year			
	1977	*1978*	*1979*	*1980*
0–6.9%	4	4	2	4
7–13.9%	3	5	8	5
14–20.9%	4	1	1	1
21–27.9%	0	1	0	1
Major Issues	7	7	9	7
Political-Military Issues	3	4	5	5

Note: An issue had to be discussed at least 7% of the time to be considered a major issue.

KEY ISSUES AND ACTORS

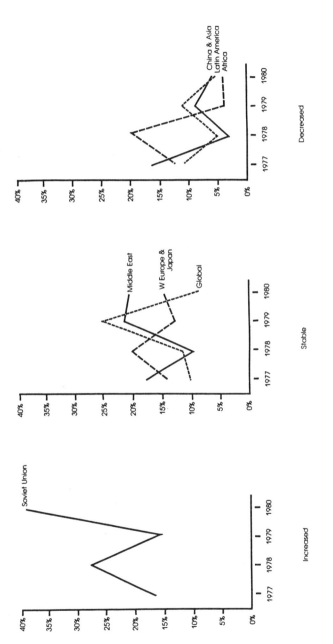

Figure 4.2   Evolution of the importance of major actors.

This narrowing of key actors is further depicted in table 4.3. In 1977 seven major actors were roughly equally addressed. The next two years resulted in greater concentration on fewer actors. Five were important overall, and two in particular assumed prominence for each year: the Soviet Union and Western Europe for 1978; global actors and Middle Eastern actors in 1979. The Carter Administration's image perceived a much greater hierarchical system in 1980. Only three actors were significant: Western Europe and Japan, the Middle East, and most importantly the Soviet Union. By 1980 the Soviet Union was preponderant in the eyes of the Administration.

The expanding presence of the Soviet Union in 1978 and 1980 is illustrated in greater depth in table 4.4. In 1977, the Soviet Union was important for only one of seven major issues: arms control. In 1978, the Soviet Union became important in five issue areas, especially arms control and Western security. This overall role remained substantial for three of nine issues in 1979—again especially in arms control and Western security. And in the final year of the Administration, Carter officials regarded the Soviets very important in five of seven issue areas, including arms control and the year's two most important problems—the Southwest Asian conflict and Western security and defense. The movement from actor diversity to a concentration on fewer actors, especially the role of the Soviet Union, reinforces the description of the Carter Administration's change in image from an emphasis on the possibilities of a global community to the threat to global stability.

Understanding Image Stability and Change

The key to understanding the change in the Carter Administration's collective image from global community to global stability is to examine the images of the three policymakers who comprised the collectivity. As the individual images evolved, the Administration's collective image also evolved. Different degrees of image change occurred for each of the three major Carter policymakers. Whereas NSC Advisor Brzezinski and especially President Carter experienced a great deal of change in their image of the international system, Secretary of State Vance's image was relatively stable over time.[3] Because determining why one person's belief system was stable and another person's image changed is extremely difficult, what follows is an explanation of the evolution of the three individual's images as developed from the discussion of image stability and change presented in chapter 2.

Three interrelated factors explain the dramatic change in Carter's and Brzezinski's image of the international system: the individual personalities, the occurrence of major events, and the impact of domestic forces. While

UNDERSTANDING IMAGES

Table 4.3

Evolution of Actor Importance

Level of Actor Importance	Year			
	1977	1978	1979	1980
0–9.9%	1	3	3	5
10–19.9%	7	3	3	1
20–29.9%	0	2	2	1
30–39.9%	0	1	0	1
Major Actors	7	5	5	3

Note: An actor had to be discussed at least 10% of the time to be considered a major actor.

Carter's personality was open to new information, Brzezinski's insecurity and rigid personality prompted his return to a previously held image. Major events played a critical role in shaping their alternative views: Soviet and Cuban interventionism in Africa was particularly crucial for Brzezinski; the Iranian hostage crisis and the Soviet invasion of Afghanistan for Carter. And finally, the development of a more pessimistic image for Brzezinski and particularly for Carter was reinforced by the changing mood of the country in a more nationalistic and conservative direction. Vance was the least affected by the international events and the changing domestic environment of the late 1970s and held the most stable image in the Carter Administration.

Table 4.4

Summary of Relative Importance of the Soviet Union for Issues

Level of Soviet Importance	Year			
	1977	1978	1979	1980
0–9.9%	6	2	6	2
10–19.9%	0	3	1	1
20–39.9%	0	0	0	1
40–50.9%	0	1	1	1
60–99.9%	1	1	1	2
Importance for Major Issues	1	5	3	5

Note: The Soviet Union had to be discussed at least 10% of the time for each issue to be considered an important actor.

President Carter

Over time, President Carter experienced the most profound image change. He entered office in 1977 with genuine conviction in the boundless possibilities for relations among human beings (Carter, 1975; Glad, 1980; Mazlish & Diamond, 1979). This faith, reinforced by his religious beliefs, inevitably colored his perspective on international behavior. Carter was the most optimistic about the Soviet Union and the future of a global community. However, by 1980 his image had completely changed. The key factors that interacted to change his image were President Carter's personal lack of knowledge in global affairs and open-minded personality, the crucial events involving the hostages in Iran and the Soviet invasion of Afghanistan, and the presidential election of 1980 during a time when the domestic climate was becoming more nationalistic. Each of these factors will be addressed more fully.

Because he was a highly motivated individual with little experience in foreign affairs, President Carter emerged as the individual most susceptible to a change in outlook. Carter had not developed many central beliefs concerning the nature of the international system when he assumed the presidency. Much of the information he did have had been gained from his brief relationship with Brzezinski and the Trilateral Commission—an organization oriented toward promoting cooperation and development among the Western industrialized democracies.[4] "Those Trilateral Commission meetings for me," Carter is reported to have said (Jordan, 1982, p. 45), "were like classes in foreign policy—reading papers produced on every conceivable subject, hearing experienced leaders debate international issues and problems, and meeting the big names like Cy Vance and Harold Brown and Zbig."

Carter's lack of knowledge and receptivity to new ideas was combined with an intense desire to know more about the world. He had a voracious appetite for information and spent much of his time studying the issues. During his first year as president he worked an average of more than seventy hours per week, spending close to half of that time reading and studying (Bonafede, 1978). According to Gary Sick, a member of the NSC staff (1985, p. 223), "President Carter was totally absorbed by the *substance* of policy. On an important issue he would immerse himself in the facts, drawing on the best expertise he could find, and would very quickly make himself into something of an expert." Carter accepted "challenges to his ideas" and was "pleased to improve his mind" (Fallows, 1979, p. 48). He once remarked, "I'm learning, I'm studying. I get over here every morning at the latest by seven o'clock and go home in time for supper at seven, and then I spend two or three hours a night working and studying and reading. It's not a laborious thing for me because I really enjoy it" (in Johnson, 1980, p. 151).[5]

In the early years of his administration, however, Carter's experience level was still such that his central belief in human nature provided the guideposts by which he evaluated the world around him. Quite naturally, this led him to harbor optimistic impressions of many of the world's actors, most notably the Soviet Union. More significantly though, it also compelled him to set high standards of behavior for nations like the Soviet Union. Therefore, whenever the Soviets acted opportunistically abroad and violated these behavior standards, Carter experienced periods of dissonance. Initially, he responded with surprise and confusion. As the pattern of contrary Soviet behavior persisted, however, surprise and confusion turned to frustration and disenchantment. Carter displayed the most uncertainty and skepticism about the nature of the Soviets in 1979 and swayed between optimistic and pessimistic statements in public. By 1980, the skepticism had hardened and Carter's image of the Soviet Union and the international system had changed.

Two events—the hostage seizure in Iran and the Soviet invasion of Afghanistan—compelled Carter to reassess his notions of the Soviet Union and the world (Burt, 1980; Weinstein & Beschloss, 1982). In an interview with Frank Reynolds on ABC-TV's *World News Tonight*, Carter confessed how the Soviet invasion affected him:

> My opinion of the Russians has changed most drastically in the last week than even the previous two and a half years before that. It's only now dawning on the world the magnitude of the action that the Soviets undertook in invading Afghanistan . . . to repeat myself, this action of the Soviets has made a more dramatic change in my own opinion of what the Soviets ultimate goals are than anything they've done in the previous time I've been in office. (U.S., President Carter, 1980e, p. 4)

It was as if Carter viewed the Soviet Union through his personal relationship with Mr. Brezhnev and thus felt that the action in Afghanistan was a direct stab-in-the-back.[6] As the literature on fear arousal suggests, Carter became more amenable to appeals for new policies in an effort to alleviate the crises. Likewise, this was also a most opportune time for Brzezinski to gain approval for specific anti-Soviet policies he had been pushing for some time in response to the events in Iran and Afghanistan.

The domestic environment acted to spur and reinforce Carter's commitment to a more pessimistic image of the international system. Americans had become more concerned with foreign affairs as the 1970s evolved, and the public's perception of the Soviet Union grew more negative with time. "By the time of the 1980 presidential election, fearing that America was losing control over its foreign affairs, voters were more than ready to exorcise the ghost of Vietnam and replace it with a new posture of American assertiveness" (Yankelovich & Kaagan, 1980, p. 696). Public opinion in America increasingly favored greater military spending and defense of American interests overseas (Russett & DeLuca, 1981; Schneider, 1983; Watts & Free, 1980). This trend was further promoted by the rise of the "new right" and neoconservatism. Numerous individuals and groups who argued for a stronger U.S. foreign policy based upon a fear of Soviet communism received considerable attention and gained legitimacy within the political system (see Crawford, 1980; Nash, 1979; Sanders, 1983; Steinfels, 1979).

Nineteen eighty was also an election year, and the public agenda was basically defined by the political right. President Carter had to campaign for reelection in a domestic environment that was increasingly inhospitable to his earlier optimistic image of the international system (see Drew, 1981; Greenfield, 1982). As described by Brzezinski in an interview, "the focus of public attention, the focus of our international debate, the focus of mass media profiles, all centered on that East-West issue" (Weinstein & Beschloss, 1982, p. 79; see also Vance, 1983). In a study of the 1980 election, Moore (1981, p. xii) concludes that "foreign policy was involved more prominently throughout the campaign than inflation, and it played a more explicit role in the behavior of candidates and the media."

President Carter never developed the requisite leadership skills that may have allowed the American public to understand and support his policies, nor to counteract the rise of conservatism throughout the domestic environment. According to Brzezinski (1983, p. 57), the major problem of the Carter Administration foreign policy performance was that "we were overly ambitious and that we failed in our efforts to project effectively to the public the degree to which we were motivated by a coherent and well-thought-out viewpoint." While Carter focused on the substance of policy, he tended to ignore the importance of form: "He seemed unwilling to devote the same degree of care and attention to the atmospherics and public relations aspects of public presentation as he did to the decision itself. Fundamentally, he seemed to believe that if a decision was correct it would sell itself" (Sick, 1985, p. 223).

The lack of strong leadership increased the possibility for public disenchantment with President Carter and his administration (see Hah & Bartol, 1983). Although Iran was basically ignored by the media throughout the 1970s, once Americans were taken as hostages the "crisis" became a major media event.[7] In fact, it became the ultimate media event—the Iran hostage crisis "had more extensive coverage on television and in the press than any other event since World War II, including the Vietnam War'' (Smith, 1986, p. 198). This exacerbated the public's perception of Jimmy Carter as a poor presidential leader by constantly reminding Americans of the hostages' plight: the national anthem was played regularly on the radio and national television news usually ended its broadcast by keeping a count of how many days the hostages had been held (It has been said that Americans displayed a nationalistic fervor that had not been seen since World War II). This mood was further accelerated by the Soviet invasion of Afghanistan.

President Carter's new, pessimistic image of the Soviet Union was consistent with the mood of the country. However, in the minds of most Americans the international prominence of the United States was considered to be at a low, and Carter was perceived to be a weak leader. Thus, the nationalistic environment surrounding the election not only promoted a change in Carter's image but contributed to his lack of support for reelection.

National Security Advisor Brzezinski

Zbigniew Brzezinski also changed his image of the international system, but his shift was less extensive and took place over a much shorter time-frame. In fact, Brzezinski's change is particularly difficult to explain due to previous modifications in his thinking and the integral role his personality played in forming his image.

As discussed in chapter 3, Brzezinski was the least optimistic about Soviet activities from the beginning of the Carter Administration, but it was not until 1978 that his view of the USSR and the possibility for positive global change became blatantly pessimistic. Nevertheless, many people, including Brzezinski, argue that he never shared a similar optimistic image of the international system as Carter and Vance—that he entered office with a pessimistic image but initially was forced to assume a more optimistic position in line with the President's preferences.[8]

Actually, Brzezinski is contradictory concerning his own image in 1977 in his memoirs. On the one hand, he argues that from the beginning he focused on the Soviet Union because of his concern with an increasingly fragmented and unstable world, suggesting that he was at odds with others in the Carter Administration. As early as January, 1977, Brzezinski (1983, p. 3) stated he was determined

to improve America's strategic position, and that meant primarily in relationship to the Soviet Union. I had become increasingly concerned about the longer-term political implications of growing Soviet military power, and I feared that the Soviet Union would become increasingly tempted to use its power either to exploit Third World turbulence or to impose its will in some political contest with the United States.

Therefore, Brzezinski (1983, p. 13) "was uneasy even in these days about the policy orientation of some of Carter's foreign policy appointments" and "feared that he would not be obtaining, especially from the State Department, the kind of realistic and hard-nosed advise which should balance his more idealistic views."

On the other hand, he acknowledges that he was integral in providing the foundation for moving away from an East-West mentality in order to integrate West-West and especially North-South issues that provided the basis of consensus within the Carter Administration. He states that it was not until 1978 that dissensus really occurred, when the "solidarity of the activist first year of foreign policy was cracking under the weight of the intensifying debate on how to handle the U.S.-Soviet relationship" (Brzezinski, 1983, p. 316). Substantive policy differences, especially between him and Vance, arose "first, over the issue of the Soviet-Cuban role in the African Horn and the likely impact of that on SALT" (Brzezinski, 1983, p. 38).

The contradiction in his portrayal of the level of consensus and his particular role within the first year of the Carter Administration may be a function of the nature of memoirs, for Brzezinski (1983, p. xiii) is honest enough to admit that "it would be absurd to pretend that mine is not a subjective account. All volumes of memoirs present a view of the events from the vantage point of the memorialist, and it is possible that I have not entirely avoided the common pitfall of enhancing my own role."

It is interesting to note, in fact, that Brzezinski's memoirs are organized into three parts that correspond highly to the depiction in this study of the Carter Administration's evolving foreign policy. The first year represented a time of shared optimism: "the first phase of Carter's foreign policy, which lasted till early 1978, was thus dominated by high expectations and ambitious goals" (Brzezinski, 1983, p. 81). The second and third years were a time of growing dissensus:

a combination of lasting achievements and bitter disappointments—required us to gradually revise our basic priorities and to concentrate our efforts on policies designed to preserve and maximize American power. Inevitably, the resulting shift generated some internal disagreements, in contrast to the more hopeful first phase. (Brzezinski, 1983, p. 193)

The final year resulted in the triumph of the need for promoting global stability: "the last phase of Carter's foreign policy involved the shaping of a new balance between the priorities of power and principle. The higher recognition of the centrality of power in world affairs emerged gradually, through intense internal debates sparked largely by the impact of Soviet expansionism and the crisis with Iran'' (Brzezinski, 1983, p. 401).

Whether Brzezinski "privately" believed in promoting a global community based on an image of global complexity in 1977 is an open question. What is important is that he acted in "public" and as a "decision-maker" within the Carter Administration as if he adhered to such a philosophy. In other words, he articulated an optimistic image of the international system along with Carter and Vance, even though he was more skeptical about the Soviets role within the international system. He continued to behave in this manner until the Somali-Ethiopian conflict triggered a change in 1978.

Previous to this, however, Brzezinski's image of the international system had undergone two other major transitions. A Polish immigrant and a prominent Sovietologist, Brzezinski developed a very pessimistic view during the 1950s and early 1960s of the Soviet Union and communism as the major threats in a bipolar international system (see, e.g., Brzezinski & Friedrich, 1956; Brzezinski & Huntington, 1963). Then in the late 1960s and early 1970s, his thinking changed, and he joined those promoting a more optimistic image of a complex global community. This is best represented by his book *Between Two Ages: America's Role in the Technetronic Era* in 1970 and his directorship of the Trilateral Commission (Brzezinski, 1970).[9] This is the image he entered the White House with. Taking into account all of Brzezinski's fluctuations of mind, Simon Serfaty remarks (1978, p. 13):

> Having ridden the realist wave of the 1960s against the remnants of Wilsonian moralism, and having next uncovered the 1970s as the decade of global equality against the tyranny of Kissingerian power politics, it was ironic to see Brzezinski now return to the issue of liberty that had flourished earlier in the 1950s.

The interaction of Brzezinski's personality and external events seems critical in explaining his loss of optimism. Brzezinski was noted for being extremely ambitious, and for having coveted a high-level foreign policy position within the U.S. government (Drew, 1978; Quinn, 1979a, 1979b, 1979c).[10] Very attuned to elite opinion, he was often in the forefront of the most popular trends of thought in U.S. foreign policy, which may explain his abandonment of his early pessimistic image and his commitment to the creation of a global community in a complex world. "What is striking . . . in Brzezinski's case," stated Serfaty (1978, p. 8), "is the ease and light-heartedness with which adjustments" have been made in his image.

Once he reached the pinnacle of power in American foreign policy Brzezinski found he no longer needed to conform to external opinion.[11] Brzezinski was considered to have a large ego and to be terribly insecure. "Ego is such a vague, overworked concept, don't you think?" stated Brzezinski,

> I prefer to perceive of myself as possessing an adequate measure of self-confidence, which is, of course, an absolute requisite for someone like me. I am very achievement oriented, and I have this pecularity in my personality that I have come to accept: By a very large margin, I prefer winning over losing—and, although I do not say this immodestly, I'm pretty good at winning. I win a great deal. I seldom lose, very seldom. (in Wooten, 1979, pp. 2–3)

Brzezinski's intense personality made his primitive beliefs of a growing and expansionist Soviet Union particularly susceptible to arousal.[12] Despite his temporary optimism, it seems clear that Brzezinski's earlier negative image of the Soviet Union was very central to his belief system and his personality. When challenged by events in the Horn of Africa, memories of the past overwhelmed and shattered his optimism for the future. This may have been reinforced by the fact that, although he gave much thought to international affairs throughout his life, he did not have much government experience.

The Soviet role in Ethiopia and the consequences for American foreign policy resulted in the first serious confrontation within the Carter Administration, especially between Brzezinski and Vance (Gelb, 1980a; Schram, 1978). As Vance stated at the time, "a different perspective with respect to the Soviet Union is the biggest set of differences between us" (Vance, 1978, p. 21). For Brzezinski, Soviet behavior in Africa was an omen of the future. In fact, in 1980, Brzezinski (1983, p. 189) attributed the events in Africa of 1978 to the failure of SALT II in the U.S. Senate and the deterioration of American-Soviet relations:

> Two years later, in March 1980, as we were reacting to the Soviet invasion of Afghanistan, I wrote in my journal: "I have been reflecting on when did things begin genuinely to go wrong in the U.S.-Soviet relationship. My view is that it was on the day sometime in . . . 1978 when at the SCC meeting I advocated that we send in a carrier task force in reaction to the Soviet deployment of the Cubans in Ethiopia. At that meeting not only was I opposed by Vance, but Harold Brown asked why, for what reason, without taking into account that that is a question that

should perplex the Soviets rather than us. The President backed the others rather than me, we did not react. Subsequently, as the Soviets became more emboldened, we overreacted . . . That derailed SALT, the momentum of SALT was lost, and the final nail in the coffin was the Soviet invasion of Afghanistan. In brief, underreaction then bred overreaction.'' That is why I have used occasionally the phrase "SALT lies buried in the sands of Ogaden.''

Not only did Brzezinski and Vance differ over substantive policy, but their personal styles of interaction exacerbated the situation when a disagreement arose over an issue. As reported by Elizabeth Drew (1978, p. 104), "Brzezinski reacts 'Don't just sit there, do something,' while Vance reacts 'Don't just do something, sit there—until you understand the consequences of what you want to do'." As Destler, Gelb, and Lake (1984) suggest, Brzezinski represented the new type of ambitious, partisan, and activist foreign policy professional elite, while Vance rose through the ranks of the foreign policy establishment during the cold war years in which one operated in a more gentlemanly, nonpartisan, and quiet fashion.[13] This made the conflict between Brzezinski and Vance more severe and undermined Carter's ability to control the situation.

Secretary of State Vance

Unlike Carter and Brzezinski, Secretary Vance's image was relatively stable throughout his three and one-half years in office. He perceived a complex international system and believed in the pursuit of a global community although this was somewhat modified in 1980. According to Destler, Gelb, and Lake (1984, p. 95), "it was an irony that Vance was to help usher in the new era. He was by birth, style, temperament, character and career, an examplar of the old Establishment." A common characteristic of an individual raised within the foreign policy establishment is to avoid theatrics and operate at a distance from the public spotlight. Therefore, Vance's image stability is difficult to assess because, although he was long on government experience, little is known about the man. He is foremost a reserved, private person. "Washington observers accustomed to sizing up people in terms of jockeying for position and the bureaucratic play have found Cyrus Vance difficult to fathom'' (Gwertzman, 1979, p. 34).

Vance's experience with the Vietnam War appears to have been central to his thinking.

From the time Vance left his post as Deputy to Defense Secretary Robert McNamara in 1966 and returned to Simpson, Thacher and Bartlett, his law firm, something happened to him. His thinking about foreign policy changed. He moved from safe centrist positions to a more liberal line, from being a man whose career had defined the center to someone who would take the point position on controversial issues he cared about. (Destler, Gelb & Lake, 1984, p. 96)

While serving as Deputy Secretary of Defense under President Johnson between 1964 and 1967, he became increasingly pessimistic about the war (Hoopes, 1969; McLellan, 1985). Yet it was not until he officially left Washington that he realized how far the American public had turned against it (Oberdorfer, 1971). The tragic consequences of America's intervention in Indochina dramatically altered and solidified his beliefs in a more optimistic direction: the United States had to promote positive ideals and constructive change, rather than rely on the negative use of military force to promote the status quo.

Vance believed passionately in the pursuit of global peace and cooperation through the use of diplomacy and the creation of international law. This was consistent with his background as a lawyer and special presidential envoy to settle important conflicts in Panama, the Dominican Republic, Vietnam, Detroit (following racial violence), Cyprus, and Korea throughout the 1960s, and was reinforced by lessons that he learned from the Vietnam War. Vance believed that negotiation and diplomacy were a key means of promoting conflict resolution.

With the Soviet invasion of Afghanistan, Vance's worldview no longer was ascendant within the Carter Administration. "Afghanistan was unquestionably a severe setback to the policy I advocated. The tenuous balance between visceral anti-Sovietism and an attempt to regulate dangerous competition could no longer be maintained. The scales tipped toward those favoring confrontation" (Vance, 1983, p. 394). Although he became more sympathetic about the need to respond to Soviet behavior throughout the Middle East, he was still reluctant to use military force.[14]

External events such as the foreign interventionism in Africa and the Iran hostage crisis only reinforced Vance's beliefs on the need to exercise restraint and respond to the causes, not the symptoms, of the conflicts. In the case of Iran, Vance preferred to rely on the use of diplomacy to release the American hostages. He was extremely skeptical about American chances of rescuing the hostages and believed that any such attempt was not only counterproductive but dangerous. Nevertheless, President Carter decided to risk a military rescue operation—in fact, the key decision came during a meeting when Vance was resting in Florida.

UNDERSTANDING IMAGES

The restoration of containment and militarization to the forefront of American foreign policy and the specific decision to rescue the hostages against Vance's advice left him with little choice. Three days before the military rescue of the hostages he submitted his resignation, becoming the first Secretary of State to voluntarily resign on a matter of principle in over sixty years.[15] He explained his reasons for his resignation following the rescue attempt:

> Even if they were extricated successfully, the Iranians would probably seize hostages the next day—either other Americans in the country or other foreigners. Further, the bloodshed that would take place in connection with the operation and the consequent death and injury to Iranians could well lead to a wider explosion across the Persian Gulf which might divide the Islamic world from the West . . . And finally, this would tend to drive the Iranians toward the Soviets rather than separating them, so certainly that wasn't in our interests as well. In addition, it would further strain our relations with our allies. (in Gwertzman, 1980, p. 1)

After leaving office, Vance (1980, p. A12) continued to argue against the "dangerous fallacy of the military solution to nonmilitary problems . . . It is an illusion to believe they are a substitute for the diplomacy and resources needed to address such problems as internal change and basic needs in other nations or a battered international economy." He thought that it was necessary to stick to the original goals of the Carter Administration. "Neither we nor the world can afford an American foreign policy which is hostage to the emotions of the moment." Nor could America afford "a longing for earlier days when the world seemed, at least in retrospect, to have been a more orderly place in which American power could, alone, preserve that order." If America abandoned its goals for pursuing global cooperation in a world of increasing complexity and diversity "the world will indeed be the inhospitable place many now fear it is."

In sum, throughout the four years of the Carter Administration, a dramatic reversal of its image of the international system took place reflecting the change and continuity in the images of the individual policymakers. The very optimistic image of a complex international system where a variety of important issues had to be addressed and a variety of different actors were important in order to promote a global community began to be challenged in 1978. By 1979, two conflicting images coexisted within the Carter Administration resulting in a highly incoherent and unstable image of the international system. And by 1980, the Carter Administration had acquired a completely new and pessimistic image of an increasingly turbulent and fragmented international system that threatened the stability of the globe.

It has been argued that the Carter Administration's new image of the international system may have been temporary—that President Carter's change in image was a political expedient in order to respond to the domestic pressures and the rise of the political right that intensified with each international crisis, especially given that 1980 was an election year. "What is not clear," wrote Leslie Gelb (1980a, p. 19), "is whether these moves actually constitute the nucleus of a new Carter foreign policy or were inspired solely by the immediate need to react to the crisis in Southwest Asia" (see also Destler, Gelb & Lake, 1984).[16] Whether or not it would have continued into the future will never be known, however, for 1980 brought the election of Ronald Reagan as the new President of the United States.[17]

Notes

1. Other regional conflict and energy were relatively minor issues, but grew in importance (other conflict: 5.2% in 1977, 7.4% in 1980; energy: 1.3% in 1977, 4.5% in 1980).

2. Eastern European actors remained unimportant throughout all four years of the Carter Administration.

3. Secretary of State Muskie's image is not examined in terms of its level of stability because of his short duration in office.

4. Members of the commission consisted of prominent people involved in politics and economics from the trilateral countries. A large number of Carter Administration officials were members of the Trilateral Commission, including: Brzezinski (the Director), Vance, Vice President Walter Mondale, Secretary of Defense Harold Brown, Secretary of the Treasury Michael Blumenthal, Ambassador to the United Nations Andrew Young, and Director of the Arms Control and Disarmament Agency Paul Warnke (Lanouette, 1978b; Sanders, 1983, pp. 171–183). For a revisionist view, see Karpel (1977).

5. An interesting anecdote about Carter was told by his chief aide, Hamilton Jordan (1982, pp. 34–35): "He once told me that in addition to the information that State Department briefing books supplied on nations and their leaders, the easiest and best way to understand a country, its history, and its vital interests, was to look at the globe—to observe the countries surrounding it, its proximity to richer and stronger nations, to international waters and ports. Before conferring with a foreign leader, Carter would often sit by his globe, poring over his briefing books and trying to imagine the political, economic, and military pressures experienced by the leader and his or her country. 'I try to put myself in their shoes,' he once told me."

6. Carter explained his statement about his drastic change in attitude toward the Soviet Union by saying, 'I've never doubted the long-range ambitions of the Soviet Union . . . But it is obvious that the Soviets' actual invasion of a previously nonaligned country, an independent, freedom-loving country, a deeply religious country, with their own massive troops is a radical departure from the policy or actions that the Soviets have pursued since the Second World War" (U.S., President Carter, 1980a, p. 111).

NOTES

7. A study by Raphael (1981–82) found that the three television networks covered Iran an average of only five minutes per year from 1972 to 1977.

8. A similar argument is made by Sanders (1983) and Smith (1986). Sanders, however, does not focus on the role of Brzezinski but on the general effort by members of the Administration to straddle the two principal competing schools of thought—the global managers versus the containers.

9. According to Norman Podhoretz, a leading neoconservative: "Zbig has been maneuvering himself toward that stance (global interdependence) for several years. It was a great symbolic moment when he changed his institute at Columbia several years ago from the Research Institute on International Communism to the Research Institute for International Change" (in Sanders, 1983, p. 180). See also Brzezinski (1976) for another example of his thinking during the 1970s.

10. Brzezinski (1983, pp. 4–5) argues that he has always preferred to be the Special Assistant to the President for National Security Affairs rather than Secretary of State, although the opposite was usually reported in the press.

11. Alexander and Juliette George (1956) distinguish between "power-seeker" and "power-holder" in their personality study of Woodrow Wilson. In Wilson's efforts to gain power in order to overcome his low self-esteem, he conformed to the dominant beliefs of individuals who could significantly influence his rise. However, once Wilson successfully gained a position of power, he would demonstrate incredible rigidity and close-mindedness after he took a stand. This may be helpful in understanding Brzezinski's evolution in image: as power-seeker he was much more receptive to other people's preferences than as a power-holder.

12. See Rokeach (1968) for a discussion of primitive beliefs and their relationship to other types of beliefs.

13. Brzezinski also discusses the decline of the establishment and the rise of the professionl elites, but ironically seems to identify himself as part of the former establishment and is critical of the new professionals. It is his opinion that the foreign policy establishment "has been replaced either by partisan dogmatists within the extreme wings of the two parties or by a new generation of foreign policy technicians who are adept at shifting from one orientation to another, without any deeper philosophical commitment" (Brzezinski, 1983, p. 545).

14. Brzezinski called Vance "the last Vietnam casualty" and stated that "Vance is so worried after the disastrous use of force in Vietnam that he lacks the will to use force again" (in Sullivan, 1985, p. 166). However, Leslie Gelb disagreed with the interpretation that Vance was mesmerized by Vietnam and was afraid to use force: "For what it is worth, those of us who worked most closely with him were all convinced that he was neither a pacifist nor a bluffer, that where he believed the use of force would make sense, he would be bold in recommending it. Meanwhile, the third world may be about to go up in flames, and we have neither the force nor the economic wherewithall to do anything about it" (Gelb, 1980c, p. 15).

15. Resignations in the U.S. government based on principle have become quite rare. The last principled resignations by a Secretary of State occurred under Woodrow Wilson. William Jennings Bryan resigned over the administration's response to the sinking of the *Lusitania* and Robert Lansing, who replaced Bryan, resigned due to policy differences with Wilson over the Versailles treaty (Felton, 1980). It has also been reported that Vance nearly resigned in 1979 over the appointment of Robert Strauss as Middle East Ambassador (Ajemian, 1979).

CONTINUITY AND CHANGE

16. Rokeach (1973) has pointed out that cognitive theories usually focus on short-term change. He makes a distinction between ''short-term'' and ''long-term'' attitudinal change, and has suggested that the latter occurs primarily when underlying values have undergone change.

17. It is interesting to note that President Carter's farewell address in January, 1981 (U.S., Carter, 1981), focused on three major themes that reflected his earlier optimism: the threat of nuclear destruction, the stewardship of the physical resources of the planet, and the preeminence of the basic rights of human beings.

FIVE | *Foreign Policy Behavior*

I T has been commonly assumed that beliefs are significant causal forces of behavior. According to Kenneth Boulding (1969, p. 423), "we must recognize that the people whose decisions determine the policies and actions of nations do not respond to the 'objective' facts of the situation. It is what we think the world is like, not what it is really like, that determines our behavior." This basic assumption has become so firmly imbedded in the attitudinal research literature that the relationship between beliefs and human behavior has not received adequate study.

The Carter Administration had a worldview that changed over time. But did the Carter Administration's foreign policy behavior initially reflect its optimistic image of a complex international system? Did it reflect the growth of dissensus during 1978 and 1979? Was the Carter Administration's behavior consistent with its pessimistic image of an unstable and turbulent international system during the final year?

A description of the Administration's foreign policy behavior is based on the development of an events data set—that is, foreign policy events reported by publicly available sources such as newspapers (see appendix B for a discussion of the research method and appendix D for a list of the major foreign policy action taken by the Carter Administration). Results are presented on a yearly basis in describing America's foreign policy behavior toward the major issues, followed by a discussion of U.S. behavior toward the major actors with a focus on the importance of the Soviet Union for the United States. This allows for a direct comparison between the Carter Administration's beliefs and behavior.

The First Year

During the first year, the Administration's image focused on responding positively to the changing international environment so as to promote a global community. In accordance with this image, a diverse, complex, and pluralistic international system was perceived in which a variety of issues were believed to be of importance. Additionally, because no actor—including the United States or the Soviet Union—was considered able or willing to dominate international behavior, numerous international actors needed to be addressed. Behavior, during this time, closely corresponded to image.

Issues

In keeping with its perception of a complex international system, the Carter Administration in 1977 directed its action toward a large number of issues. These included Administration efforts to promote normalized relations, human rights, a prosperous global economy, a comprehensive peace in the Middle East, arms control, and conflict resolution in Africa. In fact, the same issues that were most important for the Carter Administration's beliefs were most important for its behavior (.79 correlation, see table 5.1).

Human rights and the normalization of relations attracted the most action. Carter's choice as Ambassador to the United Nations, Andrew Young (a close associate of Martin Luther King and the first black to hold such a high diplomatic position), was an indication of the Carter Administration's commitment to human rights and improving relations with countries that had traditionally been ignored. During the first year, President Carter, Rosalynn Carter, Vice President Mondale, Secretary of State Vance, and Ambassador Young visited over twenty countries in order to improve U.S. relationships abroad.

The Administration made a special effort to improve its relations with the Third World. A prime example of this occurred on September 7, 1977, when after more than a decade of American-Panamanian negotiations under three previous presidents, the Panama Canal treaties were successfully negotiated and signed by President Carter. Two treaties were agreed to: one allowed for the eventual transition of the Panama Canal to Panama in 1999; the other defined the neutral status of the canal and American rights to defend the canal. The willingness of the Carter Administration to return the canal and the Canal Zone to Panama was an important indication that "big brother's" paternalism toward Latin America was an attitude of the past and that a new positive era in U.S.-Latin American relations based on equality would result. For the Carter Administration, this was of major symbolic importance for the independence and sovereignty of Latin American and all Third World countries.

Table 5.1

Issues Acted Upon, 1977

Issue	Behavior (%)	Beliefs (%)
Normalization	27.3	16.2
Human Rights	24.5	16.9
Economy	11.2	7.2
Middle East Conflict	8.4	14.4
Arms Control	7.7	15.6
African Conflict	7.7	13.1
Security + Defense	6.3	1.8
Other Conflict	4.9	5.2
Southwest Asian Conflict	2.1	0.7
Energy	0	1.3
Development	0	7.5
	N = 143	N = 597
Rank-order correlation = .79		

Note: The rank order correlation coefficient used is Spearman's Rho, which varies from 1.0 (positive) to − 1.0 (inverse relationship).

The United States also attempted to improve relations with its former adversaries. For the first time since trade relations were suspended in 1960, the United States held talks with Cuba on maritime boundaries and reached agreement on fishing rights in their overlapping fishing zone. In June the United States and Cuba each agreed to open an "interest" section and exchanged middle-rank diplomats for the first time in sixteen years. Normalization of relations with the People's Republic of China was pursued by the Administration, including a four-day visit by Secretary of State Vance to China. This action was reinforced by the U.S. decision on June 30 to formally end its membership in the Southeast Asian Treaty Organization (SEATO), an alliance originally created to contain (Chinese) communist aggression. Efforts were also made to improve relations with Vietnam, first by relaxing the trade embargo and discussing the fate of the MIAs (Missing in Actions), then through resumption of the Paris talks.

The promotion of human rights was fundamental to the Administration's foreign policy behavior as well as its image during the first year. Eastern European countries and, in particular, the Soviet Union were often singled out for their human rights abuses. For example, the United States charged Czechoslovakia with violating the 1975 Helsinki agreement provision on human rights due to its recent actions against dissidents, the first time the United States had publicly accused any government of failing to live up to the Helsinki accord. President Carter spoke out regularly against Soviet violations of human rights, going so far as to send a letter to Soviet dissident Andrei Sakharov asserting the U.S. commitment to human rights. United States foreign assistance was cut or withheld from numerous other countries for violations of human rights: including Argentina, Brazil, Chile, El Salvador, Guatemala, Ethiopia, Laos, Mozambique, the Philippines, Uganda, and Uruguay. In fact, this was the first time an American administration reduced foreign assistance to another country on humanitarian grounds. The United States also voted against loan proposals in multilateral financial institutions (e.g., the International Monetary Fund, World Bank) to numerous countries because of human rights violations (Smith, 1986, p. 53).

The Carter Administration's commitment to human rights and democracy was also evident in its behavior toward resolving the conflict in Africa. In close consultation with Great Britain, diplomatic efforts were vigorously pursued to promote black majority rule and democracy in Rhodesia and Namibia. The Byrd Amendment, which allowed the importation of Rhodesian chrome in violation of a United Nations resolution, was repealed by the United States. With regard to South Africa, the Carter Administration recalled its Ambassador and two other U.S. government officials. Furthermore, the United States, France, and Great Britain reversed a previous policy and voted for a U.N. Security Council resolution calling for a mandatory six-month renewable arms embargo against South Africa. Both actions were designed to influence South Africa to support the Anglo-American effort to resolve the conflict in Rhodesia and Namibia as well as to indicate the U.S. attitude toward the oppressive policies of apartheid. Administration action to promote peaceful change in southern Africa was also intended to improve United States relations throughout black Africa.

The global economy and the resolution of the Arab-Israeli conflict were also important areas for the Administration's foreign policy behavior in accordance with its image. Trade agreements were signed with Japan and the European Economic Community in which they accepted certain fishing rights within the United States' new 200-mile coastal fishing zone, and an agreement was signed with Canada to construct the Alaskan pipeline. President Carter attended a major economic summit of the industrialized democracies that focused on problems of inflation and unemployment held in London. The United States also signed a trade agreement with Mexico providing for bilateral tariff reduction in certain goods—the first trade agreement with Mexico in 35 years.

THE FIRST YEAR

The United States was active in trying to peacefully resolve the conflict in the Middle East. Attempts were made to achieve a comprehensive peace through the participation of all the relevant parties: Israel, Egypt, Jordan, Saudi Arabia, Syria, and the Palestinians. In October, the United States and the Soviet Union took the unprecedented step of jointly issuing a formal declaration calling for the creation of a new Middle East conference to meet in Geneva to achieve a comprehensive peace. Whereas past administrations had attempted to keep the Soviet Union out of the Middle East, the Carter Administration was attempting to work with the Soviets in order to resolve the Arab-Israeli conflict.

President Carter was a firm believer in the pursuit of arms control, and action by the United States was directed in this area. The Strategic Arms Limitation Talks (SALT II) proceeded with the Soviets despite a early set-back when Administration officials attempted to promote more reductions than the Soviets had originally agreed to at Vladivostok with the Ford Administration. Negotiations also were initiated regarding chemical and radiological weapons, conventional arms transfers to developing countries, the demilitarization of the Indian Ocean, and a comprehensive test ban on nuclear explosions.

In May, the Carter White House attempted to restrain and reduce U.S. conventional arms transfers abroad by issuing Presidential Directive (PD) 13, which included a cut in arms sales after 1977, a ban on developing advanced weapon systems intended only for export (and being the first to introduce new weapons into a region), ending production agreements with other countries for significant weapons (and prohibiting transfers of such weapons to other countries), and forbidding the U.S. government from promoting arms sales. NATO countries, Japan, Australia, New Zealand, and Israel were exempted from the restrictions. PD 13 attempted to limit weapons sales by establishing a number of guidelines governing what should be sold, to whom, and for what purpose. According to one study, ''PD 13 was the most restrictive policy on arms transfer the United States had adopted'' (Semmel, 1983, p. 91).

The Administration's early arms control efforts also promoted nuclear nonproliferation. The President instituted a number of measures to prohibit the spread of nuclear weapons: the development of the plutonium-based fast breeder reactor was delayed, the reprocessing of plutonium was stopped, guidelines were issued for the reprocessing of spent (uranium) fuel rods on a case-by-case basis, and legislation was submitted to tighten controls of American exports of nuclear technology (resulting in the Nuclear Non-Proliferation Act of 1978). In May, President Carter signed the Treaty of Tlatelolco prohibiting the possession, use, and fabrication of nuclear arms in Latin America.

FOREIGN POLICY BEHAVIOR

Carter Administration foreign policy action appears to have diverged from its international image only in two issue areas—Western security and Third World development. While Western security was relatively unimportant for the Carter Administration's image (discussed 1.8% of the time), the number of foreign policy actions (6.3%) suggested that it was concerned with strengthening the military in order to maintain Western security: an agreement was reached with Oman for U.S. base facilities, the MK–12A nuclear warhead was scheduled for development to upgrade the Minuteman Inter-Continental Ballistic Missile (ICBM) system, and authorization was requested to produce the neutron bomb. However, to characterize the Carter Administration as a major promoter of American defense forces during the first year would be deceptive since most of these actions were implemented in accordance with decisions made by previous administrations. In fact, most of Carter's decisions were consistent with his belief that the military should be downplayed as an instrument of American foreign policy.

Probably the most important decision made by President Carter concerning defense was his decision to cancel the production of the B–1 bomber, which was intended to replace the aging B–52 bomber as the main weapon in the Air Forces's arsenal. President Carter decided to withdraw U.S. ground troops from South Korea, another indication of his effort to avoid excessive reliance on the military and to signal displeasure with the repressive military regime. In May, Major General John Singlaub was recalled and removed from his command as Chief of Staff of U.S. forces in Korea following an interview in which he said that President Carter's announced policy of withdrawal would lead to war—the first such dismissal since former President Truman fired General MacArthur in 1951. President Carter also attempted to restrain covert activities and abuses by the Central Intelligence Agency (CIA). For example, upon entering office CIA payments that had been going to Jordan's King Hussein for over twenty years were stopped. Overall, the Administration's defense policy was based on PD–18, a "top secret" five-page memo premised on a very optimistic image of the world and an impression of the Soviet Union as an "incomplete superpower" (Kraar, 1978).

Third World development, the second divergent issue area, was important in Carter's quest for a global community. However, no action was reported in this area during the first year or, for that matter, throughout the Administration's entire term of office. This omission may be due to the fundamental flaw of the data set. As discussed in appendix B, the source of information used for determining the Carter Administration's foreign policy behavior, *Deadline Data* (and the media in general), has a tendency to under-report events that focus exclusively on the Third World. Actual efforts were made to promote Third World development that were not reported in *Deadline Data*. For example, the Carter Administration attempted to increase significantly U.S. funding for the multilateral development banks and became actively involved in a number of issues that had been a focus of the North-South debate—for example, the Law of the Sea (see, Hollick, 1981; U.S., Congress, 1978, pp. 101–116). Nevertheless, the Carter Administration's foreign policy action toward Third World development may not have reflected its beliefs.

Actors

During Carter's first year, not only did United States foreign policy behavior address a variety of important issues; it also directed behavior to a wide variety of actors. Six of the eight actor categories were the targets of United States action a minimum of 10 percent of the time. Those actors that were the most important for beliefs tended to be important for behavior (.44 correlation, see table 5.2). The relative importance of the actors varied depending on the issue for both the Carter Administration's beliefs and behavior. In fact, so far was the tilt away from an East-West orientation that the majority of American foreign policy behavior was directed at Latin America, China and Asia, and Western Europe and Japan.

Carter Administration officials did not believe the Soviet Union should be the predominant focus of its attention. The Soviet Union was only one of many

Table 5.2

Actors Acted Toward, 1977

Actors	Behavior (%)	Beliefs (%)
Latin America	23.4	11.3
China + Asia	16.8	16.4
Western Europe + Japan	16.1	14.3
Middle East	11.7	17.9
Soviet Union	11.7	16.6
Africa	10.9	12.5
Global	6.6	10.5
Eastern Europe	2.9	0.5
	N = 137	N = 391
Rank-order correlation = .44		

Note: The rank-order correlation coefficient used is Spearman's Rho, which varies from 1.0 (positive) to −1.0 (inverse relationship).

important actors in 1977: in terms of its importance in the belief system of the Administration it was rank-ordered second, receiving 16.6 percent of the attention; in terms of behavior toward the Soviet Union it was ranked-ordered fourth, receiving attention 11.7 percent of the time (see table 5.3). In 1977 the Carter Administration did not believe that the Soviet Union had a major role to play for most of the issues addressed. The Soviets were a minor actor for both the Administration's beliefs and behavior in five of the seven most important issue areas: the Middle East conflict, conflict in Africa, normalization, the global economy, and Third World development. The only issues for which they were important were arms control and, to a lesser extent behaviorally, human rights.[1]

So optimistic was the Carter Administration about the Soviet Union that, paradoxically, relations got off to a rocky start. U.S. behavior in 1977 proved conflictual two-thirds of the time (see table 5.4). The United States challenged the Soviet Union in the areas of arms control and, in particular, human rights. The SALT II negotiations suffered a setback when the Carter Administration attempted to get Soviet approval for greater reductions in strategic forces than previously agreed to. The Carter Administration was particularly vocal and active relative to the issue of human rights, unlike previous administrations, which tended to ignore human rights or work behind the public stage. These actions, along with those affecting U.S. defense forces and movement toward a comprehensive peace to the Arab-Israeli conflict, were in accordance with

Table 5.3

Importance of the Soviet Union, 1977

Major Issues	Behavior (%)	Beliefs (%)
Arms Control	27.3	69.8
Human Rights	14.7	5.7
Middle East Conflict	8.3	6.8
Economy	6.3	2.9
Normalization	2.6	7.6
African Conflict	0.0	4.4
Development	0.0	6.7
Rank-order correlation = .52		
For All Issues, %	11.7	16.6
Rank-order (relative to other actors)	4	2

the Carter Administration's image in which there was no need to emphasize or fear the Soviet Union.

To summarize, during the first year a high level of congruency existed between the Carter Administration's optimistic image of the international system and its foreign policy behavior. The importance of the Soviet Union and the role of military force were deemphasized while diplomatic, economic, and moral policies of promoting a cooperative international environment were accentuated. Foreign policy behavior was concerned with a variety of important issues and actors, and such diversity coincided with its image of global complexity.[2] Overall, a strong positive relationship existed between the beliefs and the behavior of the Carter Administration throughout the first year.

The Second Year

The original Carter Administration image was modified with time as differences in individual images clearly emerged due to events in Africa. While President Carter and Secretary Vance became somewhat skeptical about Soviet activities, they continued to retain their basically optimistic image of the Soviet Union and adhered to the development of a global community in a complex environment. However, NSC Advisor Brzezinski's image of the Soviet Union became pessimistic. He began to focus on the threats to the "arc of crisis" and placed greater emphasis on political-military issues and the need to respond to Soviet foreign interventionism. This change in collective image resulted in less congruency with Carter's foreign policy behavior at the collective level. Though action was still directed at a variety of major issues and

Table 5.4

Type of Action Toward the Soviet Union

	Year			
Type of Action	*1977*	*1978*	*1979*	*1980*
Very Conflictual,%	6.3	0	0	5.7
Conflictual, %	62.5	50.0	61.9	92.5
Neutral/Mixed, %	12.5	7.1	4.8	0
Cooperative, %	6.3	42.9	23.8	1.9
Very Cooperative, %	12.6	0	9.6	0
	N = 16	N = 14	N = 21	N = 57

Note: Given the limited number of cases, the frequency distributions should be used as a rough indicator.

actors, inconsistencies emerged relative to the specific issues and actors when comparing the Carter Administration's beliefs and behavior.

Issues

The Carter Administration directed its foreign policy behavior toward a variety of major issues in 1978, concentrating its activity on many of the same issues as the previous year and adhering to overall policies based on optimism. However, due to Soviet and Cuban involvement in Africa, the Carter Administration began to adopt new positions toward some issues that were inconsistent with its optimistic image. Therefore, moderate congruency existed between the Carter Administration's beliefs and behavior toward the most important issues (.49 correlation, see table 5.5), although this was lower than the previous year.

Differences in policymaker images emerged within the Carter Administration resulting in a major policy debate over what to do concerning Cuban and Soviet interventionism in the Horn of Africa. Brzezinski suggested and supported a number of political-military moves, including: sending a U.S. naval task force to the area; assisting third parties in sending troops to support Somalia (e.g., the Sudanese, Egyptians, Iranians, or the Saudis); and reinstating the

Table 5.5

Issues Acted Upon, 1978

Issue	Behavior (%)	Beliefs (%)
Normalization	23.7	8.9
Economy	15.8	12.4
Middle East Conflict	14.5	7.4
Human Rights	13.2	11.6
Security & Defense	10.5	11.9
African Conflict	9.2	21.0
Arms Control	5.3	16.0
Other Conflict	5.3	2.7
Energy	1.3	2.0
Southwest Asian Conflict	1.3	0.9
Development	0	5.1
	N = 77	N = 886

Rank-order correlation = .49

Note: The rank-order correlation coefficient used is Spearman's Rho, which varies from 1.0 (positive) to −1.0 (inverse relationship).

concept of "linkage" in American-Soviet relations. Most Administration officials, including Carter and Vance, opposed these policies (Drew, 1978, pp. 111–118; Gelb, 1980c; Kaiser & Oberdorfer, 1978; Oberdorfer, 1978).

Although opposed to direct American intervention, many Administration members were nonetheless concerned about Soviet and Cuban adventurism and felt frustrated at their inability to effectively respond to the situation. It was during this time that the White House began to criticize Congress for "tying the Administration's hands" in Africa. The specific complaint made was that congressional restrictions against aiding the rebel forces in Angola prevented the United States from undertaking any efforts to weaken the government that was supported by Cuba and the Soviet Union.

Ultimately, the Carter Administration's behavior in the Horn of Africa proved consistent with its optimistic image. Although aroused by Soviet and Cuban interventionism, the Administration elected to downplay the issue and refused to supply a limited amount of defensive arms to Somalia until Somali regular armed forces withdrew from Ethiopian territory and Somalia provided assurances that the weapons would not be used in the disputed area of the Ogaden. Accordingly, the Carter Administration decided not to become militarily involved—it limited its action to publicizing the issue.[3]

Concern over Soviet and Cuban interventionism had other consequences for U.S. foreign policy behavior—leading to various inconsistencies with the Administration's more optimistic image. In response to foreign intervention in the Katanga province of Zaire, President Carter accused Cuba of training and equipping the rebels (who invaded from neighboring Angola). Furthermore, the United States made an overt commitment; it sent 18 C–141 air transports to Zaire to assist in the airlift of Franco-Belgian troops who sought to stop the invading force. In so doing, the Carter Administration chose to emphasize the external threat and respond with direct military support rather than minimize the strategic importance of the issue and emphasize local sources of the regional conflict—a behavior that would have been much more in accord with its optimistic image.

Subsequent to Soviet and Cuban activities in Africa, American-Cuban efforts to normalize relations began to deteriorate. A similar situation evolved with Vietnam following its invasion of Kampuchea and the signing of a Soviet-Vietnamese friendship treaty. Therefore, although the Carter administration verbalized that it was committed to the normalization of relations throughout the globe, Soviet, Cuban, and Vietnamese activities resulted in some contradictory behavior.

While bilateral relations suffered in some areas, the Carter Administration persisted in its efforts to promote better relations with other actors throughout the globe. Secretary Vance formally returned to Hungary the Crown of St. Stephen, taken by the U.S. Army at the end of World War II—a lingering irritant in U.S.–Hungarian relations. President Tito met with President Carter, the first communist leader he received, in an attempt to strengthen relations with Yugoslavia. The U.S. Senate narrowly approved the Panama Canal treaties—a very controversial step within the domestic arena, but of tangible and symbolic importance to Latin America and much of the world. Carter also visited Nigeria, making him the first American president to visit a black African country.

Most importantly, the United States grew closer to China. National Security Advisor Brzezinski visited China; the United States agreed to sell airborne geological equipment to China (denied to the Soviet Union because of potential military uses); and the United States agreed to no longer block Western European arms sales to China. Finally, on December 15, President Carter announced that establishment of formal diplomatic relations would take effect at the beginning of the new year. As a result, the United States would officially withdraw from its defense treaty with the Republic of China (Taiwan), no longer recognize Taiwan as the official government of all of China (maintaining unofficial links), and limit the sale of sophisticated military weaponry to Taiwan—at the same time, providing assurances for a peaceful resolution of the "two-Chinas" problem. This was an important step by the Carter Administration because it took thirty years to restore official diplomatic relations with the most populous country in the world following the "fall of China" in 1949.

The Administration was also active in the international economic arena. The United States agreed with Japan on means to reduce Japan's $10 billion trade surplus and implemented joint measures with West Germany to stabilize the dollar and coordinate economic policies. As a result of instability in the foreign exchange market near the end of the year, the United States coordinated its action with Japan and European Economic Community countries to contain the fall of the dollar. The United States also began to monitor its exports to communist countries more closely: Poland and Rumania would get "more favorable" treatment and Hungary would get "favorable discrimination" in comparison to the Soviet Union, Bulgaria, East Germany, and Czechoslovakia. Furthermore, the United States would emphasize an "evenhanded" approach to technology transfers to the Soviet Union and China.

In 1978, attempts at resolving conflict in the Middle East became a prime concern of the Carter Administration. Initial efforts for a meeting in Geneva for a comprehensive peace were unsuccessful, but Carter persevered. His most noted foreign policy achievement occurred when he successfully mediated peace and a partial resolution of the Arab-Israeli conflict. For thirteen days in September, Carter conferred with Egyptian President Anwar Sadat and Prime Minister Menachem Begin and, though the negotiations were often tortuous, the three leaders were able to agree to the Camp David accords. The accords were based on two documents: one was an agreement between Egypt and Israel to conclude a peace treaty within three months based on an Israeli withdrawal from the Sinai peninsula and full diplomatic relations (in which Egypt would become the first Arab country recognizing Israel's right to exist); the other document provided the framework for Egypt, Israel, and other interested parties (i.e., Jordan, Syria, and the Palestine Liberation Organization) to grant autonomy to Palestinians in the Gaza strip and the West Bank after five years. The Camp David accords represented a major accomplishment consistent with the Carter Administration's belief that the Arab-Israeli conflict needed to be peaceably resolved.

Human rights remained another priority. During 1978, United States protests continued against trials of Soviet dissidents and military assistance was suspended to Chile in response to the assassination of former Chilean foreign minister Orlando Letelier. Military assistance was also suspended to the Somoza Government in Nicaragua, a critical action affecting the civil war. This reversed a long tradition of U.S. military assistance to Nicaragua. More refugees were allowed into the United States in light of many of the people affected by regional conflicts, especially refugees from Indochina, but also political prisoners from Cuba and victims of Lebanon's civil war. The Carter Administration remained committed to bringing peace and majority rule to the people of southern Africa. Negotiations under Anglo-American leadership continued in Rhodesia, and Western diplomatic efforts (Canada, France, Great Britain, the United States, and West Germany) were made in Namibia.

Carter Administration efforts continued in the area of arms control. The eighth round of SALT II talks was completed, and most of the issues between the U.S. and the Soviet Union were resolved by the end of the year. Arms control talks also incorporated a new area in 1978—antisatellite weapons. Concerning arms transfers, President Carter announced an $8.6 billion ceiling on U.S. arms sales abroad outside the Western Europe-Japan region for 1978 and a $8.4 billion limit for 1979—each ceiling amounting to an 8 percent cut from the previous year.

Finally, the Administration took some of its most controversial steps in the area of U.S. defense policy. President Carter pledged 8,000 more U.S. troops in Europe in the next eighteen months. Yet, at the same time, the President decided to defer production of the neutron bomb, which was previously set to be deployed in the European theater (creating an irritant in U.S.-

German relations). U.S. military forces stationed in Asia were reduced in number. In South Korea, 800 U.S. ground troops were withdrawn during the year, although this represented a slowdown in the planned withdrawal (of 3,400 troops for the year). The United States also reduced its military personnel in Taiwan by half (to 750). Finally, President Carter vetoed a weapons authorization bill because it contained provisions for building a $2.1 billion nuclear aircraft carrier, which he felt was unnecessary for national security and wasteful of U.S. tax dollars.

Actors

Overall, in 1978 there was a moderate level of consistency between the Carter Administration's beliefs and behavior toward the actors. United States foreign policy behavior was directed at a variety of international actors. No single actor received a disproportionate amount of action relative to others. In fact, at least 10 percent of America's foreign policy behavior was directed at six of the eight groupings of actors. This behavior by the Carter Administration was consistent with its perception of a pluralistic international system. However, unlike 1977, there was little relationship between those actors that Carter believed were most important and those actors receiving most of the foreign policy action (.18 correlation, see table 5.6).

The Soviet Union was the most important actor (the recipient of 17.1 percent of America's behavior in 1978 versus 11.7 percent in 1977; see table

Table 5.6

Actors Acted Toward, 1978

Actors	Behavior (%)	Beliefs (%)
Soviet Union	17.1	27.6
China + Asia	15.8	3.1
Middle East	14.6	10.3
Western Europe + Japan	13.4	20.4
Eastern Europe	12.2	2.0
Latin America	12.2	4.9
Global	9.8	11.9
Africa	4.9	19.9
	N = 82	N = 554
Rank-order correlation = .18		

Note: The rank-order correlation coefficient used is Spearman's Rho, which varies from 1.0 (positive) to − 1.0 (inverse relationship).

5.7). Nineteen seventy-eight was a period when Cuban and Soviet involvement in Africa aroused major concern and the Soviet Union became the predominant object of Administration foreign policy beliefs and behavior. The Soviets became more integral to the major issues addressed by the Carter Administration. They were very important to the Carter Administration's beliefs and behavior for three issues: arms control, Western security, and human rights. For two other issues, the global economy and the Middle East conflict, the USSR was a relatively minor actor—other actors were more vital. Discrepancies in beliefs and behavior existed only for two issues: the conflict in Africa[4] and the normalization of relations. Overall, the relative importance of the Soviet Union for the major issues was similar for the Carter Administration beliefs and behavior (.68 correlation).

Although the Administration acted boldly during 1977, it became more cautious in its dealings with the Soviet Union in 1978. During the second year, bilateral relations continued along a troublesome path due to Soviet action in Africa. Two patterns emerged in United States foreign policy action vis-à-vis the Soviet Union. For the most part, American behavior was based upon its optimistic outlook on the Soviet Union—protests continued against trials of Soviet dissidents (Shcharansky and Ginzburg), Carter deferred production of the neutron bomb, SALT II and arms control progressed, and the United States was reluctant to become involved in the Horn of Africa crisis. However, skepticism over Soviet intentions due to its activities in Africa was also

Table 5.7

Importance of the Soviet Union, 1978

Major Issues	Behavior (%)	Beliefs (%)
Arms Control	50.0	78.2
Western Security	50.0	53.5
Human Rights	20.0	16.3
Global Economy	8.3	7.6
Normalization	0.0	19.7
Middle East Conflict	0.0	1.9
African Conflict	0.0	18.8
Rank-order correlation = .68		
For All Issues, %	17.1	27.6
Rank-order (relative to other actors)	1	1

reflected in U.S. behavior. The United States proceeded with the Camp David peace process without Soviet participation, assisted the French-Belgian airlift to support Zaire, began to monitor exports to the Soviet Union, and expressed disapproval over the Soviet-Vietnamese friendship treaty. These two contradictory patterns of behavior by the Carter Administration—one based on optimism, the other on pessimism—were reflected in its mixed behavior toward the Soviet Union: 50 percent conflictual and 42.9 percent cooperative (see table 5.4).

U.S. defense spending behavior was relatively consistent with the Administration's optimistic image of the Soviet Union. At the beginning of every year the president submits his proposed annual budget to Congress, including his request for the military. Defense spending is a significant indication of the behavioral orientation of the United States toward the Soviet Union because American military forces are overwhelmingly targeted toward the Soviet Union and defense budget totals are based upon assessments of Soviet intentions and capabilities.

The first Carter Administration budget, fiscal year 1979 submitted in early 1978, requested a modest 3 percent increase in defense spending, but at a much slower rate than previously requested (see table 5.8). As stated by President Carter, it was "consistent with campaign pledges to the American people, it is $8 billion below the defense budget projected for 1979 by the previous administration" (U.S., OMB, 1979, pp. 5–6). This slowdown in spending is evident by examining the smaller percentage of the federal budget devoted to national defense compared to the previous year—23.5 percent for 1979 versus 25.5 percent for 1978. Therefore, it can be argued that, although a modest increase occurred in aggregate numbers, the Carter Administration slightly reduced the size of the defense budget for fiscal year 1979 relative to the previous administration's policies.

In conclusion, the Carter administration's foreign policy behavior was moderately consistent with its optimistic image of the international system in 1978. Relations with China were normalized, the Panama Canal treaties were approved, peace was achieved between Egypt and Israel in the Middle East, measures were taken to strengthen the global economy, the U.S. defense posture was modified, and efforts in the area of arms control and human rights continued. Soviet and Cuban interventionism in Africa affected the Administration's behavior; the Soviet Union became more important to the Carter Administration's image, and this was reflected in much of its behavior toward the Soviet Union. Nevertheless, the United States played a relatively passive role during the Ethiopian-Somali conflict consistent with its belief that direct military involvement was counterproductive.

Table 5.8

Defense Spending

Fiscal Year Budget	Previous Year Outlay[a]	Proposed Outlay[a]	Increase (%)		Federal Budget (%)
			Year	*Real*	
Ford 1978	100,075	112,262	12.2	—	25.5
Carter 1979	107,626	117,779	9.4	3	23.5
Carter 1980	114,503	125,830	9.9	3	23.7
Carter 1981	130,368	146,241	12.2	5	23.8
Carter 1982	161,088	184,399	14.5	6	24.9

[a]Millions of dollars.

Note: All figures at the time were based on estimates.

Source: U.S., Office of Management and Budget. *Budget of the United States* (fiscal years 1978–1982).

Some inconsistency between the Carter Administration's beliefs and behavior also occurred, especially pertaining to the relative importance of the actors involved and the differences in the ranking of issues. Furthermore, the Carter Administration occasionally displayed much more conflictual behavior, as in providing airlift assistance to put down the rebellion in Zaire and halting the process of normalization with Cuba and Vietnam. The inconsistency that existed between collective beliefs and behavior appears to have reflected the modified optimistic image of the international system that resulted during the second year due to the differences in images that emerged among the major foreign policymakers within the Administration.

The Third Year

During the third year, two divergent views coexisted within the Carter Administration as a result of differences in individual images of the international system. Vance saw a complex system that offered an opportunity to promote positive global change and a new world order. Brzezinski perceived an increasingly turbulent, unstable system conducive to Soviet interventionism, and in light of this, felt the United States needed to promote the West's security and defense. Carter wavered between being more optimistic in accordance with Vance and being pessimistic more in accord with Brzezinski's view.

The foreign policy behavior during the third year reflected this precarious balance of images through two dominant trends. On the one hand, international behavior was directed at a variety of major issues and actors in accordance with its optimistic perspective of global complexity. Yet at the same time, Administration officials became more concerned with maintaining a strong defense posture and protecting national security, especially near the end of 1979 when challenged by the seizure of American hostages in Iran. Overall, these two patterns in beliefs and behavior produced virtually no congruency when the collective beliefs of the Carter Administration were compared with its collective behavior for 1979.

Issues

Many Carter actions were consistent with the pursuit of global community. The Administration remained active in trying to improve U.S. bilateral relationships (see table 5.9). President Carter traveled to Mexico City for an official visit, and the two countries eventually agreed to the sale of Mexican natural gas to the United States, ending a two-year conflict over prices. The United States reestablished relations with Uganda after the fall of Idi Amin (they were originally suspended in 1973 because of human rights violations). Congress passed and President Carter signed into law a bill implementing the Panama Canal treaties, a victory for Carter in light of the domestic opposition surrounding the treaties.

U.S. relations with China continued to improve. First Deputy Premier Teng Hsiao-ping became the first high-level communist Chinese official to visit the United States and Vice President Mondale reciprocated by traveling to Peking. The United States and China agreed to an outstanding claims settlement, which cleared the way for the establishment of normal trade relations. The United States, in fact, extended ''most-favored-nation'' status and agreed to provide $2 billion in U.S. trade credits over the next five years. In addition, the United States and Taiwan finally agreed on a formula to maintain unofficial relations.

The Carter Administration attempted to follow through on the Camp David accords of the previous year in order to peacefully resolve the Arab-Israeli conflict. President Carter travelled to Egypt and Israel, successfully bringing about the final resolution of the differences over the peace treaty. The treaty was signed by Begin, Sadat, and Carter on March 26 in Washington, D.C.—Egypt had officially withdrawn from the Arab-Israeli conflict, and Israel officially recognized the rights of Palestinians in the Gaza strip and the West Bank. In order to insure the peace agreement between Egypt and Israel, the United States committed itself to supply large amounts of foreign aid (over $5 billion to the two countries over the next three years) and provide aerial surveillance of the Sinai (for three years). A similar aid package was con-

Table 5.9

Issues Acted Upon, 1979

Issue	Behavior (%)	Beliefs (%)
Normalization	18.9	9.7
Southwest Asian Conflict	18.2	2.2
Middle East Conflict	14.7	15.0
Human Rights	14.0	11.2
Other Conflict	8.4	8.1
Security & Defense	7.7	11.4
African Conflict	7.0	8.4
Energy	4.9	4.4
Arms Control	3.5	10.0
Economy	2.8	8.7
Development	0	10.8
	N = 143	N = 712

Rank-order correlation = − .01

Note: The rank-order correlation coefficient used is Spearman's Rho, which varies from 1.0 (positive) to − 1.0 (inverse relationship).

structed for other Arab countries as an incentive for them to enter into the Camp David peace process.

The Administration also maintained an active stance in promoting human rights and democracy. The Carter Administration recalled the U.S. Ambassador and cut diplomatic, military, and economic relations with Chile in retaliation for its refusal to extradite officials in connection with the murder of Chilean exile leader Orlando Letelier. President Carter announced that the United States would double the number of incoming Indochinese refugees from 7,000 to 14,000 per month. In August, a minor incident occurred at the Kennedy International Airport in which the United States delayed an Aeroflot plane to determine if the recently defected Aleksandr Godunov's wife was returning to Moscow on her own free will. In October, the United States ordered the Ambassador to South Korea home for consultation to protest the expulsion of opposition leader Kim Young Sam from the National Assembly. During the same month, the United States said that it was "surprised and disappointed" at the conviction of the PRC dissident leader Wei Jingsheng, the first public rebuke of China since normalization.

The Administration's greatest efforts to promote human rights and democracy were made in addressing regional conflicts in Africa and Central

America. In Rhodesia, the United States continued to push for majority rule and full political participation for all parties in an effort to resolve the growing African conflict. The Case-Javits amendment instructed the Administration to lift economic sanctions against Rhodesia following the April elections, although it excluded the Patriotic Front. President Carter, however, did not lift the sanctions, declaring that it would not be in the interest of the U.S. because the elections were neither fair nor free. This aided the critical negotiations that were going on and eventually were resolved in London under British auspices. Only after an agreement was signed by all the parties—including the Patriotic Front—for a peaceful transition through free elections to majority rule, did the United States then announce an end to the twelve-year-old trade sanctions in support of the new state of Zimbabwe.

A relatively peaceful transition from white minority rule to black majority rule had been achieved by the Anglo-American initiative. Western diplomatic efforts attempted to achieve a similar breakthrough over Namibia throughout the year. This action was supported by U.S. sanctions against South Africa that went beyond the U.N. arms embargo: including suspending all nuclear cooperation with South Africa, curtailing all official sports contact, limiting Eximbank and Commodity Credit Corporation credits, and restricting visas for high-ranking South African military and police officers. The Carter Administration continued to condemn racial injustice, seeking to promote black majority rule in southern Africa.

In Nicaragua, the United States took a strong position against the status quo and in support of human rights and majority rule. During 1979, an internal situation that had long been festering broke out into an intense civil war between the Somoza government and the Sandinistas. The United States had been the traditional backer of the Somozas in Nicaragua going all the way back to the 1930s. Nevertheless, when the civil war reached its critical stage in June, the United States embargoed all U.S. arms shipments to Nicaragua, and the White House called on other countries to do the same. In the Organization of American States (OAS), the United States voted for the ousting of the Somoza regime, called for a cease-fire and a "transitional government of national reconciliation," and supported deployment of an OAS peace-keeping force to restore order and democracy. The Carter Administration was concerned with the communist left and preferred broader representation in the new government beyond just the Sandinistas. But the situation in Nicaragua was completely out of U.S. control, and the Latin American countries did not support the U.S. plan for an OAS peace-keeping force. Nevertheless, after the fall of Somoza, the United States established diplomatic relations with the new

THE THIRD YEAR

Sandinista government, sent emergency food and medical aid, and promised them economic assistance to support the growth of democracy.

The Carter Administration focused less attention in promoting arms control and a prosperous global economy, but significant progress was still made. The SALT II agreements signed by Carter and Brezhnev on June 18 in Vienna provided limitations on strategic nuclear weapons at levels slightly lower than the ceilings set at Vladivostok (e.g., total launchers were reduced from 2,400 to 2,250). After intensive hearings, a majority of the Senate Foreign Relations Committee in November recommended full Senate approval for the treaties. As for nonproliferation, the United States reduced aid to Pakistan, and also indicated disapproval for its repressive policies, following Pakistani purchase of equipment that could enable it to develop an atomic bomb (although arms sales were not affected).

In the economic realm, in April the Tokyo round of multilateral trade talks which began in 1974 under the auspices of the GATT (General Agreement on Trade and Tariffs) were brought to fruition. Where agreement was reached over the reduction of tariffs during the Kennedy round of the early 1960s, the Tokyo round produced important agreement over the regulation of nontariff barriers. Two major summits were held, at Guadeloupe and Tokyo, attended by heads of the industrial democracies; they focused on the West's energy position and the need to strengthen the international economy. The Western countries, including the United States, agreed to cut their oil demand (by 5 percent) and oil imports to dampen the inflationary effects of the recent increases in the price of oil. Furthermore, President Carter outlined a six-point domestic energy program, calling for an immediate ceiling on oil imports (at 1977 levels), a 50 percent cut in oil imports by 1990, a $82 billion plan to develop alternative domestic energy sources, and major steps to promote conservation.

Other actions by the Carter Administration reflected a more pessimistic image of the international system. Its concern with the threat posed by the Soviet Union resulted in more action toward other regional conflicts and efforts to bolster the West's security and defense forces. When conflict between North Yemen and South Yemen broke out, resulting in South Yemen becoming more closely allied to the Soviet Union, the United States quickly sided with North Yemen. President Carter ordered U.S. naval forces to the Arabian Sea, sent two AWACs planes to Saudi Arabia in a show of support (including 200 U.S. Air Force personnel), and subsequently invoked national security powers to speed delivery of $300 million in arms to North Yemen without the prior approval by Congress. Another crisis erupted in South Korea following the assassination of President Park in October. On this occasion the

United States responded by placing U.S. armed forces in South Korea on a higher state of alert and ordering an aircraft carrier and radar warning planes into the area to help deter outside interference, even though a month previously opposition leader Kim Dae Jung had been sentenced to death by a military tribunal.

As Carter policymakers became more concerned with dampening these regional conflicts and the threats to U.S. interests, they became more committed to a stronger defense. In the strategic realm, President Carter approved the full-scale development and deployment of the M-X missile system to replace the Minuteman ICBMs—based on a mobile launcher with more powerful and accurate nuclear warheads. The United States also instituted plans for the development of a 100,000-man Rapid Deployment Force (RDF) for the Third World, focusing on the Middle East and the Persian Gulf region. In South Korea, the Administration halted the program of withdrawing U.S. troops following new intelligence that concluded that North Korean armed forces were stronger than previously thought—thereby reversing its original position.

The revolution in Iran took the Administration by complete surprise and became a major focus of contention.[5] Historically, the United States was responsible for the 1953 coup that restored the Shah to power, providing him with total support for twenty-five years until instability overtook the country in late 1978. Where traditionally the United States would have backed the Shah of Iran in promoting stability and order, the Iranian revolution illustrates the two opposing images competing for control of American foreign policy. Both optimistic and pessimistic patterns in foreign policy behavior were evident.

Brzezinski initially favored complete support for the Shah to impose a military crackdown on the opposition and then, realizing that the Shah had lost control of events, supported a military coup to reimpose order and stability throughout the country. Vance preferred the formation of a national coalition government in order to promote a moderate solution given the likely fall of the Shah, later extending this to include a role for Khomeini and the Islamic fundamentalists. President Carter wavered between these two positions, initially supporting the Shah but reluctant to recommend the need for a crackdown, followed by support for a national coalition government although never foreclosing the possibility of a military coup (Sick, 1985; Sullivan, 1980; Taubman & Burt, 1980). The net result was that the United States initially deemphasized any direct action and eventually advised the Shah to leave the country in an effort to soften the repercussions of the revolution and promote a moderate national coalition.

The seizure of the American hostages in November, however, produced a more confrontational style. The United States ordered the immediate suspen-

ate suspension of oil imports from Iran, froze all official Iranian assets in the United States, ordered the Iranian embassy in Washington to cut back its staff, ordered the Justice Department to begin deportation proceedings against Iranian students who were in the country illegally, ordered naval forces to the Arabian Sea, and sought the support of the United Nations for obtaining the release of the hostages. These coercive measures were meant to complement the use of diplomacy in attempting to get the Americans released. Clearly the Administration's behavior toward the situation in Iran throughout the year reflected the two divergent worldviews that competed within the Administration. Initially, the Carter Administration responded to the Iranian revolution by supporting a moderate transition government reflecting a more optimistic orientation, but later coercive measures as well as diplomacy were used to try to get American hostages released, which reflected a more pessimistic image.

Actors

In 1979 contradictory behavior was exhibited toward the actors. The Carter Administration narrowed its focus of attention to a more select group of international actors. Whereas in 1977 and 1978 at least 10 percent of its behavior had been directed toward six different actors, in 1979 only five actors were major targets of Administration behavior (see table 5.10). Unlike 1978, the Soviet Union did not receive the most attention. In fact, a majority of

Table 5.10

Actors Acted Toward, 1979

Actors	Behavior (%)	Beliefs (%)
Middle East	29.7	21.9
China + Asia	19.3	9.3
Soviet Union	14.5	15.5
Western Europe + Japan	12.4	13.1
Latin America	10.3	11.2
Global	7.6	25.9
Africa	6.2	3.1
Eastern Europe	0.0	0.2
	N = 145	N = 420
Rank-order correlation = .50		

Note: The rank-order correlation coefficient used is Spearman's Rho, which varies from 1.0 (positive) to −1.0 (inverse relationship).

American foreign policy behavior was directed at Middle East actors and toward China and Asia.

The Soviet Union was one of many important actors in 1979. It was rank-ordered third for beliefs and third for behavior (see table 5.11). The Soviets were important for beliefs and behavior in arms control and the conflict in Southwest Asia. For normalization, the conflict in Africa, the Middle East conflict, Third World development, and human rights, other actors were much more important for both beliefs and behavior. However, inconsistencies in Carter Administration beliefs and behavior toward the Soviet Union surfaced over Western security and defense, other regional conflicts, and the global economy. Overall in 1979, a relatively low level of congruency existed between beliefs and behavior concerning the relative importance of the Soviet Union for the major issues (.41 correlation).

The inconsistency between beliefs and behavior toward the Soviet Union becomes clearer when examining specific American behavior toward the Soviets. During 1979 American action toward the Soviet Union was cooperative one-third of the time while three-fifths of its action was conflictual (see table 5.4). Two different patterns developed. For the most part, Soviet-American relations improved considerably during the beginning of the third year, but

Table 5.11

Importance of the Soviet Union, 1979

Major Issues	Behavior (%)	Beliefs (%)
Arms Control	66.7	77.8
Other Conflict	37.5	12.1
Global Economy	25.0	3.0
Western Security	18.2	61.1
Southwest Asian Conflict	11.5	12.5
Normalization	3.7	6.3
Middle East Conflict	0.0	0.0
African Conflict	0.0	3.2
Development	0.0	0.0
Human Rights	0.0	0.0
Rank-order correlation = .41		
For All Issues, %	14.9	15.5
Rank-order (relative to other actors)	3	3

then quickly deteriorated. The United States lifted the embargo on the sale of a computer to the Soviet news agency Tass for use during the Olympic games and negotiated an unprecedented direct agreement to exchange two Soviet spies for five Soviet dissidents. The high point came in June when Carter and Brezhnev met in Vienna for the signing of the SALT II agreements. The United States subsequently agreed to sell the USSR an additional ten million metric tons of wheat for the next fourteen months.

Soviet-American relations, however, began to suffer in September with the revelation of a Soviet combat brigade in Cuba. The incident was originally exaggerated by Senator Frank Church, then seized upon by the media, and blown out of proportion by the Administration's handling of the situation. The initial response by the Administration was to state that it was a "very serious matter," that the status quo was "not acceptable," and to threaten retaliatory measures. Eventually, it was acknowledged that nothing had really changed in Cuba—that the Soviet brigade had been there for years—and the commotion died down. Nevertheless, in October shortly after the Cuban brigade incident, President Carter rebuffed an arms control proposal by President Brezhnev to reduce tactical nuclear weapons in Europe. And following the capture of American hostages in Tehran, the United States warned the Soviet Union against exploiting the situation to its advantage.[6]

In 1979, the Carter Administration's request for defense spending seemed relatively consistent with the ambivalent image of the Soviet Union. The Carter Administration's defense budget for Fiscal Year 1980, submitted in January 1979, requested a modest 3 percent increase from the previous year (see table 5.8), reflecting the continual need to strengthen U.S. defense forces but not a preoccupation with the Soviet threat to the West.

In sum, during 1979 the Carter Administration's foreign policy behavior exhibited two major trends, which reflected the two different images that coexisted within the Administration. The Carter Administration promoted policies that coincided with its image of a complex international system and its efforts to move toward a global community, especially with regard to the general improvement of bilateral relations, majority rule and human rights in southern Africa and Central America, and the promotion of the Middle East peace process. At the same time, the Carter Administration acted to strengthen American defense forces and demonstrated support for its security interests in response to different regional conflicts. This was much more consistent with a pessimistic image of the international system. These contradictory patterns were clearly reflected in the Carter Administration's initially optimistic and then increasingly pessimistic behavior in response to the situation in Iran.

In comparing the two patterns of behavior with the two patterns in image at the collective level, very little overall congruency resulted. The diversity in Administration behavior did not directly reflect the diversity in beliefs. There was no relationship concerning the relative importance of the issues between beliefs and behavior ($-.01$ correlation). At the same time, a modest relationship for the relative importance of the actors did exist (.50 correlation). This meant that the Carter Administration addressed many of the same actors in its collective beliefs and behavior; however, the actors addressed for any issue varied dramatically between beliefs and behavior.

Overall, there were two patterns in the Carter Administration's beliefs—one optimistic, the other pessimistic. This was reflected in two similar optimistic and pessimistic patterns in its behavior toward the issues and actors. In combining the two contradictory patterns at the aggregative level, however, this resulted in little congruency between the Carter Administration's collective beliefs and collective behavior. The overall inconsistency between the foreign policy behavior of the Carter Administration and its image of the international system is quite understandable given the internal differences and disagreements that developed and were never resolved within the Administration in 1979.

The Fourth Year

By the beginning of 1980, global change was no longer thought to be positive—the complex contemporary world was too turbulent and dangerous. The Carter Administration had now come to believe in and act upon a policy of global stability that was status-quo oriented, emphasizing the prevention of Soviet expansionism and the maintenance of the West's security: in Europe, in the Far East and, of immediate concern, in Southwest Asia.

Issues

In 1980, the Administration oriented its foreign policy behavior around the events in Southwest Asia: the holding of American hostages in Iran, and the Soviet invasion of Afghanistan. Both sets of events resulted in the need to promote the security and defense of the West. This resulted in a great deal of consistency between the Carter Administration's beliefs and behavior toward the issues (.90 correlation, see table 5.12).

The Carter Administration implemented a number of punitive measures to compel Iran to release the American hostages. Following the initial measures taken at the end of 1979, the United States severed diplomatic relations with Iran, placed a formal embargo on all exports to Iran, and attempted to get

Table 5.12

Issues Acted Upon, 1980

Issue	Behavior (%)	Beliefs (%)
Southwest Asian Conflict	37.5	22.6
Security + Defense	17.4	18.0
Middle East Conflict	12.0	12.0
Normalization	8.2	9.6
Other Conflict	7.6	7.4
Human Rights	7.6	9.7
Economy	4.3	2.8
African Conflict	3.3	3.5
Arms Control	1.1	7.3
Energy	1.0	4.5
Development	0.0	2.6
	N = 184	N = 1,099

Rank-order correlation = .90

Note: The rank-order correlation coefficient used is Spearman's Rho, which varies from 1.0 (positive) to − 1.0 (inverse relationship).

support for sanctions against Iran from its allies throughout the world. As pressure continued to mount, President Carter finally relented and ordered a military operation to resolve the crisis.

Actually, planning for the rescue attempt began immediately following the taking of the Americans. Secretary Vance, however, was against any effort to use direct military force to resolve the problem. The official decision was made by President Carter during a meeting on April 11 while Vance was on vacation in Florida (Felton, 1980; Sick, 1985; Vance, 1983, p. 409; Wicker, 1980). The rescue operation was a fiasco, and only in the final moments of the Carter presidency was agreement reached with Iran to repatriate the American hostages.

Following the Soviet invasion of Afghanistan, the White House became preoccupied with containing the Soviet threat to the Persian Gulf and the West and instituted a number of measures against the Soviet Union. The United States cut grain shipments and trade ties to the Soviets, halted the sale of high technology items, placed a curb on Soviet fishing in U.S. waters, reduced the number of Aeroflot flights into the United States, cancelled most cultural, economic, and scientific exchanges, deferred the opening of new consulates, expulsed seventeen Soviet consular officials, and froze the official Soviet diplomatic presence in the United States (the first time a ceiling had been imposed on Soviet diplomatic personnel). Carter also prohibited American teams from participating in the Olympic Games held in Moscow and supported plans for a separate international sports festival to demonstrate the seriousness of U.S. concern and action.

These actions signaled a revival of the old U.S. strategy of containment with an emphasis on a global political-military response to the Soviet threat in Southwest Asia. The United States reaffirmed its 1959 defense commitment to Pakistan in case of external aggression and offered them $400 million in military and economic assistance over the next two years, reversing its policy of cutting assistance to prevent nuclear proliferation and human rights abuses. Oman, Kenya, and Somalia agreed to provide access to military facilities so the United States could project its military forces into the Persian Gulf (in return for military aid). A number of major improvements were also made to the American military base on the island of Diego Garcia in the Indian Ocean (Wilson, 1980).

In the Middle East, the United States and Egypt conducted a series of joint military exercises as a show of force. President Carter ordered amphibious assault forces into the Arabian Sea to demonstrate U.S. ability to project ground forces into the Persian Gulf region. Most significantly, it was revealed that by the middle of January the United States had begun a clandestine CIA (Central Intelligence Agency) operation to supply Afghan rebels with light infantry weapons to strengthen their resistance against Soviet forces (Bernstein, 1981). This was the Administration's first major covert paramilitary operation after reorganizing the Central Intelligence Agency and deemphasizing its paramilitary covert operations during the first three years.

To reinforce this strategy, the Administration prodded its allies worldwide to support the containment of Soviet expansionism. The United States got the European Common Market, Canada, and Australia, three major foreign grain exporters, to agree not to sell wheat to the Soviet Union that would replace the grain cut by the United States. NATO countries mutually agreed to modernize their nuclear forces in Europe by deploying Pershing IIs and cruise missiles in response to the recent Soviet placement of mobile SS–20 missiles in Eastern Europe. Saudi Arabia was provided AWACs planes and was asked to provide Pakistan with large amounts of foreign assistance. In Africa, Carter went so far as to send former boxing champion Muhammad Ali to tour the area in hopes of gaining African backing for the Olympics boycott—a trip that failed miserably.

The United States also took major steps to revamp its defense forces. President Carter proposed a plan to restore military draft registration. In addition, he signed Presidential Directive 59, instituting a new, more aggressive, official strategy in case of nuclear war, giving priority to attacking military targets and leadership posts in the Soviet Union rather than destroying cities and industrial complexes, which was the basis of mutual assured destruction (Szulc, 1980). The United States accelerated development of an experimental aircraft— the Stealth bomber—that was expected to be virtually invisible to Soviet radar. The growth of the Rapid Deployment Force was expedited to give the United States the capability to militarily respond to various regional trouble-spots, especially in the Middle East and Southwest Asia.

As a result of this resurrection of containment, arms control efforts were curtailed (addressed only 1.1 percent of the time). After the invasion of Afghanistan, public skepticism grew concerning any agreements with the Soviet Union. Therefore, President Carter withdrew the SALT II treaty from Senate consideration to prevent what appeared to be certain defeat. Arms control talks on antisatellite weapons, chemical weapons, a comprehensive test ban, and the demilitarization of the Indian Ocean were suspended. Arms sales limitations collapsed, and no moves were made in the nonproliferation area, except for U.S. approval to sell enriched uranium fuel to India.

Another byproduct of the deterioration of U.S.-Soviet relations was a closer U.S.-Chinese relationship. Agreements were signed on trade in textiles, consular services, shipping, and U.S. grain sales. Secretary of Defense Brown visited China, the first Pentagon chief to visit the mainland since 1949. Actions such as the agreement to sell China a ground station to receive information from the Landsat Earth Resources Satellite laid the groundwork for greater cooperation with China in defense matters and marked an end to the overall U.S. policy of "evenhandedness" toward China and the USSR. The United States allowed China to buy American air-defense radar helicopters and transport planes, and authorized U.S. companies to build electronics and helicopter factories in China. American foreign policy had definitely tilted in favor of China and against the Soviet Union.

A few efforts were made to normalize relations with other countries in 1980. For example, following President Tito's death, President Carter provided support for Yugoslavia's independence and policy of nonalignment. However, the conflict in Southwest Asia and the threat of Soviet expansionism to Western security not only diminished the importance of arms control and normalization for the Carter Administration, less action was directed toward other issues that were previously important, such as conflict in Africa and the global economy. No progress was made in resolving the conflicts in Namibia, South Africa, or elsewhere in Africa. Beyond some joint agreements, no new developments proceeded in the international economic area.

Though preoccupied with the Soviet threat in Southwest Asia, the Administration nonetheless attempted to continue some of its earlier efforts in the areas involving the Middle East conflict and human rights. Substantial time was invested in attempts to repair damage to the Camp David accords inflicted by Israel's continued settling of the West Bank and the Sinai, and its annexation of the Arab sector of Jerusalem. The United States undertook a public relations campaign against Israeli activities, and President Carter held talks with King Hussein of Jordan but failed to entice him to enter the peace process concerning Palestinian autonomy. The Carter Administration, nevertheless, maintained faith in the Camp David accords and signed a fourteen-year agreement with Israel to guarantee to supply them with oil in case of an emergency.

More surprisingly perhaps, the Carter Administration continued to promote human rights and democracy. A U.S. embassy was opened in Zimbabwe, recognizing the independence of the new country, thus demonstrating support for racial justice and majority rule in southern Africa. President Carter also met with Robert Mugabe, the new Prime Minister and former guerilla leader, and agreed to grant $2 million for the rehabilitation of government medical clinics damaged by the war. In South America, the United States halted all economic assistance to Bolivia after a military coup nullified a democratic presidential election. Refugees from Cuba were welcomed into the United States (though not from Haiti). In Poland, President Carter provided symbolic support for Solidarity and warned the Soviet Union not to militarily intervene to crush the movement. However, even with this behavior Carter Administration actions in the area of human rights in 1980 were much more sporadic than in previous years.

The Carter Administration's behavior toward the conflict in Central America increasingly reflected its pessimistic image as the fighting in El Salvador intensified. The internal situation in El Salvador had been festering for years and, following the Nicaraguan revolution, armed conflict and civil war escalated in intensity. The Administration sided with the government but also supported internal reform, the maintenance of human rights, and movement to democracy. In fact, the United States threatened to cut economic and military assistance to the country if the civilian-military junta, which came to power in October 1979 and attempted to implement reforms, was overthrown by rightists. The reformist junta eventually collapsed and was replaced by a traditional military junta. In December, following the killing of four American nuns, the United States suspended $25 million in foreign aid to the government of El Salvador. However, as the internal situation deteriorated the Carter Administration reversed its policy from trying to reform the El Salvadoran government to fully supporting it. Aid was immediately reinstated after the

THE FOURTH YEAR

Carter Administration concluded that the guerillas posed a major threat to the survival of the "moderate" Salvadoran government.

Actors

During 1980 the Carter Administration's foreign policy behavior was directed at only three major groupings of actors: the Soviet Union, the Middle East, and Western Europe and Japan. The other actors were relatively unimportant to the United States in its efforts to contain the threat to Western security, especially in the Persian Gulf area. This concentration on a few key actors was totally consistent with the administration's pessimistic image in which the world was no longer perceived as a pluralistic international system but as a globe that was increasingly hierachical in nature (.86 correlation, see table 5.13).

During 1980 United States foreign policy behavior focused on the Soviet Union. It was rank-ordered first for beliefs, receiving 39.1 percent of the attention, and first for behavior, receiving 29.6 percent of the action (see table 5.14). The Soviet Union was the critical actor for four major issues, including the two most important perceived by the Carter Administration: the conflict in Southwest Asia, Western defense and security, other regional conflict, and arms control. It was a relatively minor actor for the Middle East conflict and human rights. Only for the major issue of normalization was there a minor discrepancy between beliefs and behavior in the relative importance of the

Table 5.13

Actors Acted Toward, 1980

Actors	Behavior (%)	Beliefs (%)
Soviet Union	29.6	39.1
Middle East	27.4	20.8
Western Europe + Japan	15.1	15.1
China and Asia	8.4	6.2
Latin America	7.8	5.3
Africa	4.5	3.6
Global	3.9	8.9
Eastern Europe	3.4	1.1
	N = 179	N = 663
Rank-order correlation = .86		

Note: The rank-order correlation coefficient used is Spearman's Rho, which varies from 1.0 (positive) to −1.0 (inverse relationship).

Soviet Union. Overall, belief-behavior congruency for the Carter Administration toward the Soviet Union for the major issues was extremely high in 1980 (.89 correlation).

American-Soviet relations suffered deeply in 1980, reflecting the increasingly pessimistic image of the Soviet Union. The Carter Administration revitalized a containment strategy in order to stifle and neutralize what was perceived to be a growing Soviet global threat. In 1980, therefore, virtually all of the Carter Administration's action toward the Soviet Union, 98.2 percent, was conflictual in nature (see table 5.4).

Defense spending requests in January 1980 and 1981 were also very consistent with the Carter Administration's pessimistic image of the Soviet Union (see table 5.8). For the 1981 fiscal year budget, President Carter proposed "significant increases in the resources necessary to assure our national security," entailing a 5 percent real increase (U.S., OMB, 1981, p. 7).[7] The last budget of the Carter Administration, fiscal year 1982 submitted in the beginning of 1981, included a sizable increase in the investment of U.S. defense forces—over 6 percent after inflation. The increases for fiscal year 1980 and in particular 1981 were actually much higher because supplemental requests were made by the Carter Administration after submission of the original budget.[8] During 1980, especially as the election approached, the President was fond of saying that "we've had a steady increase in our commitment to the strength of our national defense, as measured by budget levels and

Table 5.14

Importance of the Soviet Union, 1980

Major Issues	Behavior (%)	Beliefs (%)
Arms Control	50.0	89.8
Western Security	45.7	63.9
Southwest Asian Conflict	45.3	56.3
Other Conflict	35.7	36.2
Human Rights	7.1	5.2
Normalization	6.7	17.5
Middle East Conflict	0.0	7.1
Rank-order correlation = .89		
For All Issues, %	29.6	39.1
Rank-order (relative to other actors)	1	1

also measured by the tone and actions that I have taken'' (U.S., President Carter, 1980a, p. 109). Obviously, President Carter's point of view and emphasis concerning defense spending had changed remarkably since 1977.

During its final year, the Carter Administration's foreign policy behavior was very consistent with its pessimistic image of the international system. The United States directed its behavior toward punishing the Soviet Union for its intervention into Afghanistan in an effort to contain future threats of Soviet expansionism to global stability. American foreign policy behavior focused on responding to the threat of instability in the Middle East and Southwest Asia—the third central strategic zone within the arc of crisis. The Carter Administration made major efforts to increase its defense forces, to strengthen its military presence and capability to protect the Persian Gulf region, and to obtain support from other countries, especially in Western Europe and the Middle East. In sum, the Carter Administration's major foreign policy actions during 1980 were in accord with its newly acquired image of the international system—to promote global stability in an increasingly fragile and turbulent international system.

Notes

1. As indicated in chapter 3, an issue had to be addressed 7% of the time and an actor had to be addressed 10% of the time to be considered significant.

2. On May 23, 1977, President Carter requested the initiation of ''what became a three-year effort to discover the long-term implications of present world trends in population, natural resources, and the environment and to assess the Government's foundation for long-range planning'' (U.S., Council on Environmental Quality, 1980, p. vii). Unlike previous administrations, the Global 2000 Study was an indication of the Carter Administration's concern with the future and the need to respond to the variety of problems that the United States and the world were likely to confront.

3. Although the conflict in Africa was a major focus of the Carter Administration's image (receiving 21% of the attention), U.S. foreign policy action toward the conflict in Africa did not reflect the same level of belief system concern (receiving 9.2% of the attention) as represented by the quantitative indicators. This inconsistency between beliefs and behavior is misleading for two reasons. First, the Carter Administration displayed little overt physical behavior in response to the Ethiopian-Somalian conflict. Second, as addressed in the method section in appendix B, since the behavior the United States did produce was primarily verbal, it was therefore included in the public statements that were utilized for determining the Carter Administration's belief system. The belief-behavior discrepancy for the conflict in Africa represents a problem faced by all events data sets. By defining behavior as observable action, foreign policy decisions involving ''no'' overt action are ignored. In this case, the fact that the United States did not physically respond to the events surrounding the Horn of Africa was extremely significant and consistent with the optimistic image displayed by the Carter Administration.

4. See the second footnote in this chapter.

5. The frequency distributions were much higher for the Carter Administration's behavior toward Southwest Asia (18.2%) in comparison with its image (2.2%) primarily because no major public addresses were made by Administration officials after October of 1979 for that year. Therefore, the Iran hostage crisis and its affect on the Carter Administration were not incorporated in its image of the international system during the year through use of the quantitative content analysis.

6. During October, Brzezinski had drafted a top-secret memorandum describing a three-phase program, *Top Secret Umbra*, to counter Soviet and Cuban global activities. "As part of the scheme, Brzezinski ordered a questionnaire sent to all U.S. ambassadors requesting data on Cuban activities in their areas for use in a world wide propaganda campaign" (Anderson, 1979). Secretary Vance was a major opponent of the program, but President Carter was said to be sympathetic.

7. Budgetary figures are expressed in terms of "outlays" and "budget authority." Outlays refer to what is actually spent for that year. Authority refers to what has been obligated for that year but actually may not be spent until some time in the future (e.g., when developing a major weapons system). Therefore, budget authority is usually a larger figure than budget outlays. Under the Carter Administration, budget authority compared to budget outlays showed smaller increases during the first two years (9.0% vs. 9.4% in 1979; 8.1% vs. 9.7% in 1980) and larger increases for the last two years (14.2% vs. 12.2% in 1981; 15.2% vs. 14.5% in 1982). This reinforces the trend in greater defense spending over time under the Carter Administration.

8. This is illustrated in table 5.8 by comparing the $125 billion proposed for FY 1980 and the actual outlays for 1980 of $130 billion and for FY 1981, when $146 billion was initially proposed but over $161 billion was actually spent.

SIX | *The Carter Years and Policymaker Beliefs in Perspective*

FOUR fundamental stages emerged in the Carter Administration's evolution of its image of the international system, each of which has important implications for understanding American foreign policy in the late 1970s. The first stage occurred in the first year, when the primary Carter policymakers shared a similar perception of a very complex and diverse international system. A variety of issues were deemed to be of global significance and, therefore, worthy of attention. The system was portrayed as highly pluralistic, and no actor, including the United States or the Soviet Union, was considered willing or able to dominate international behavior. Of the three officials under study, President Carter maintained the most optimistic image of the Soviet Union and the future of the international system, while National Security Advisor Brzezinski was the least optimistic. As a result of this generally shared image, the Carter Administration was primarily concerned with ushering in an era of cooperation and peace—a quest for global community.

During the second year the consensus in collective image began to collapse. Vance and Carter remained optimistic about the future of American foreign policy and the world. However, individual differences emerged as Brzezinski became more pessimistic about the Soviet Union and the future of the international system. The third stage was reached in 1979, when dissensus and disagreement became the norm. Intra-administration schisms intensified when a major split developed between Vance and Brzezinski. During this time Carter also grew more skeptical and wavered between Vance and Brzezinski, resulting in the escalation of policy conflict that plagued the Carter Administration.

The final stage was observed in 1980 when the Administration's image changed completely. The resignation of Vance and the turnabout in Carter's perception restored a homogeneous outlook to the White House during the final year. The original image of a complex global system was disavowed and supplanted with a new consensus image of a turbulent international system threatened by Soviet expansionism and in need of global stability.

Four stages also existed concerning the level of congruency between the Carter Administration's image of the international system and its general foreign policy behavior. During the first year there was a considerable degree of consistency between beliefs and behavior that reflected the high-level of shared images that existed between Carter, Vance, and Brzezinski. A variety of important international issues and actors were addressed in accordance with the prevailing optimistic image of global complexity. The use of military force was deemphasized; instead political, economic, and social instruments were relied upon in pursuit of a global community.

As individual differences arose in 1978, the Administration's foreign policy behavior displayed less congruency with its beliefs—the relationship was moderate. During 1978, Brzezinski's image began to diverge from President Carter's and Secretary Vance's, and while a wide variety of significant international issues and actors were addressed, the relative importance of the issues and actors for beliefs and behavior became less consistent at the collective level. Political-military concerns intruded upon a more complex and optimistic orientation.

By 1979, the consensus in collective image totally collapsed. Contrasting outlooks were pursued by Vance and Brzezinski simultaneously, with Carter reluctant to fully subscribe to either. The resulting foreign policy behavior was highly incoherent and unstable. Given the disagreement that existed within the Administration, policy behavior could not flow naturally from the divergent beliefs. Inconsistency between collective beliefs and collective behavior was the consequence, especially over the significance of what issues should be addressed and which issues were actually addressed.

During the final year, Carter foreign policy behavior fully reflected its change in image. The Iranian hostage crisis and the Soviet invasion of Afghanistan prompted Vance to resign and prompted a new homogeneous international image. The foreign policy concerns of the Administration became clear-cut: global containment was revived to counter Soviet expansionism, with an immediate focus on Southwest Asia. For 1980 the overall relationship between the Carter Administration's image and its major foreign policy behavior was extremely high.

Understanding the Administration's Foreign Policy

The findings of the study reveal the four schools of thought or positions described in chapter 1 to be only partially correct about the Carter Administration's foreign policy. No position was completely incorrect or confirmed; however, the third school of thought comes closest to accurately portraying the evolution of Carter foreign policy.

The first position argued that no coherent worldview existed. This certainly does not accurately describe 1977 or 1980, when the image of the international system was shared within the collectivity. And while it is true that Brzezinski began to diverge from Carter and Vance in 1978, it was not until 1979 that dissensus and incoherence truly developed. The second position asserted that an optimistic worldview existed. This, however, was no longer true by 1979 and was completely transcended in 1980. That a pessimistic worldview eventually developed out of dissensus was the contention of the fourth school of thought. However, this ignores the consensus that existed during the early part of the Carter Administration, especially in its first year. Only the third position, which maintained that the Carter Administration had a cohesive worldview that changed from optimism to pessimism over time, proved generally accurate.

The Carter Administration did initially share an optimistic image of the international system, and this image changed to one of pessimism. But in fact, the evolution of the Carter Administration's image was more complex than any single author recognized. The change in the Administration's image was both evolutionary and abrupt. While there was a consensus within the Carter Administration in 1977 about the quest for global community in a complex world, Carter was the most optimistic and Brzezinski was the least optimistic about Soviet intentions. Consensus was shattered in 1978 when Brzezinski became pessimistic in response to events in the Horn of Africa. The breakdown of consensus accelerated in 1979 as a result of President Carter's increasing skepticism concerning Soviet activities and inability to resolve the differences between Vance's and Brzezinski's competing images. A new consensus emerged by early 1980 oriented toward global stability when Carter turned completely pessimistic and Vance resigned due to the Iran hostage crisis and the Soviet invasion of Afghanistan.

Historical Perspective

Examining Carter foreign policy improves our general understanding of American foreign policy. Most American scholars have concluded that U.S. foreign policy has been relatively stable since the end of World War II, devoted to preventing the spread of communism through a policy of containment. They argue that different administrations have not altered the fundamental thrust of the containment policy, but have only fine-tuned the approach due to the particular styles and preferences of the political leaders (see, e.g., Brown, 1983; Gaddis, 1982; Kegley & Wittkopf, 1979).[1]

This study demonstrates that the Carter Administration represented a major break from this tradition, especially in its first two years. The Carter White House was not preoccupied with maintaining global security through a policy of containment, but with promoting a global community based on an idealistic image of the international system. In order to better understand the discontinuity that the Carter Administration represented in American foreign policy, one must analyze the philosophical values that were the basis of the Carter Administration's image. The Carter Administration's change in image of the international system represented a movement from one philosophical tradition (or paradigm) to another—from liberal idealism to realpolitik. Initially optimistic and idealistic, the Administration's image became extremely pessimistic by the fourth year, an evolution consistent with the principles of realpolitik.

The *idealist* tradition in international affairs reached its height in Western civilization during the first half of the twentieth century. Following the terrible destruction wreaked by the First World War, many individuals believed it was necessary to construct a peaceful and cooperative world order. The pursuit of a just global community is based upon an optimistic vision of mankind. Idealists believe that the human race is fundamentally "just" and "selfless." Global change, thus, can be steered in a positive direction for the benefit of all. Liberal idealists often point to democracy and capitalism—both based on the principle of human individualism and liberty—as the dual paths to such a global community. They believe that societies governed by authoritarian means and without free market economies are the major contributors to international warfare (the latter is much more important to classical liberals). Furthermore, they contend that as the world becomes more complex and interdependent the development of appropriate institutions and global processes—such as international organizations and international law—become more necessary to insure global peace and prosperity.

HISTORICAL PERSPECTIVE

The *realpolitik* tradition has dominated international policy-making since the beginning of the nation-state system. Although briefly superseded by the idealist tradition during the 1920s and 1930s, realpolitik was resurrected in the West with the beginning of the cold war. Those adopting this view, often called "realists," believe human beings are fundamentally "shortsighted" and "selfish." The existence of a particular type of national and economic system, although important, is not considered consequential in determining political behavior. Rather, states (and all international actors) act to promote their "national interest." Power is the ultimate arbiter of international behavior, and international stability can be maintained only by a precarious "balance of power."[2] Realpolitik focuses, not on what might be, but on the immediate environment. Satisfied actors emphasize the promotion of their national interests without fundamentally upsetting the status quo and the stability of the system. Realists are particularly concerned with preventing the rise of unsatisfied and, therefore, "revolutionary" actors who would attempt to change the system.

In sum, the idealist and realist traditions represent two different empirical and normative visions of the same international environment (see Carr, 1964; Kennan, 1951; Morgenthau, 1946; R. Osgood, 1953; Waltz, 1954).[3] Idealists are very hopeful about the future and the potential for building a better world—they have been called "children of light." Realists are skeptical about reform and are concerned with maximizing gains and minimizing costs for themselves in the contemporary environment—they are the "children of darkness" (Niebuhr, 1944).

In one of Zbigniew Brzezinski's last speeches as a public official, he argued that "the distinctive character of the Carter foreign policy is that it has very deliberately tried to blend what traditionally have been two conflictual major strands in American thought about foreign affairs"—realism and idealism:[4]

One is the inclination to stress a commitment to the status quo, to emphasize the primacy of power and to pursue policies which perhaps can be subsumed with the word *realpolitik*, a hard-nosed, realistic, foreign policy. . . . The other—Wilsonian idealism—has stressed moralism and morality as the central factors that ought to shape American foreign policy. Inherent in it is a suspicion of power and in some respects even a rejection of power. Inherent in it is the notion that traditional military power is no longer relevant in our age, but that instead America should identify itself with certain widespread human aspirations and that this is the best way to preserve our interests. (U.S., NSC Assistant Brzezinski, 1980c, p. 1)

Brzezinski was correct in saying that both philosophical traditions were integral to the Administration. However, idealism and realism were rarely pursued simultaneously. Whereas the Carter image of the international system at the beginning was based upon a liberal idealist vision, by the fourth year realpolitik became the dominant orientation.[5]

Carter's effort to create an improved world order in which mankind would benefit made his approach to foreign policy extremely different from previous administrations. The containment of communist expansion throughout the globe in order to promote global security had been the basis of American foreign policy in every post-World War II administration from Harry Truman to Lyndon Johnson. Containment and deterrence of communism were pursued through military spending and the development of nuclear weapons, the creation of alliances, the placement of military troops and facilities around the world, the overt use of military troops such as in Korea and Vietnam, the use of covert activities, the provision of foreign assistance to allies, and the effort to isolate economically the Soviet Union and its allies.

With Vietnam and the rise of Henry Kissinger, American foreign policy under Nixon and Ford was refined: from the containment of communism to insure global security to an emphasis on the promotion of global stability. The major threat was not communist expansion and hegemony but global instability, which Soviet expansionism could only exacerbate. Therefore, the key was to move the Soviet Union from a revolutionary global actor into a legitimate, status quo actor. This was to be done through a policy of detente based on the concept of linkage: accommodation when the Soviet Union was acting in accord with American desires, containment when the Soviets were expansionist. The conduct of American foreign policy under the tutelage of Kissinger represented realpolitik at its height during the postwar years.

The Vietnam War shattered the consensus of the foreign policy establishment that provided the foundation to America's policy of global containment throughout most of the 1950s and 1960s. As a result of Vietnam, the foreign policy elite splintered into competing schools of thought (see Hodgson, 1973; Holsti & Rosenau, 1984; Rosati & Creed, 1987).[6] The lesson of Vietnam for many of these foreign policy elites was to reject the policies of globalism, containment, and militarism, and replace them with a global managerial approach emphasizing interdependence and accommodation. Vietnam led to the revival of a true liberal internationalist orientation. People who identified with such an orientation became part of the Carter Administration and provided the foundation for the Administration's foreign policy, especially during its early years (see Destler, Gelb & Lake, 1984; Sanders, 1983).

Upon entering office the Carter Administration represented a major break with the past by rejecting containment as the basis of its foreign policy. The people who staffed the Carter Administration no longer saw a bipolar international system that pitted Soviet communism against the U.S.-led "free world" in a global cold war. Unlike previous administrations, the Carter Administration was not preoccupied with containing communism in order to promote global security or with influencing Soviet behavior in order to promote global stability. In its place came the first truly moral and idealistic vision in U.S. foreign policy since the end of World War II.

The Carter Administration saw a much more complex international system in which—rather than defending and protecting the status quo—the United States would take the lead in moving the international system in a direction consistent with global change in order to promote the building of a global community. As stated by President Carter in his memoirs (1982, p. 143):

> I was familiar with the widely accepted arguments that we had to choose between idealism and realism, or between morality and the exertion of power; but I rejected those claims. To me, the demonstration of American idealism was a practical and realistic approach to foreign affairs, and moral principals were the best foundation for the exertion of American power and influence.

The Administration's image of global complexity and a quest for global community did not stay in its pure form for long. During 1978 and 1979, the early image was modified: Brzezinski rejected it, and President Carter grew more skeptical. By 1980, the idealistic image of a complex global community was lost: the world was perceived to have become increasingly fragmented and unstable. A pessimistic image had completely replaced the earlier optimism in accordance with realpolitik. No longer did the Administration look to the future—global change was likely to be detrimental to U.S. interests. Instead, Carter foreign policy became status-quo oriented in order to prevent Soviet expansionism and to promote global stability. Consequently, in 1980 the Carter Administration reinstated the policy of containment against the Soviet Union. This became the foundation of its foreign policy, making it much more consistent with America's post-World War II orientation.

The Carter Administration's foreign policy in 1980 fell somewhere in between the cold war policies of the 1950s and 1960s and the Kissinger policies of the 1970s. The Carter Administration's foreign policy goals were more reminiscent of the Nixon and Ford Administration's foreign policy, while its foreign policy action more closely resembled the foreign policy that predominated under the administrations of Truman to Johnson.

The Carter Administration wanted to contain Soviet expansionism in order to promote global stability. The Carter Administration did not fear that the security of the United States was threatened by the growth of communism, which was the preoccupation during the 1950s and early 1960s. A tight bipolar international system had been replaced by a more complex and turbulent world. Therefore, the concern was with the increase in international instability and chaos due to shortsighted actions of the other great power—the Soviet Union—which indirectly threatened the United States. In order to promote global stability, the Carter Administration reinstituted a policy of containment. Where Kissinger attempted to manipulate Soviet behavior through selective containment and accommodation, the Carter Administration returned to the earlier policy of global containment emphasizing a military build-up, the threat of force, alliances, and economic sanctions in order to punish and deter future Soviet expansionism.

Thus, the Carter Administration's image of the international system not only changed throughout its four years in office, but fundamentally changed in terms of basic philosophical values. The change from one set of philosophical values to another lies at the heart of the changes that occurred in the foreign policy behavior of the Carter Administration over time. The change in philosophical values from liberal idealism to realpolitik under the Carter Administration also lends perspective to continuity and change in contemporary American foreign policy.[7]

Implications for the Study of Images

The findings also have important implications for the role of beliefs in the overall study of foreign policy. The evolution of the Carter Administration's image during its four years in office was based upon the images held by the individual policymakers themselves. As individual images changed, the collective image changed. From this, it appears that a direct relationship exists between the level of shared images among individuals and the level of image cohesiveness and image stability for the collectivity.

During times of high consensus there is a minimum of internal disagreement, thus resulting in a highly cohesive collective image—that is, the group maintains a relatively consistent and coherent image. Shared individual images also produce stability in the collective image due to the reinforcement of the same central beliefs through individual interaction within the group. If,

IMPLICATIONS FOR STUDY OF IMAGES

however, individual differences in image begin to emerge and widen, the group's collective image becomes increasingly unstable. When this occurs, a competition of beliefs is likely within the group with an overall negative effect for the cohesiveness of the aggregate belief system.

In attempting to understand the content and evolution of beliefs that are held by a group of political leaders, the following two propositions are offered:

Proposition 1. The greater consensus in image among decisionmakers, the greater the likelihood that the collective image will be cohesive.
Proposition 2. The greater consensus in image among decisionmakers, the greater the likelihood that the collective image will be stable.

The nature of individual images and their interrelationships determines the level of image cohesiveness and stability for the collectivity. These two propositions are more clearly explained by examining the evolution of the Carter Administration's image of the international system.

During the first and last years in office Carter Administration officials had a coherent and consistent portrait of the world and America's role within it. During the first year President Carter, Secretary Vance, and Assistant Brzezinski shared an optimistic image of a complex international system in which global change could be promoted in pursuit of global community. During the fourth year President Carter, Secretary Muskie, and Assistant Brzezinski shared a pessimistic image of a fragmented international system in which Soviet expansionism needed to be contained in pursuit of global stability. Both 1977 and 1980 were years of high consensus when the collective image was most cohesive and achieved its highest degree of stability.

Conversely, the Administration's image became increasingly incoherent and was in a state of transition during the second and third years. Individual differences emerged and finally polarized. Brzezinski first became pessimistic due to Soviet activities in 1978. This was followed by an even more pessimistic Brzezinski in 1979 and accompanied by a wavering Carter. Therefore, the collective image began to lose its cohesiveness and stability in 1978 and became completely incoherent and unstable in 1979. The second and third years were a time when individual differences in images intensified to the point where the conflicting images directly competed with each other for dominance within the administration.

The study also reveals the importance of the group leader in affecting the collective image. As the president is the most important individual in the conduct of American foreign policy, the Carter Administration's collective image was heavily dependent on the image held by President Carter. This was especially visible when dissensus appeared within the Administration during the second and third years. In 1978, because Carter's image remained optimistic and this view was also shared by Vance, the optimistic orientation prevailed and provided the foundation for the collective image. However, in 1979 Carter's image began to vaccilate—sometimes optimistic, sometimes pessimistic. Because the President no longer fully subscribed to a consistent image, the two opposing images represented by Vance and Brzezinski were allowed to compete for ascendancy. This was the time when dissensus, incoherence, and instability in the administration's image reached their apex—no worldview predominated. It was also the time when the bureaucratic politics model of decision-making became most applicable for explaining Administration foreign policy actions.

Thus, it is the nature of the individual images and their interrelationships that determine the level of image cohesiveness and stability for the collectivity. The higher the level of consensus among the decisionmakers the greater the likelihood that the collective image will be coherent and stable. Within the United States, the president is the single most important individual in affecting the American foreign policy process and, consequently, the administration's overall collective image.

In addition to being crucial for the cohesiveness and stability of an administration's collective image, the level of image consensus among the participants is also fundamental for determining the degree of congruency that exists between beliefs and behavior for the collectivity. When individuals in a group share similar images, the impact of the aggregate image on external behavior will be high. A homogeneous group will be more unified in presenting a cohesive image to the public and abroad. This will also be a time when the collective image is most stable since there is little disagreement concerning the most important issues and actors that need to be addressed. Therefore, a high level of consensus in image among the decisionmakers will promote policy behavior that is consistent with its collective image.

When individuals within a collectivity have different images, the impact of the aggregate image on external behavior will be much lower. Dissensus within the collectivity makes it literally impossible for the group to reach an optimal decision and agree on a common course of action. Decisions may be reached only through compromise (as suggested by the bureaucratic politics model of decision-making) or through some type of decision rule, such as majority vote or the final decision of the leader of the group. Once arrived at, the ultimate course of action may bear little resemblance to decisions reached at previous points in time. Disagreement among individuals also presents the opportunity for slippage to occur during the implementation stage. Therefore, the lack of a dominant image within the

IMPLICATIONS FOR STUDY OF IMAGES

group is likely to produce little congruency with behavior produced by the collectivity over time.

In attempting to explain the relationship between an actor's foreign policy beliefs and behavior, the following proposition is offered:

Proposition 3. The greater the consensus in image among decision-makers, the greater the likelihood that foreign policy actions will be congruent with beliefs.

The focus on shared images versus conflicting images is fundamental for explaining an actor's collective image and its relationship to behavior.

That the level of consensus affects behavior is demonstrated by the foreign policy behavior of the Carter Administration. The Carter Administration's belief system was most consistent with its foreign policy behavior during the first and last years, when its image of the international system was shared by the major officials and relatively cohesive and stable throughout the year. The incongruency between beliefs and behavior began during the second year and reached its apex during 1979, when the Carter Administration's image was in transition and increasingly incoherent—first Brzezinski and then Carter experiencing changes in individual images. Overall, the Carter Administration's foreign policy behavior over four years cannot be adequately explained or understood without reference to its collective image of the international system (table 6.1 provides a summary).[8]

As discussed in chapter 2, little attention has been paid to the study of collective beliefs in political psychology—the focus has been on a single individual's beliefs (or beliefs at the mass level). Rarely has a psychological or belief system approach been integrated within a collective or decision-making context or empirically applied to a group of individuals or collectivity. To correct this deficiency, therefore, it is imperative that one study the beliefs of individuals and groups. This is especially important in order to broaden and

Table 6.1

Summary of Major Findings and Relationships

Year	Image Consensus ⟶	Image Cohesiveness	Image Stability ⟶	Behavior Congruence
1977	high	high	high	high
1978	moderate	moderate	moderate	moderate
1979	low	low	low	low
1980	high	high	high	high

deepen our understanding of foreign policy and international behavior since most decisions in politics and foreign policy are a function of many individuals who act as part of a group or collectivity.

More work needs to be done on the concept of collective images. This point needs to be emphasized because although the relationships that were found between image consensus, image cohesiveness, image stability, and behavior all seem rather obvious, there is little systematic literature discussing and linking these concepts at the group or collective level in international relations or political psychology.[9] It is hoped that this analysis contributes to the study of individual and collective beliefs in political psychology, at the same time addressing the controversy about American foreign policy during the Carter Administration.

Notes

1. There are different interpretations as to the nature of the continuity in American foreign policy. As indicated in chapter 1, a revisionist literature has also developed. The revisionist literature associated with the political left emphasizes, not the containment of communist expansion, but that the goal of American foreign policy has been to consistently maintain and promote American capitalism throughout the world (see, e.g., Berkowitz, Bock & Fuccillo, 1977). The revisionists of the political right emphasize the American failure to contain the growth of communism due to major American figures of high finance who have consistently pursued policies to create global socialism under their control (see, e.g., Allen, 1971).

2. *Balance of power* is a concept that has meant many things to many people. Claude (1964) and Haas (1953) have pointed out that balance of power may refer to a relationship of equilibrium as well as a hegemonic relationship.

3. There is a third philosophical tradition that has become important with time in international politics—radical idealism. Liberal idealists and realists are basically content with a nation-state international system: realists are status-quo oriented, liberal idealists are reformers. Radical idealists, on the other hand, want the global system to be transformed, either through the promotion of international integration and the creation of some type of world government, or based upon a neo-Marxist revolutionary transformation. Radical idealism, however, has not had much of an impact in Western industrialized democracies at the policy-making level. For a very interesting analysis of international politics and the cause of war based upon these three philosophical traditions, see Claude (1964) and Nelson and Olin (1979).

4. This theme is consistent with the one made in his memoirs, as indicated by the title *Power and Principle*.

5. A similar argument is made by Smith (1986). An interesting article (Winter, 1978) assesses the relationship between Reinhold Niebuhr's philosophy and President Carter's.

6. American foreign policy under Nixon and Ford attempted to bridge the disagreements between the two most popular schools of thought: the conservative internationalists, who had provided the foundation for America's cold war policies during the 1950s and 1960s, and the liberal internationalists, who were to provide the foundation for the Carter Administration's foreign policy.

NOTES

7. It is important to point out that many analysts who agreed that the Carter Administration had an optimistic worldview argue that the Carter Administration continued to pursue a policy of containment, but emphasized an alternative means of containing Soviet communism. Therefore, there was continuity in American foreign policy in its ends, although change in its means. This interpretation is not supported by this study which found that the Carter Administration did not pursue a policy of containment as *the basis* of foreign policy—the major goal was not to contain Soviet communism. Therefore, the Administration represented a change in American foreign policy since World War II.

8. Although no definitive conclusions can be drawn from use of a longitudinal case study, case studies, nevertheless, can contribute to the development of theory (see, e.g., Lijphart, 1971).

9. The relationship between image consensus, image cohesiveness, image stability, and belief-behavior congruency has already been suggested in chapter 2 and may appear obvious to the reader. However, given the limited amount of work on the concept of collective (or group) beliefs, these linkages were not obvious to me when I conducted the research and is why I spend some time elucidating these points.

SEVEN | *The Power of Beliefs*

THIS study has addressed the controversy over the foreign policy of the Carter Administration by examining the beliefs of political leaders. This perspective assumes that an understanding of the Carter Administration's foreign policy called for the application of insights that political psychology had to offer concerning beliefs and their impact on human behavior. As we have seen, the evolution of the Administration's image of the international system and its relationship to foreign policy behavior was found to be principally a function of the level of consensus that existed among individual policymakers' images over time. Crucial to the entire analysis is the position that the study of beliefs is an important explanatory and predictive source for international behavior.

Explanatory Power

Efforts to apply psychological approaches explicitly to the study of international relations began in the early 1930s. Continuing throughout the 1940s and early 1950s, psychological concepts were utilized in an attempt to improve one's understanding of the nature of war and peace.[1] Rarely, however, were these studies based on an international relations foundation. Instead, they began at the level of the individual and directly applied psychological concepts to the study of international relations.

This well-intentioned attempt by many psychologists to apply different concepts and approaches to the study of international behavior bestowed a bad name on the psychological literature as a whole (Holsti, 1977, pp. 16–20; Jervis, 1976, pp. 3–10). Most political scientists found these studies lacked

EXPLANATORY POWER

realism and believed that they were not relevant to the study of international relations (e.g., Waltz, 1954). The problem was clearly stated by Herbert Kelman (1965a, p. 6): "only if we know where and how these individuals fit into the larger process, and under what circumstances they operate, are we able to offer a relevant psychological analysis."

Although this initial effort to incorporate psychological approaches into the analysis of international behavior failed to influence the field, some scholars gradually began to question the lack of psychological input into the study of international relations. Quincy Wright (1955, p. 433), in his magnum opus, *The Study of International Relations*, proposed that psychology belongs at the "core" of the discipline:

> International relations cannot, therefore, be confined to intergovernmental relations and conclusions based on the assumption that they can fail to provide an adequate foundation for prediction and control. The minds of individuals who constitute the world's population, the influences that affect them, and the influences they exert, both domestic and foreign, must be taken into account by examining their minds.

Beginning in the mid-1950s, the importance of psychological approaches to the study of international relations grew in importance due to the interaction of the "peace research" movement and the development of the "behavioral" revolution (Kelman, 1965a; Kelman & Bloom, 1973). A number of psychologists, sociologists, economists, anthropologists, and other social scientists became interested in applying the knowledge and techniques of their disciplines to the problems of war and peace. At the same time, many scholars became interested in making the field of international relations more empirical and scientific. In comparison to the early efforts by psychologists, the late 1950s and 1960s represented the beginning of a qualitative leap forward for psychological approaches and their application to the study of international relations. It was the era of the initial application of psychological approaches from an international relations perspective:

> Writings have shown increasing theoretical and methodological sophistication, with greater awareness of the complexities one encounters in moving across different levels of analysis. And, most important, two groups of specialists have emerged and interacted closely with one another: students of international relations, with a political science background, who are thoroughly grounded in social-psychological concepts and methods; and social psychologists (as well as students of other disciplines outside of political science) who have systematically educated

themselves in the field of international relations. (Kelman & Bloom, 1973, p. 263)

The result has been that psychological aspects of international relations have begun to be closely examined, both explicitly and systematically. Nevertheless, the question that needs to be addressed is how helpful are these approaches, in particular the role of beliefs, in explaining international behavior.

The Problem of Determining Causality

This analysis has demonstrated that there was a close relationship between the Carter Administration's beliefs and its foreign policy behavior. The higher the level of consensus in beliefs among policymakers, the greater the cohesiveness and stability of the group's image and, consequently, the higher the congruency for collective behavior. Congruency was found to have been very high during the first and last years of the Carter Administration. The relationship found between beliefs and behavior does not imply that the Carter Administration's beliefs about the international system necessarily caused its international behavior. Three conditions must be fulfilled in order to have a causal relationship between beliefs and behavior: covariation (beliefs and behavior must be related in time), temporal precedence (changes in beliefs must precede changes in behavior), and nonspuriousness (no other factors beyond beliefs can be responsible for the behavior).[2]

This study of Carter's foreign policy really only investigated and satisfied the first condition. Beliefs and behavior were highly congruent during the first and fourth year. They were moderately congruent in the second year and basically incongruent during the third year. But even the low levels of congruency reveal a direct relationship between beliefs and behavior: when a group's image is not shared by individuals and is therefore not cohesive and stable, congruency with behavior should not be expected. Therefore, as discussed in the previous chapter, the level of consensus in an image for a collective group is directly related to the level of congruency between beliefs and subsequent behavior.

Temporal precedence was not directly examined; the same time periods were compared for describing the relationship between the Carter Administration's image of the international system and its foreign policy behavior. Temporal precedence is extremely difficult to determine primarily for two reasons. First, in order to establish temporal precedence, beliefs must occur before behavior. It is almost impossible, however, to determine how much time it takes for beliefs to fully affect behavior. Therefore, although a time lag can be incorporated in the analysis, it cannot be certain if the duration of the time lag between beliefs and behavior is an appropriate one.

The second major problem in determining whether beliefs originated before behavior is the interactive nature of beliefs and behavior. Not only do beliefs affect behavior, but behavior also affects beliefs. According to Daniel Heradstveit (1979, p. 123), "beliefs and action are interactive. Beliefs determine action, while, on the other hand, action determines beliefs. Action is the testing ground for beliefs and may cause beliefs to be modified, changed, or given up altogether. But then the newly formed beliefs again become determinants of consequent action." This results in the "chicken and egg" dilemma—cause and effect are complementary and, thus, difficult to isolate.

Many scholars tend to underestimate or ignore the validity problems involved in determining causality. The difficulty of determining temporal precedence in this study is further exacerbated because both individual and collective beliefs of a very general nature were analyzed. Also, major public statements were irregularly given relative to foreign policy behavior. Therefore, the temporal relationship between beliefs and behavior for the Carter Administration was quite complex, involving a multitude of different time lags and interactions.

The major obstacle, however, in determining causality is the requirement of nonspuriousness, i.e., no external factors beyond beliefs can account for the resultant behavior. "Ideally, the theorist should be responsible for the identification of all other factors which may induce changes in the major concepts being considered. He should demonstrate that, even after all these factors have been taken into account, the major concepts still covary. But, in reality, these demands can seldom be met" (Lin, 1976, p. 22). The requirement of nonspuriousness makes it literally impossible for social scientists to attribute causality with any degree of confidence.

Other factors obviously affected the Carter Administration's foreign policy behavior in addition to its image of the international system. Once differences in principal policymaker images developed, the Administration's international image became so complex and incoherent that it was difficult to translate the belief system into concrete programs and foreign policy behavior. This gave other individuals and organizations throughout the bureaucracy greater opportunity to affect the implementation of policy. Even when it appeared that the beliefs of the Carter Administration were affecting behavior, such as during 1977 and 1980, other elements may have been operating, such as the influence of Congress.

This study, therefore, satisfies only one of the three requisite conditions for demonstrating that beliefs may have caused behavior. Nevertheless, a more promising and fruitful path in explaining international behavior is not to focus on beliefs as a causal variable, but as an intervening variable.

Beliefs as a Causal Nexus

Beliefs can easily be treated as an intervening variable—in other words, as a filter through which other factors pass. This type of approach allows for the integration of a variety of important causal factors and "views explanatory variables not as in competition with one another in accounting for foreign policy behavior but as combining to produce a more adequate explanation than any one variable or cluster of closely related variables could do alone" (East, Salmore & Hermann, 1978, pp. 18–19).

"Background factors never directly cause behavior," stated Gordon Allport (1931, p. 173), one of the founders of attitudinal research in psychology, "they cause attitudes (and other mental sets) and the latter in turn determine behavior." Beliefs are naturally positioned between the environment and behavior. Attitudes, according to Milton Rokeach (1973, p. 3), "more than any other concept . . . are an intervening variable that shows promise of being able to unify the apparently diverse interests of all the sciences concerned with human behavior."[3] Using beliefs as an intervening variable overcomes the charge, so often heard in international relations, that psychological approaches are fundamentally reductionist in nature.[4]

This study was based upon a framework that integrates theoretical work developed at four different levels: the individual, group, societal, and the international environment. A belief system approach was developed in which the concept of international system was incorporated as part of the psychological environment in order to better understand the Carter Administration's foreign policy beliefs. This belief system approach was integrated within a decision-making context in order to determine which individuals were to be examined as part of the collectivity—the President, National Security Advisor, and Secretary of State. The role of personality, external events, and domestic forces were analyzed as a result of their relevance for explaining image stability and change in the evolution of the individual and collective images of the Carter Administration (see figure 7.1).

The major advantage of using beliefs as the causal nexus is the synthesis of both environmental and psychological factors for the explanation of international behavior. As described by Fred Greenstein (1975, p. 7), behavior "is a function of both the environmental situations in which actors find themselves and the psychological predispositions they bring to the situation." However, in previous international relations work, the tendency has been to rely on a psychological approach or an environmental factor for explaining international

EXPLANATORY POWER

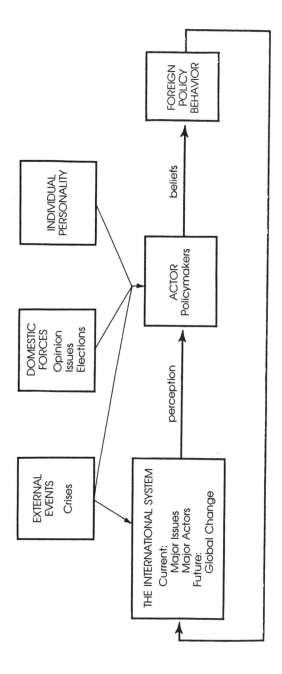

Figure 7.1   Summary of causal nexus approach.

behavior. Rarely have the two general approaches been integrated into a larger framework. Most belief system approaches have focused on describing the content and importance of beliefs; they have tended to "de-emphasize the multitude of interwoven factors" (Ben-Zvi, 1976–77, p. 90).

This approach is not without its weaknesses—the most important being its fundamental emphasis on the "psychological environment." The "objective environment" is not directly incorporated unless it is perceived to exist. The difference between the psychological and objective milieu is clearly described by Harold and Margaret Sprout (1965, p. 11):

> So far as we can determine, environmental factors (both nonhuman and social) can affect human activities in only two ways: such factors can be perceived, reacted to, and taken into account by the human individual or individuals under consideration. In this way, and in this way only . . . environmental factors can be said to 'influence', or to 'condition', or otherwise to 'affect' human values and preferences, moods, and attitudes, choices and decision. On the other hand, the relation of environmental factors to performance and accomplishment . . . may present an additional dimension. In the latter context environmental factors may be conceived as a sort of matrix or encompassing channel, metaphorically speaking, which limits the execution of undertakings. Such limitations on performance, accomplishment, outcome, or operational result may not— often do not—derive from or depend upon the individual's perception or other psychological behavior.

Given the fact that individuals perceive the environment differently, certain objective or material conditions may affect behavior and not be subsumed within the psychological environment. Certain aspects of the objective environment may be misperceived, ignored, or hidden (see figure 7.2).

This study focused on the significance of the subjective or psychological environment for explaining international behavior. Beliefs were used as an intervening variable in which a variety of important theoretical factors were integrated so as to better understand and explain the Carter Administration's foreign policy. Obviously, objective conditions above and beyond the psychological environment must also be taken into account. Nevertheless, beliefs do serve as an important source of international behavior.

Explanation and International Behavior

The growing interdisciplinary nature of international relations has forced scholars to focus on different theoretical approaches and different levels of analyses. This has led to considerable disagreement over the contribution of

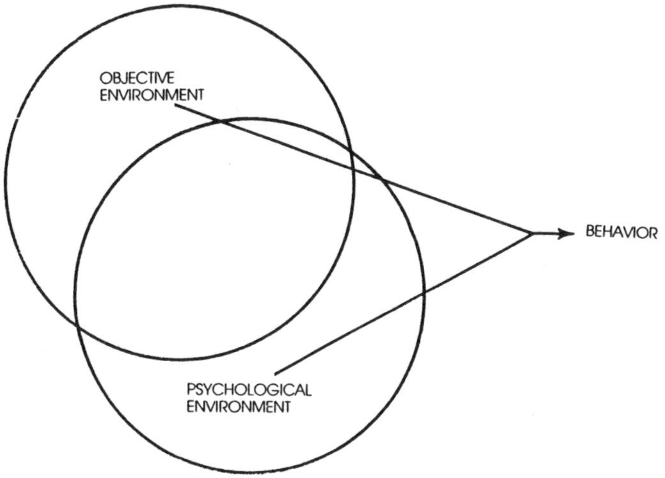

Figure 7.2   **Relationship between the psychological and objective
environment.**

various theoretical approaches to the explanation of international behavior.
The tendency has been for scholars to emphasize the particular theoretical
approach that they subscribe to as the most productive for understanding
international behavior. As described by Snyder and Diesing (1977, pp.
21–22):

> In our teaching and research, we are like travelers in a houseboat, shut-
> tling back and forth between separate "islands" of theory, whose related-
> ness consists only in their being commonly situated somewhere in the
> great "ocean" of international behavior. Some theorists take up perma-
> nent habitation on one island or another, others continue to shuttle, but
> few attempt to build bridges, perhaps because the islands seem too far
> apart.

Occasionally, efforts have been made to rank-order different approaches
and to suggest those that might be most fruitful for analyzing behavior (e.g.,
Kegley & Wittkopf, 1979; Rosenau, 1966). In any case, an overwhelming
amount of attention has been spent on "levels of analysis" questions: what are
the different levels of analysis, what levels have the greatest explanatory
power, and, consequently, what theoretical approaches are most relevant?

THE POWER OF BELIEFS

Continuous debate has existed over the role of psychological approaches in contributing to an understanding of international behavior. Those sympathetic to the study of beliefs have argued it is fundamental in analyzing international behavior; opponents have maintained that political beliefs have little or no consequence in affecting international behavior. A more fruitful way, however, to evaluate the potency of different theoretical approaches is not to focus on the level of analysis, but rather on the "unit of explanation"— the phenomena that one is attempting to explain. Not much attention has been spent on the conceptualization of "international behavior" and its relation to international relations theory.[5] It is quite likely that the relative potency of different theoretical approaches will vary depending upon the type of international behavior that is to be explained.[6]

A simple taxonomy of international behavior should be helpful in contributing to the question of theoretical relevance. Very simply, there are three general types of behavior that serve as a principal focus of study in international relations: foreign policy behavior, interaction behavior, and systemic behavior (see Coplin & Kegley, 1975). Foreign policy behavior refers to the actions that result from a single state or actor into the international arena. Interaction behavior describes the interchange of behavior that takes place among two or a few international actors. Finally, systemic behavior refers to interaction that occurs throughout the entire international system (or a major subsystem, such as within a geographic region).

I propose the following relationship between belief system approaches and international behavior (see figure 7.3):

Proposition 1. Belief system approaches are most relevant for explaining foreign policy behavior,
Proposition 2. Belief system approaches are moderately relevant for explaining interaction behavior, and
Proposition 3. Belief system approaches are least relevant in contributing to an understanding of international systemic behavior.

Most of the belief system literature—whether elite image studies, operational code, or cognitive mapping—have in fact concentrated on the foreign policy of a single state, followed by an examination of the interaction behavior of two or three states. Therefore, the abundance of belief system literature in international affairs is consistent with the propositions. To propose that beliefs are "least" relevant for contributing to an understanding of systemic behavior does not imply that beliefs are irrelevant. Rather, a belief system approach can also provide a valuable contribution to an explanation of international behavior at the systemic or global level.

EXPLANATORY POWER

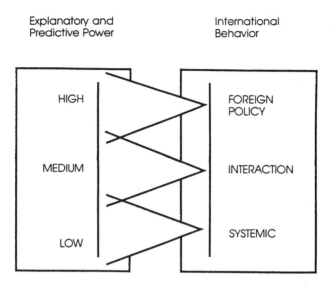

Figure 7.3   Impact of beliefs on international behavior.

Most of the macro theory about the evolution of the international system—whether the theory of hegemonic stability, long cycles theory, or world systems theory—either ignores the internal dynamics of actors or assumes rationality. Some of the literature depicts state action in a highly deterministic fashion, a function of the structure and process of the international system.[7] Other work examining the evolution of the international system, however, suggests that an individual actor retains freedom of action to affect the system. Robert Gilpin (1981), for example, has developed a model of international systems change that clearly describes the essential role of independent state action upon the entire system. He argues that the international system does not deterministically transform itself with time. Rather, systemic stability or change is the result of the development and outcome of major international events, especially war. Two factors principally influence the impact of events and the evolution of the international system: the attributes of the international system and the action of international actors, especially the role of major states. However, Gilpin, like most systemic theorists, assumes rationality as the basis of state behavior and looks solely to environmental factors as the explanatory source of war and change.

As demonstrated by Ned Lebow (1981, p. 4), "the proximate causes of conflict may even be as important as the underlying ones if a crisis can determine whether long-standing tensions are ultimately eased or lead to war." This explains the disproportionate amount of attention that the study of international crises has received. For how crises are resolved "can determine whether war breaks out or peace is maintained. They can also intensify or ameliorate the underlying sources of conflict in cases where war is averted" (Lebow, 1981, p. 334). The integral role crises play in effecting war and change in the international system requires that we examine the internal dynamics of state behavior, as well as environmental constraints, as a source of explanation.

International crises occur at times when the impact of independent actors is at its highest and when the role of the individual is maximized (see Greenstein, 1975; M. Hermann, 1978; Holsti, 1977; Jervis, 1976). During such times, the application of a psychological approach can be particularly enlightening for understanding crisis bargaining and its eventual resolution. Therefore, although a belief system approach may be most fruitful for explaining foreign policy and then interaction behavior, it may also be an important source of explanation for international systemic behavior as well.[8]

Predictive Power

The study of beliefs not only contributes to an explanation of international behavior, but it also has considerable predictive power. The conditions that must be met for prediction are in many respects less rigorous than for explanation. Causality does not have to be demonstrated; the only requirement is that beliefs must covary with behavior over time. According to Falkowski (1979, p. 9), "if we find that certain statements of attitudes tend to be highly related to subsequent behavior, are we not increasing our ability to predict even if we are not totally clear how the two variables are causally related?"

To say that the examination of individual beliefs contributes to the prediction of behavior is not to imply that all types of behavior can be predicted in a comprehensive fashion. "It is of course naive to believe that the study of doctrines will enable us to predict specific events or concrete decisions," states Brodin (1972, p. 111). "No such thing is intended. By prediction is simply meant the effort to evaluate which of a number of alternative outcomes stand out as more likely or more probable than others." Knowledge of the beliefs of political leaders allows one to predict the parameters in which behavior is likely to occur. What is actually predicted is the "choice propensities" of decisionmakers (George, 1979, 1980). As described by Tweraser

(1974, pp. 69–70), "by identifying the beliefs the actor uses to bound reality, we have an essential tool to predict the range of actions within which his probable choice will be contained and to exclude unlikely ones" (see the belief-behavior discussion in chapter 2).

The following factors must be taken into consideration in attempting to predict behavior from beliefs: (1) the level of stability in beliefs over time, (2) whether or not there may be competing beliefs, (3) the context in which behavior is predicted from beliefs, and (4) the nature of alternative policy actions that are available.

In attempting to predict behavior, it is essential to know whether beliefs have changed with time. It has been found that as long as a subject's attitudes did not change much, predictions of its behavior over a three- or even six-month period could be made quite accurately (Schwartz, 1978). In this study, the Carter Administration's image of the international system was only stable during the first and last years, fluctuating during the intermediate years. Therefore, in order to maximize prediction it is important to update the description of the content of beliefs because change may occur. The longer the time elapses between the determination of beliefs and the prediction of behavior, the greater the chance for inaccuracy.[9]

The second major factor affecting prediction is that there may be competing beliefs that may be significant in affecting behavior. The competition among beliefs may occur within the belief system of a single individual or as a result of different images held by different individuals. In the first case, it is important to determine the existence of different "situational thresholds" in order to establish which central beliefs are likely to become operative (Campbell, 1963; Cottam, 1977; Deutscher, 1973; Schuman, 1972).[10] In the latter case, when individuals have different images, the distribution of power within the decision-making unit must be examined in order to determine which beliefs are dominant for the group. Both cases seemed to be operating within the Carter Administration in 1979. Isolating the most central beliefs was extremely difficult due to the coexistence of two contrasting worldviews held by Vance and Brzezinski within the administration and because of Carter's inconsistent state of mind. These factors explain why the Carter Administration's foreign policy behavior for that year was so erratic.

Prediction is also affected by the context from which beliefs are derived. It is important to be conceptually clear as to what type of behavior is to be predicted from what type of beliefs. Not all beliefs are equally useful for predicting all forms of behavior. For example, more specific beliefs are better able to predict more specific behavior; likewise, more general beliefs are more appropriate for predicting more general behavior (Fishbein & Ajzen, 1975;

Herberlein & Black, 1976). With regard to collective beliefs and collective behavior, a similar context also requires that the beliefs that need to be examined should be derived from those individuals most directly involved in affecting the behavior to be predicted. For example, an examination of the Carter Administration's image of the international system based upon the beliefs of its most significant decisionmakers is most appropriate for predicting the general parameters of its major foreign policy behavior. As already discussed concerning the importance of situational thresholds, behavior is more likely to be successfully predicted from beliefs if they share a similar setting.

The fourth major factor affecting prediction concerns the variety of alternative behaviors possible. Even if the above three conditions are met, it is possible that the actor could still be constrained from performing his preferred alternative. The existence of external constraints is due to the critical impact of the objective environment. Regardless of the intention, if an actor does not have the capability to act, the appropriate behavior cannot be performed. Therefore, the objective environment, as difficult as it is to accurately perceive, may further narrow the choice propensities that are available to decisionmakers beyond those created by their belief systems.

In sum, the analysis of beliefs can be extremely valuable in predicting future behavior. A number of prerequisites must be satisfied to insure the existence of covariation and, therefore, to maximize the predictive power of beliefs (see, e.g., Ehrich, 1969): beliefs must be relatively stable; in case of competing beliefs, those most central must be determined; beliefs must be derived relative to the appropriate situation or context; and the objective environment may reduce the possible alternatives of behavior available to an actor. If these factors are taken into consideration, a belief system approach should be able to contribute substantially to the prediction of human behavior.

Policy Relevance

The study of beliefs of political leaders can also be very useful in assisting policymakers. However, in the study of international relations a considerable gap has developed between the social scientist and the policy practitioner. This is especially the case in the United States, where it is almost as if two separate worlds have developed, where an individual interested in international affairs must choose to be either policy-oriented or scholarly-oriented.[11] Even though the two orientations are far from mutually exclusive, recent efforts to bring the two groups together have not been all that successful. Richard Merritt (1974,

POLICY RELEVANCE

p. 128) describes the low-level of meaningful communication that occurs between foreign policy practitioners and academic scholars:

> A generation of policy studies scholars using new methodologies and systematic approaches seems scarcely to have made a dent in the armor of entrenched bureaucrats dealing with foreign policy on a day-to-day basis. Whether the fault, if fault it be, lies with the obtruseness of the behavioral scientists or the abtruseness of policymaking officials is not at issue here. More to the point is that breakthroughs are needed to bridge the communication gap.

There has been a considerable debate over the question of policy relevance in international relations research. Some scholars have argued that attention should be devoted to the building of theory in an effort to promote knowledge (Young, 1972) and that in any respect international relations research has few empirical generalizations useful to the policymaker (Whiting, 1972). Other scholars have argued that there is a need for policy-relevant theory as a product of scientific research in international relations (George & Smoke, 1973; Wright, 1955).

My feeling is that while the sympathies of the former position are understandable, there is no need to neglect the concerns of the policymaker who is, after all, the one actively involved with international behavior. According to William Fox (1986, p. 36), "we are not simply tourists on this planet . . . Our collective job is *not* to whisper in the ear of today's dictator, but it is to help those in and out of government with present or future influence on the policy process understand some of the expected middle-run and long-run consequences of alternative policy choices." Furthermore, as stated by Coplin and Kegley (1975, p. 6), "despite the common contention that scholars should not recommend policies or advocate particular conditions, almost all do, including those most committed to social science methodology." From the policymaker's perspective, international relations theory and research can be most helpful by assisting in the explanation and prediction of international behavior and, therefore, strengthening the foundation from which policy is prescribed.

The study of international relations can contribute to the policymakers' diagnosis and predictions of policy issues and problems. In this way the decisionmaker may be able to avoid the use of oversimplified theories and be able to extend and enrich his models of international behavior. "If the social sciences cannot revolutionize the work of the foreign policy analyst, they may sharpen his existing tools and suggest new ones. . . . These insights can broaden and deepen the foreign policy analyst's capacity for creative judgement—which will remain the central element of his art" (Horelick, Johnson, & Steinbruner, 1973, p. 2).

Although most research in international relations may be relevant to the public official, the study of beliefs is extremely useful. Most policymakers already operate implicitly from a belief system approach.

> We are all philosophers or theorists of sorts. . . . Or rather we all use political theories, if we have any conscious political life at all, if we think at all about politics. For a political theory is an explanation of what politics is all about, a general understanding of the political world, a frame of reference. Without one we would be unable to recognize an event as political, decide anything about why it happened, judge whether it was good or bad, or decide what was likely to happen next. (Bluhm, 1971, p. 61)

An important role for the academic to play in the policy world is to challenge the assumptions held by policymakers. Cottam (1977, p.11) argues that "at the very least this should sensitize decision makers to the importance of looking at the assumptional underpinnings of each of several differing policy-preferential positions. Optimally, it would persuade them to make explicit, to explore, to evaluate, and, one hopes, to revise their own assumptional positions." In this way the study of beliefs provides policymakers with a better understanding of the international and decision-making environment for making policy.[12]

Some governmental organizations and policy research institutions in the United States have found international relations research to be quite useful in contributing to their understanding of international behavior. Social-psychological approaches, including a focus on beliefs, have been favorably received and utilized in a number of agencies—especially in the Central Intelligence Agency (and the intelligence agencies in general). This is still, however, a far cry from having international relations research used extensively throughout the policy-making community.

Policy prescription may be important not only for the decisionmaker but also for any individual within the general political system. In this respect, knowledge of the beliefs of political leaders are very important in affecting political action and determining the type of policies that have the opportunity of being approved and implemented. Efforts to change reality and the possibility of future success will increase if individuals prescribe policy that is empirically well-grounded and viable.

There is, however, no guarantee that people will use social scientific theory wisely and productively. The question of good or bad policy is a normative one and dependent on the values of the individual. Whatever one's preferences, beliefs are fundamental in affecting behavior and creating a future world order. Personally, I share Kenneth Boulding's (1969, p. 431) simultaneous fear and hope that

> we live in an international system so unstable that it threatens the very existence of life on earth, our main hope for change may lie in the rapid growth of sophistication, especially at the level of the images of the powerful. . . . We have no secure place to stand where we are, and we live in a time when intellectual investment in developing more adequate international images and theories of the international system may bear an enormous rate of return in human welfare.

Only by affecting the human mind is it possible to approach a cooperative world where community and freedom can flourish.

Notes

1. For an overview of this early literature, see Kelman (1965a), Klineberg (1950), and Pear (1950).

2. These three conditions for determining causality are based on positivist epistemology, which has come to dominate inquiry in the social and physical sciences.

3. The significance of utilizing beliefs as a causal nexus has been recognized in the study of international relations. Robert Isaak (1974, p. 274), in a very interesting philosophical argument, has argued that phenomenology "can be used to solve the level-of-analysis problem and to de-reify popular abstractions such as 'nation-state as actor' and 'the international system'." This is a similar position taken by Richard Snyder (1958), in his path-breaking work on decision-making, and Herbert Kelman (1965b).

4. It should not be assumed that this belief system approach is the only viable causal nexus approach that can promote integration and synthesis. This approach rather is one of a variety of potential ways of integrating the theoretical literature on international relations (see Andriole, Wilkenfeld & Hopple, 1975; Brecher, Steinberg & Stein, 1969; Smith, 1966; Snyder, Bruck & Sapin, 1962).

5. Individuals involved with the events data movement have spent considerable attention on the concept of behavior, especially with regard to maximizing validity and reliability when operationalized. However, they have not really delved much beyond methodological questions and analyzed the concept of behavior at a more abstract, theoretical level.

6. In other words, a focus on unit of explanation may result in different theoretical approaches being complimentary and demonstrate that the disagreement over different levels of analysis may be a "psuedo-debate."

7. For example, Modelski (1972, pp. 6–7) states:

> The principal merit of the systems approach was to establish a viable characterization for phenomena of global interdependence, and to signal the need for a greater understanding of particular interdependencies. For to say that the world now forms an international system is at

THE POWER OF BELIEFS

the same time to assert that various parts of that system not only interact but also cohere, that changes in one part of the system inevitably set in motion changes in other parts. This serves as a corrective to the unsubstantiated images of chaos, if not anarchy, that were frequently associated with perceptions of international politics.

8. In one of the earliest and most significant analyses of international behavior, Kenneth Waltz (1954) examined the role of international relations theory at three different levels: man (the first image), state (the second image), and the international system (the third image). He concluded his study by stating the following: "The third image describes the framework of world politics, but without the first and second images there can be no knowledge of the forces that determine policy; the first and second images describe the forces in world politics, but without the third image it is impossible to assess their importance or predict their results" (Waltz, 1979, p. 238). See also McClelland, 1968; Rosecrance, 1963; Schelling, 1978; Spanier, 1975.

9. It is important to remember that "only when central beliefs change should there be a corresponding change in behavior" (Rokeach, 1973, p. 232).

10. This is why Rokeach (1966) distinguishes between attitudes toward objects and attitudes toward situations. He argues that both types of attitudes must be integrated in order to predict behavior because an attitude-object is usually always encountered within some situation about which we have formed an attitude.

11. The studies by Couloumbis and Moore (1971) and Hicks, Couloumbis, and Forgette (1982) on the influence of academicians on U.S. foreign policy practitioners are particularly enlightening.

12. This may be a very optimistic vision as suggested by Thomas Hart (1976) in his study of Swedish national security elites. He found that politicians and bureaucrats were considerably close-minded to new information, while academicians were more open-minded. Hence, "one marvels that decision-makers can ever find researchers interested in studying what the former find interesting, or that researchers can ever find politicians interested in listening to their findings" (Hart, 1976, p. 217). However, the cognitive gap may not be as deep in the United States because many Ph.D.'s in international affairs tend to choose a more policy-oriented career.

APPENDIX A | *The Administration's Foreign Policy Process*

I am primarily concerned with explaining the broad foreign policy behavior of the Carter Administration throughout its four years in office by focusing on its image of the international system. In concentrating on the most significant and general foreign policy behavior, it is most appropriate to conceptualize the executive branch as an actor represented by the most important decisionmakers. Under the Carter Administration, the most important officials in the area of foreign policy were President Jimmy Carter, National Security Advisor Zbigniew Brzezinski, and Secretary of State Cyrus Vance (later replaced by Edmund Muskie). By analyzing the images held by the major policy-making officials of the Carter Administration one can better understand the general foreign policy behavior that resulted.

The foreign policy-making apparatus during the Carter Administration was analogous to the operations that existed during the first year of the Nixon Administration, when Henry Kissinger was the National Security Advisor. The Carter foreign policy system was centralized within the White House, yet it was relatively open and retained a high degree of flexibility. The foreign policy process revolved around the National Security Council (NSC) system and two principal advisors: the Assistant to the President for National Security Affairs and the Secretary of State.

Though originally the National Security Council was intended to be used as the main decision-making body under the Carter Administration (Presidential Directive/NSC-2, 1977b), the council fell into disuse relatively early on. In fact, the NSC rarely met throughout the four years of the Carter Administration and was not considered a decision-making body. Two formal groups within the NSC system were primarily responsible for the working operation of the foreign policy process: the Policy Review Committee (PRC) and the Special Coordinating Committee (SCC).

The Policy Review Committee was established to "develop national security policy for Presidential decision in those cases where the basic responsibilities fall primarily within a given department but where the subject also has important implications for other departments and agencies" (U.S., Department of State, 1979, p. 2). The PRC functioned as an ad hoc committee at the Secretarial level under the guidance of a specific department Secretary selected by the President depending upon the issue involved. Secretary of Defense Harold Brown was usually the designated chairman for those issues that were directly concerned with the military and defense such as the neutron bomb and arms for the Middle East. Secretary of State Vance chaired the PRC when more political-military issues were involved, including the Middle East negotiations, the Panama Canal treaties, the southern African conflict, and improvement of Far Eastern relations (Bonafede, 1977; Drew, 1978; Lanouette, 1978a).

The Special Coordinating Committee was established to "deal with specific crosscutting issues requiring coordination in the development of options and the implementation of Presidential decisions" (U.S., Department of State, 1979, p. 2). The SCC was chaired by National Security Advisor Zbigniew Brzezinski and dealt with such matters as arms control (e.g., SALT), oversight of intelligence activities, and crisis management (e.g., the Horn of Africa).

At the lowest level of the NSC system were two types of groups that did much of the legwork for the PRC and SCC and were responsible for issues of lesser significance: Interdepartmental Groups and Ad Hoc Groups. Interdepartmental Groups (IGs) dealt with the five major geographic areas (Africa, Latin America, East Asia, the Middle East and South Asia, and Europe) and general political-military affairs. Interdepartmental Group membership was recruited from the Assistant Secretary level and operated under the direction of the Policy Review Committee. Ad Hoc Groups focused on particular problems that were not covered by the guidelines in reference to the three groups mentioned. The chairmanship and membership in Ad Hoc Groups were determined by the President.

The formal policy process was activated when the President issued a Presidential Review Memorandum (PRM) that identified the issue and required that policy research be undertaken by the appropriate committees and agencies. Once the study was completed and transmitted to the President, he would decide on a particular course of action. At this point, a Presidential Directive (PD) was issued that described the President's decision and

APPENDIX A

instructed the bureaucracy as to the procedures for implementation (Presidential Directive/NSC-1, 1977a).

Obviously, the policy-making process was considerably more confusing and cumbersome than just portrayed (see Brzezinski, 1983; Kirschten, 1980; Korb, 1979). The President had to decide or agree on which issues were to be reviewed, which groups and individuals were to be involved, and who would be in charge of the Policy Review Committee (or a given Interdepartmental or Ad Hoc Group). Papers had to be prepared and revised, and meetings scheduled to discuss and debate the issue in question, all of which usually consumed a considerable amount of time and effort. The paperwork had to be organized and synthesized, the report completed and then sent to the President, usually with a brief summary and a one- or two-page memorandum attached on top. The President had to arrive at some type of decision and then the wheels of implementation, if required, had to turn.[1]

President Carter relied principally upon two individuals, Zbigniew Brzezinski and Cyrus Vance, in making the foreign policy process viable and effective. Brzezinski, as Assistant to the President for National Security and head of the National Security Council staff, was primarily responsible for coordinating the internal operations of the system. Secretary of State Vance was the chief negotiator and major spokesman for the Carter Administration.

National Security Assistant Brzezinski and Secretary of State Vance were the most heavily involved individuals and closest advisors to the President in the area of foreign affairs. They were in close contact with the President and with each other throughout the course of the day. Brzezinski usually briefed the President in the morning concerning the major developments that were occurring in the world as they affected U.S. foreign policy. In the evening, Vance often sent a report directly to the President summarizing his views for the day. Many important decisions were discussed during President Carter's weekly "foreign policy breakfasts" on Fridays with Brzezinski, Vance, and Vice President Walter Mondale (sometimes attended by chief aide, Hamilton Jordan). Brzezinski presided over a "weekly luncheon" with Vance and Secretary of Defense Harold Brown. President Carter was also usually available in the Oval Office to see his advisors or discuss policy with them over the phone (Burt, 1978; Drew, 1978; Gwertzman, 1979).

Therefore, within the Carter Administration, the most significant policymakers who dealt with foreign affairs were the President, National Security Assistant Brzezinski, and Secretary of State Vance (later replaced by Edmund Muskie). All three individuals were heavily involved in most of the major foreign policy decisions that were made across the board. Other policymakers were no doubt significant (e.g., Andrew Young, Harold Brown), but their

184

APPENDIX A

roles were much more restrictive in terms of the level of their involvement and the breadth of issues covered.

Notes

1. At the beginning of the Administration, President Carter initiated a study, as part of a larger reorganization project, examining to what extent defense, foreign, and arms control policy could be more fully integrated. The "Odeen Report" is particularly insightful concerning the Carter Administration's decision-making process, pointing out numerous problems and supplying recommendations for strengthening the policy-making apparatus (National Security Policy Integration, 1979).

APPENDIX B | *Research Method*

The approach used for determining and analyzing the Carter Administration's foreign policy beliefs and foreign policy behavior is described below. First, the concept of worldview as used in this study is defined. Secondly, the content analysis for determining the foreign policy beliefs of the Carter Administration is described. Finally, the method for determining the Administration's foreign policy behavior and for comparing the belief-behavior relationship is discussed.

The Determination of Beliefs

The term "worldview" in this study is defined in terms of an image of the international system. The determination of the Carter Administration's image of the international system is based upon a content analysis of public statements made by the major administration officials.

Worldview as Image of the International System

The perception of the international system is directly significant to the choice of policy. It is almost inconceivable to imagine that policymakers choose policy and have their governments act without any reference to the basic structures and processes that they believe exist in the international system. Therefore, worldview in this study refers to an image of the international system.

There is a need to study international systems and their impact on international behavior through the perceptions and beliefs of political leaders. A strong relationship between international images and U.S. foreign policy behavior has been previously suggested. In a work analyzing Dean Rusk's philosophical perceptions, Stupak (1971) concluded, "there is little doubt that while Rusk was Secretary (of State) he made operational decisions based on his belief that world affairs were occurring in a conflictual bi-polar framework." Alexander George and Robert Keohane (1980) argue that United States policymakers during the cold war viewed the world as bipolar— polarized, resembling a zero-sum contest, and highly unstable. "These beliefs about the nature of the international system importantly reshaped American perceptions of threats to the national interest and the resulting requirements for foreign policy" (George & Keohane, 1980, p. 232). Specifically, this led U.S. leaders

> to place a higher value on preventing distant areas, normally of peripheral interest, from coming under the control of anti-western elites, local communists, or the influence of major communist powers . . . to rely almost exclusively on the policy of deterrence via military strength . . . left largely unused were the panoply of other means that statesmen normally employ for moderating conflict potential in relations with other countries.

The conception of an international system is a significant ingredient in any discussion concerning a policymakers' foreign policy beliefs. Although the concept of international system has occasionally been integrated within a belief system approach, the literature has not "dealt systematically or extensively with questions of system structure and process" (Byers & Leyton-Brown, 1977, p. 608). This is the major criticism of the belief system literature by structuralists such as Kenneth Waltz (1979, p. 60):

> Reductionist theories explain international outcomes through elements and combinations of elements located at national or subnational levels. That internal forces produce external outcomes is the claim of such theories. . . . The international system, if conceived at all, is taken to be merely an outcome.

Focusing on an image of the international system is a refinement of previous elite image studies. In order to determine a policymaker's image of the international system there are two elements that are of primary interest: images of the "current" international system and of a preferred "future" international system.

To determine a policymaker's *current* image of the international system it is necessary to examine the perception of the two elements that are fundamental in describing systemic structure and process: actors and issues (see Dean & Vasquez, 1976; Mansbach & Vasquez, 1981).[1] More specifically, there are four actor dimensions and one issue dimension that are an integral part of current image: determining a policymaker's perception of the more important actors, the capabilities of the actors, the intentions of the actors, how the actors are (normatively) evaluated, and, most significantly, identifying the most important issues in which the actors are involved.[2]

By examining how actors are perceived along the four dimensions and incorporating the concept of issues, it is possible to construct a policymaker's image of the contemporary international system. The underlying structure of the international system is revealed by determining the more important participants and their perceived capabilities. The intentions and evaluations of the actors are significant for determining whether the interactive relationships are perceived to be conflictual or cooperative. Finally, the structure and process of the international system may vary depending upon the nature of the issue—different actors will be perceived as being important depending on the particular issue. Therefore, it is possible for an image of the current international system to vary along a continuum of simplicity to complexity with differing implications for their foreign policy and international behavior.

It is not sufficient to be concerned with a policymaker's image of only the contemporary international system. To fully understand an actor's foreign policy behavior, it is important to incorporate its perception of a *future* international system that it would like to promote. As integral as the perception of a future global system is to the entire belief system, little attention has been directed to the importance of preferred future images.[3] According to Jensen (1966, p. 199), "While some policy-makers may be hesitant to admit it, prediction or conjecture plays an important part in the policy process . . . Despite the importance of prognostication, very little systematic work has been done on the preconceived notions of policymakers about future events." One of the major problems preventing much thought and analysis concerning the future is the numerous constraints that exist on a daily basis forcing individuals to be oriented toward the present and immediate future (deRivera, 1968, pp. 65–104).

Given the likelihood that most individuals do not have much of a long-term future perspective, our concern must be with a very general future image. Does one have some type of conceptualization about a future global system? If so, what international structures and processes do they believe will and should operate? Closely intertwined with their future image is their perception of global change. If they have a negative image of global change they are likely to be more status-quo oriented. Those who see global change in a positive light may prefer to promote an international system that is quite different from the one that they perceive exists currently.

The focus of this psychological approach is on the policymaker's image of the international system. In sum, an image of the international system can be described by addressing the following questions:

What is the current nature of the international system?
>What are the most important issues?
>Who are the most important actors and why?
What type of future international system is preferable?
>Is global change desirable?

How decisionmakers perceive the general structures and processes of the current international system and how they view the future of the international system will have a direct effect on their choice of policy and on their subsequent foreign policy behavior (figure B.1 summarizes the relationship).

The Content Analysis

The delineation of the Carter Administration's image of the international system is based upon a content analysis of public statements made by major Administration officials throughout their official careers—from 1977 to 1980. Content analysis is "an attempt to infer the characteristics and intentions of sources from inspection of the messages they produce" (Osgood, Suzi & Tannenbaum, 1957, p. 275; see also Budd, Thorp & Donohew, 1967; Holsti, 1969; Janis, 1965; Krippendorff, 1980). It is both a sophisticated and delicate technique for determining the beliefs of individuals by examining patterns in the content of the messages.

> Strictly speaking, an individual does not express a "belief system." On the contrary, the respondent only expresses preferences regarding the question put to him. It is the analyst who infers some pattern and imposes structure upon the responses which are given. The identification of a belief system, therefore, is something the analyst derives through the utilization of statistical and other means. (Mennis, 1971, p. 149)

In this study, the public statements of President Carter, National Security Advisor Brzezinski, and Secretary of State Vance—later replaced by Edmund Muskie—were analyzed to identify the patterns in the content of the messages in order to determine their images of the international system.[4]

As with any research method, there are a number of problems that must be addressed to insure a high degree of validity.[5] In this context it is important to recall Philip Converse's (1964, p. 206) remark that "belief systems have

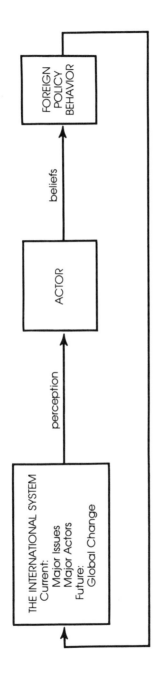

Figure B.1   Summary of an actor's image of the international system.

never surrendered easily to empirical study or quantification.'' Two major problems that complicate the utilization of content analysis exist: access and inference.

In determining the beliefs of public officials, three direct sources of information are available to the analyst: transcripts of private discussions, interviews with the participants, and official public statements.[6] Obviously, it would be optimal to have access to and integrate all three sources to maximize coverage of a public official's verbal behavior.

Closely related to the issue of access is the more significant problem of inference. Whatever documentary data one utilizes, the inference of beliefs from the content of the message is problematic. J. David Singer (1968, p. 145) depicts the major pitfall of content analysis: ''there are few more serious errors in science, or in policy, than to assume that the official and the operative ideologies are identical; yet it occurs with alarming frequency.'' A continuous debate has ensued regarding whether most communications are representative of an actor's beliefs or whether they are purely manufactured and targeted to persuade a specific audience. The ''representational'' and ''instrumental'' models have both been offered to describe the fundamental process of communication (George, 1959; Osgood, 1959; see also Jervis, 1969). As suggested by I. S. Pool (1959) most communications are likely to contain both elements—representational and instrumental.

The problems of access and inference with regard to documentary data are serious ones and must be minimized. Therefore, although there are no easy rules on how to proceed to insure a valid content analysis, the investigator must ''approach available documentary evidence with the same skills and skepticism as the well-trained historian'' (Holsti, 1977, p. 48). In addressing these problems, it might be helpful to distinguish between three overlapping types of beliefs: private beliefs, public beliefs, and operational beliefs. *Private beliefs* are what an individual believes qua individual—the underlying beliefs. *Public beliefs* are beliefs that an individual expresses in a social environment. *Operational beliefs* are those beliefs to which an individual subscribes as a decisionmaker. Since this study examines the beliefs of political leaders in their role as government officials, it is of fundamental importance to concentrate on a policymaker's operational beliefs. The operational beliefs that individuals utilize as policymakers are most likely to be comprised of a composite of both private and public beliefs (see figure B.2). Whether a particular private or public belief (assuming a difference) is likely to motivate an individual as a decisionmaker depends principally upon the state of mind of the decisionmaker and the nature of the situation.

Given the contemporary topic of the Carter Administration, I must rely primarily on their public statements and, consequently, their public beliefs (White House transcripts or internal memoranda of the Carter Administration are not fully available and interviews, although they may be insightful, would be based on recollections of the past).[7] Nevertheless, public beliefs may be more meaningful in describing the beliefs that motivate public officials as decisionmakers, especially for the Carter Administration.[8] Four general reasons can be offered to support the use of public statements as valid indicators of the operational beliefs of political leaders.

First, official declarations often act as a "constraint" on political leaders through the statements' impact on other actors within the environment (Snyder, 1958). Statements by public officials "contribute to the creation of a number of expectations both within and without the country" and "influence the basis upon which other actors make their decisions" (Brodin, 1972, p. 105).[9] Thus, the situations that public officials respond to are affected by their public statements.

Second, public officials are under constant scrutiny, and they must maximize their "credibility" if they are to exercise leadership and stay in power. This is particularly true in democratic societies with a strong tradition of free speech and a free press where, in the opinion of Richard Snyder (1958, p. 32), "it seems highly unlikely that a decisional unit could survive constant falsification of motives." Public officials create political difficulties for themselves if they constantly mislead others.

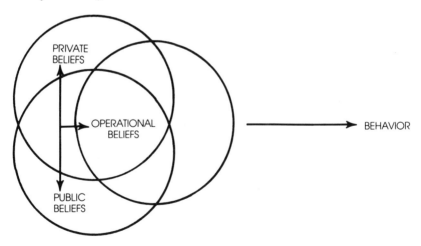

Figure B.2   Beliefs and their relationship for behavior.

APPENDIX B

Official decision-makers are likely to be subjected to a certain amount of pressure to act in accordance with previous declarations. The risk of negative sanctions tends to deter the decision-maker from courses of action he fears could be interpreted as inconsistent with an already established policy or previous commitments. (Brodin, 1972, pp. 107–108)

The third reason why public statements are important sources of the operational beliefs of individuals is that "an actor may influence himself by his own declarations" (Snyder, 1958, p. 32). This is in accordance with cognitive dissonance theory (Festinger, 1957) and Bem's (1967, 1972) theory of self-perception. Cognitive dissonance is a particular type of consistency theory that states that if an individual acts in a way that is incongruent with his beliefs, he will restore cognitive consistency by adjusting the most vulnerable link—his beliefs (since his behavior has already taken place and cannot be revoked). Self-perception theory complements the concept of cognitive dissonance by taking the position that a person derives one's beliefs from observing one's own behavior. And as stated by Richard Snyder (1958, p. 31), "much of the action which results from decision-making is verbal."

Finally, Carter Administration officials were very open and forthright in their public statements. According to diplomatic historian Gaddis Smith (1986, p. vi), "the archival record for the 1970s will not be available to historians for decades. But it is my conviction that the Carter Administration was unusually open about its purposes and activities. Members of the Administration spoke candidly and in detail to the press, to congressional committees, and to the public." This is particularly the case for President Carter. Jimmy Carter was incredibly open and forthright when he spoke publicly—especially during press conferences (see Weintraub, 1986). In this respect, he was a most unique politician and political leader.

To insure that the analyzed statements of the Carter Administration are valid and highly expressive, two complementary approaches have been employed. A quantitative content analysis was performed on the most significant and general public statements. In addition, a qualitative content analysis of all Carter Administration's public statements was conducted.

Sixty significant public statements were quantitatively content analyzed.[10] Significant public statements on the topic of foreign policy were the most useful for determining the policymakers' beliefs about the international system. Public addresses are particularly revealing because, unlike press conferences, for example, speeches are initiated by the official. The significance level of public statements was determined by the development of two criteria: the level of formality and transcript appearance. The more formal the audience

APPENDIX B

(e.g., joint session of Congress) and the occasion (e.g., State of the Union), the more significant the speech (see Gilbert, 1975). Perceived importance is also indicated if a speech is transcribed in a major forum (e.g., *State Department Bulletin*).[11] Table B.1 depicts the breakdown of the number of major speeches that were examined by policymaker and by year (appendix C provides a list of the public speeches made by the Carter Administration officials).

The themes within each public speech were coded in order to determine which were the most important international issues and actors actually perceived by the Carter Administration (see table B.2 for a breakdown of thematic statements by policymaker and year). In developing the initial coding manual a pre-test was conducted to determine the universe of issues and actors that were perceived by the Carter Administration. The actual coding of the public speeches was based on an open-ended approach; if a unique issue or actor was mentioned it was coded into a new category. Specifically, the public statements were coded in accordance with the image of the international system described above: for the issue perceived, the actors perceived to be involved relative to the issue, and various actor attributes (its capabilities, its intentions, and its evaluation).[12]

An open-ended coding approach was crucial in determining what issues and actors the Carter Administration perceived to exist in the international environment. A coding scheme that lacked this flexibility would code public statements into preconceived categories that probably would not have reflected the actual perceptions of the policymakers. Once all the public statements were coded, the specific issue and actors were consolidated (recoded) into eleven general issues categories and eight general actor categories as reflected in the perceptions of the poicymakers.[13] The general issue and actor categories were subsequently examined based upon a descriptive analysis of frequency distributions.

Table B.1

Number of Major Statements by Officials

Individual	Year 1977	1978	1979	1980	Total
Carter	7	7	2	6	22
Brzezinski	1	1	5	3	10
Vance	4	7	7	3	21
Muskie	—	—	—	7	7
Total	12	15	14	19	60

APPENDIX B

Table B.2

Thematic Statements by Officials

Individual	Year			
	1977	*1978*	*1979*	*1980*
Carter, %	52.1	38.6	12.4	26.3
Brzezinski, %	15.9	9.5	29.8	13.0
Vance, %	32.0	51.9	57.9	26.5
Muskie, %	—	—	—	34.2
	N = 597	N = 886	N = 712	N = 1099

Note: N refers to the number of thematic statements.

A qualitative content analysis was also conducted in order to fully determine the Carter Administration's image of the international system. In addition to the most significant statements, other public statements such as interviews, press conferences, and other speeches were qualitatively analyzed to determine the issues, the actors, and the nature of global change perceived by the Carter Administration throughout the international system.[14] As suggested by Alexander George (1959, p.7), "qualitative analysis of a limited number of crucial communications may often yield better clues to the particular intentions of a particular speaker at one moment in time than more standardized quantitative methods."

In determining the Carter Administration's image of the international system, a two-step process was used. The salient issues and actors perceived by the Carter Administration were derived by the quantitative content analysis while their particular significance for the image was based on the qualitative content analysis. In other words, the qualitative analysis provided an important context for understanding the quantitative findings. The quantitative content analysis had its greatest validity and usefulness in providing general findings to the Carter Administration's beliefs and behavior at the collective level—primarily due to the limited number of statements made by Carter in 1979 and by Brzezinski in 1977, 1978 and 1980 (see table B.1 and table B.2). The qualitative content analysis was most helpful for determining the individual images and comparing their similarities and differences, as well as for describing the content of the beliefs concerning the future of the international system (given the few references made by the principal policymakers).

Together, qualitative and quantitative content analyses serve as important complements in maximizing valid inferences of the beliefs of political leaders

APPENDIX B

(Cook & Reichardt, 1979). This also helps to minimize the debate between the representational and instrumental schools of thought concerning what inference can legitimately be made. According to Krippendorff (1980, p. 49), "content analysis research designs have to be *context sensitive.*" Therefore, the content analyses "should use qualitative and quantitative methods to supplement each other. It is by moving back and forth between these approaches that the investigator is most likely to gain insight into the meaning of his data" (Holsti, 1969, p.11). By conducting both quantitative and qualitative content analyses, the determination of the Carter Administration's image of the international system was maximized.

The Determination of Behavior

The Carter Administration's foreign policy behavior was determined by the development of an events data set, which was analyzed in terms of issues and actors. In this way, the Carter Administration's image of the international system was directly compared to its foreign policy behavior in order to determine the level of congruency between beliefs and behavior.

The Events Data Analysis

The description of the Carter Administration's foreign policy behavior was based upon the creation and analysis of an events data set—an aggregation of a large number of nonroutine international behaviors (McClelland & Hoggard, 1969).[15] The emphasis in analyzing events data is not with describing a specific event in detail, but in portraying a more comprehensive picture of an actor's total behavior over some length of time or in comparison with other actors' foreign policy behavior. This makes possible the description of more generalized patterns of behavior and allows for the possibility of higher-level explanatory and predictive power.

Events data sets usually have been developed through the use of publicly available sources, especially newspapers. As described by Charles Kegley (1975, p. 93), " 'data making' is a process whereby the supply of existing diplomatic records and documents are converted into scientifically useful data through systematic examination, classification, and tabulation." The use of newspaper coverage has been considered a good indicator of general international behavior for a variety of reasons: policymakers rely on newspapers, they are convenient and accessible, and the press is relatively competent in recognizing nonroutine events.

APPENDIX B

Events data analysis, however, is not without its detractors, and controversy in the comparative study of foreign policy has arisen over the relative validity of various specific events data sets. Because different events data sets have made use of different sources, some events data are more valid and more useful than others—this is dependent upon the type of international behavior that one is attempting to explain (see Azar, Cohen, Jukam, & McCormick, 1972; Howell, 1983).

In constructing an events data set as the basis for depicting the Carter Administration's foreign policy behavior throughout its four years, I have used *Deadline Data on World Affairs* as the data source. While a number of studies have pointed out that *Deadline Data* has certain weaknesses in the coverage of events—especially its low yield of total events and its tendency to deemphasize the activities of smaller nations (Burgess & Lawton, 1972, 1975; Hoggard, 1974)—it is quite appropriate for this particular study. Ironically, since this study focuses on "major" U.S. foreign policy behavior, the very weaknesses for which it is criticized actually increase the validity for using *Deadline Data*. Not only does *Deadline Data* emphasize the foreign policy behavior of the larger states, but it principally focuses on the most important international events (Burrows, 1974). This is an additional reason why it serves as an appropriate source for depicting the major foreign policy behavior that emanated from the Carter Administration (see appendix D for a list of the actions taken by the Carter Administration).

The events data set was developed by coding the reported U.S. foreign policy actions according to the issues and actors addressed. The coding scheme was analogous to the technique utilized for determining the Carter Administration's image of the international system.[16] Each American foreign policy action was coded for the issue involved, for the actors involved relative to the issue, and for the type of behavior—cooperative or conflictual—directed toward the actor.

Quantitative and qualitative analyses then were performed on the events data set of issues and actors in order to determine the content of the Carter Administration's foreign policy behavior. A quantitative analysis was conducted similar to the quantitative content analysis performed on the major public statements—based upon a description of frequency distributions. Because no monitoring instrument is perfect, "the events reported by the press therefore should not be interpreted as a full and accurate summary of all the foreign policy actions that have occurred everywhere. Rather, these records are best seen as indicators of what happened, as a sample of the behavior that has been undertaken" (Kegley, 1975, pp. 96–97; see McClelland, 1983). Accordingly, the quantitative analysis was complemented by a qualitative analysis of the major foreign policy events that occurred and supplemented by the use of traditional historical and documentary material.

The Belief-Behavior Link

The development of an events data set allows for a comparison between the evolution of the Carter Administration's image of the international system and its foreign policy behavior. In order to make a legitimate comparison of the impact of beliefs on behavior, two different sources of data must be utilized—one for beliefs, one for behavior. Therefore, a second source of information different from what was used for determining beliefs must be utilized for describing behavior (Holsti, 1977; Singer, 1968).

> The seeming circularity of generating a personality construct from behavior and using the construct to explain behavior does not in fact involve a tautology as long as we do not use the same item of behavior to infer a disposition and then use the inferred disposition to explain the item of behavior. (Greenstein, 1975, p. 65)

Accordingly, the verbal behavior (i.e., the public statements) of the three major policy-making officials used for describing the Carter Administration's image of the international system was specifically excluded as a source for the events data set.

Once the two separate data sets had been developed, a comparison between beliefs and behavior was possible. George (1979) has outlined two basic techniques for determining the impact of beliefs on behavior: the "congruence" procedure and the "process-tracing" procedure. The congruence procedure examines the relationship or level of consistency between the content of the beliefs and the content of the decision outcome. Process-tracing "seeks to establish the ways in which the actor's beliefs influenced his receptivity to and assessment of incoming information about the situation, his definition of the situation, his identification and evaluation of options, as well as, finally, his choice of a course of action" (George, 1979, p. 113). Process-tracing is better able to determine causality, but is oriented around a specific case study and requires a large amount of detailed information about the decision-making process. The congruence procedure focuses primarily on the level of association between beliefs and behavior, requires a minimal amount of data (per case), and allows for greater generalizations over time.

In this study, I have attempted to determine the level of congruency between the Carter Administration's image of the international system and its major foreign policy behavior. This was done by conducting a rank-order correlational analysis between the data sets on beliefs and behavior.[17] In addition, the relationship between beliefs and behavior was analyzed in a qualitative fashion (for example, by comparing the frequency distributions conducted on the separate data sets). The rank-order correlational analysis of the two sets of data was most revealing for describing patterns at the aggregate level while the qualitative comparison was most appropriate for indicating more specific relationships and providing a context for better understanding the quantitative findings.

Notes

1. As suggested by Rokeach (1968), belief systems are organized around (1) objects, and (2) situations.

2. A focus on actor capabilities, intentions, and evaluation is derived from previous belief system work on ''image of the opponent'' (see Holsti, 1962; Stuart & Starr, 1981–82).

3. A major exception is the variety of research on global futures, as represented by the World Orders Models Project and the Club of Rome. For example, Falk (1975) has described a number of alternative future international systems. Johan Galtung (1980) in *True Worlds* has provided a rather detailed sketch of his image of a preferred international system.

4. This study is based upon a comparative case study method and is longitudinally oriented in that I examine one ''general'' case over time by disaggregating the Carter Administration's foreign policy into four separate time categories. Each case is based upon a different year—an excellent break point due to the annual ''State of the Union'' address in which the president usually attempts to set the blueprint and tone for the year.

5. Most scholars socialized within the positivist tradition have tended to emphasize the reliability of their methodological procedures—insuring that the information they collect is accurate. The equally, if not more, important issue of the validity of a study—whether the data is relevant and appropriate to their research question—has often been ignored and needs to be directly addressed.

6. Beliefs of individuals have also been derived from examining their overt behavior. However, this procedure is self-fulfilling and tautological by assuming that beliefs cause behavior. This problem of ''circularity'' may be difficult to avoid even when a conscious effort is made. As suggested by Holsti (1977, p. 50), although we want to determine the relationship between a policymaker's behavior and his belief system, we may ''already know a great deal about his decision-making behavior and there is the danger that the analysis of beliefs will be contaminated by that knowledge.''

7. The use of public statements poses a potential problem concerning ''authorship.'' This is, however, a minimal problem for Carter Administration officials, where major speeches were often written by the principal policymaker, especially Secretary Vance and NSC advisor Brzezinski. Furthermore public addresses were cleared by the White House—very often personally by President Carter (see Marder, 1978; Quinn, 1979a; Weinstein & Beschloss, 1982). See also Weintraub (1986) concerning the source and spontaneity of his public statements.

8. What we are studying, states Brodin (1972, p. 105), ''is the official view, and that no assumptions are made about the extent to which this view reflects the private beliefs of the decision-makers in question.'' Goldmann (1982, p. 236) clearly describes the empirical nature of the relationship between private and public beliefs: ''The common dichotomy between 'real' and

APPENDIX B

'declared' motives is misleading: the degree of similarity and the amount of interaction between arguments for a policy that are given to different audiences and between these arguments and private thoughts, is an empirical question.''

9. This may be important in the formulation and implementation of policy throughout the bureaucracy. For example, within the Department of Defense (DOD), a publication (entitled *Selected Statements*) is prepared every two months to bring to the attention of key DOD personnel excerpts of public statements made by major U.S. policymakers reflecting official governmental policies pertaining to national security matters.

10. Because I am concerned with very broad beliefs of the Carter Administration—its image of the international system—the statements must have a relatively general orientation. Therefore, I included those statements that had a broad issue area and geographic coverage.

11. Ironically, the National Security Advisor, unlike the President and the Secretary of State, has no forum for expressing his foreign policy views. Although the original role for the NSC Advisor was to be managerial, he has nonetheless become a major foreign policy advisor, and the lack of a formal forum may result in an incomplete public record with time (see Destler, 1980–81).

12. Over 3,300 themes were found. Intracoder reliability in coding the speeches consisted of a .84 agreement score.

13. Charles Hermann (1978) describes this procedure on the raw data as the "data reduction approach". The final issue categories integrated two dimensions: substance or function and geographic location. The integration of the two dimensions was important to the Carter Administration policymakers images of the issues. They actually perceived, for example, that the conflict in Africa was a separate issue from the conflict in the Middle East.

14. Most of the additional public statements were located, e.g., in *American Foreign Policy Basic Documents, 1977–1980*, Department of Defense *Selected Statements, Department of State Bulletin, Public Papers of the Presidents*, and *Weekly Compilation of Presidential Documents*. Other primary and secondary sources were incorporated where appropriate to shed light on the Carter Administration's image of the international system.

15. Behavior is defined as discreet, observable action (C. Hermann, 1978; Fishbein and Ajzen, 1975).

16. In constructing the events data set, I relied heavily on previous work on events data, especially the CREON project (see C. Hermann, East, Hermann, Salmore & Salmore, 1974). Intracoder reliability consisted of a .87 agreement score.

17. A rank-order correlational analysis compares the rank-orderings of one category of variables with the rank-orderings of another category of similar variables to determine the level of similarity or difference between the two sets.

APPENDIX C | *Major Statements by Administration Officials*

President Carter

1977

Jan 20   "Inaugural Address." Made in Washington, D.C.

Mar 17   "Peace, Arms Control, World Economic Progress, Human Rights: Basic Priorities of U.S. Foreign Policy." Made before representatives to the U.N. in the U.N. General Assembly Hall.

Apr 14   "Pan American Day Address." Made before the Permanent Council of the OAS at the Pan American Union, Washington, D.C.

May 22   "A Foreign Policy Based on America's Essential Character." Made at the commencement exercises of Notre Dame University, South Bend, Ind.

Jul 21   "The U.S.-Soviet Relationship." Made before the Southern Legislative Conference at Charleston, S.C.

Oct 4   "U.S. Role in a Peaceful Global Community." Made before the 32nd U.N. General Assembly.

Nov 28   "U.S. Responsibility Toward Peace and Human Rights." Made before a meeting of the General Council of the World Jewish Congress, Washington, D.C.

1978

Jan 4   "New Agenda for Democracy." Made before the Palais Des Congress, Paris, France.

Jan 19   "State of the Union." Made before a joint session of Congress.

APPENDIX C

Mar 17	"National Security Interests." Made at Wake Forest University in Winston-Salem, N.C.
Apr 1	Remarks at the National Arts Theatre, Lagos, Nigeria.
Jun 7	"The United States and the Soviet Union." Made at the U.S. Naval Academy's commencement exercises.
Sep 18	"A Framework for Middle East Peace." Made before the Congress.
Oct 1	"The United States and Its Economic Responsibilities." Made at the opening session of the 26th World Conference of the International Chamber of Commerce in Orlando, Fl.

1979

Jan 23	"State of the Union." Made before a joint session of Congress.
Feb 20	"America's Role in a Turbulent World." Made at the Georgia Institute of Technology in Atlanta.

1980

Jan 4	"Soviet Invasion of Afghanistan." Made to the nation.
Jan 23	"State of the Union." Made before a joint session of Congress.
Feb 19	"National Security Goals." Made before the annual convention of the American Legion in Washington, D.C.
Apr 10	"U.S. Course in a Changing World." Made before the American Society of Newspaper Editors in Washington, D.C.
May 9	"U.S. Interests and Ideals." Made before the World Affairs Council in Philadelphia.
Aug 21	"National Security Policy." Made before the annual convention of the American Legion in Boston.

Secretary of State Vance

1977

Apr 30	"Human Rights and Foreign Policy." Made at law day ceremonies of the University of Georgia School of Law in Athens, Ga.
Jun 29	"America's Role in Consolidating a Peaceful Balance and Promoting Economic Growth in Asia." Made before the Asia Society in New York.
Jul 1	"The United States and Africa: Building Positive Relations." Made before the annual convention of the NAACP in St. Louis.
Nov 10	"The Goal of Real Peace." Made before the Council of Jewish Federations and Welfare Fund convention in Dallas.

APPENDIX C

1978

Jan 13   "Foreign Policy Decisions for 1978." Made before the Los Angeles World Affairs Council in Los Angeles.

Feb 8   "General Overview of 1977 Activities." Made before the Subcommittee on International Operations of the House Committee on International Relations.

Apr 10   "Arms Control and National Security." Made before the American Society of Newspaper Editors in Washington, D.C.

May 12   "Issues Facing the United States in Africa." Made before the Subcommittee on African Affairs of the Senate Committee on Foreign Relations.

Jun 19   "Elements of U.S. Policy Toward the Soviet Union." Made before the House Committee on International Relations.

Jun 20   "U.S. Relations with Africa." Made before the 58th annual meeting of the U.S. Jaycees in Atlantic City.

Dec 9   "The U.S.-European Partnership." Made before the Royal Institute of International Affairs in London.

1979

Jan 25   "American Foreign Policy in a Changing World." Made before a conference of 100 national black leaders across the country.

Feb 8   "Overview of Major Foreign Policy Issues." Made before the Subcommittee on State, Justice, Commerce, the Judiciary, and Related Agencies of the Senate Appropriations Committee.

Mar 30   "America's Commitment to Third World Development." Made before the Northwest Regional Conference on the Emerging International Order in Seattle, Wash.

May 1   "Meeting the Challenges of a Changing World." Made before the American Association of Community and Junior Colleges in Chicago.

Jul 23   "America's Growing Relationship with the Developing World." Address, as prepared for delivery, before the National Urban League in Chicago.

Sep 24   "Common Needs in a Diverse World." Made before the 34th session of the U.N. General Assembly in New York.

Sep 27   "Currents of Change in Latin America." Made before the Foreign Policy Association in New York.

1980

Feb 1   "Meeting the Challenge in Southwest Asia." Made before the Senate Appropriations Committee.

APPENDIX C

Mar 3   "Afghanistan: America's Course." Made before the Council of Foreign Relations in Chicago.

Mar 27   "U.S. Foreign Policy: Our Broader Strategy." Made before the Senate Foreign Relations Committee.

Secretary of State Muskie

1980

Jun 9   "The Middle East: Outlook for Peace." Made before the Washington Press Club in Washington, D.C.

Aug 7   "Human Freedom: American Values." Made before the United Steelworkers of America in Los Angeles.

Aug 7   "America's Strength: Ideals and Military Power." Made before the G.I. Forum in Los Angeles.

Aug 8   "The U.S. and Its Allies: New Patterns of Cooperation." Made before the Commonwealth Club of California and the World Affairs Council of Northern California in San Francisco.

Sep 18   "Essentials of Security: Arms and More." Made before the World Affairs Council in Pittsburgh.

Oct 6   "Dealing with the World's Realities." Made before the Economic Club of Memphis and the Memphis in May International Festival, Inc., in Memphis.

Oct 11   "The Challenge of Peace." Made at Notre Dame University in South Bend, Ind.

National Security Advisor Brzezinski

1977

Oct 25   "American Policy and Global Change." Made to the Trilateral Commission in Bonn, Germany.

1978

Dec 20   Remarks to the Foreign Policy Association in Washington, D.C.

1979

May 1   "The Wider Meaning of National Security." Made at the annual convention of the American Society of Newspaper Editors in New York.

Aug 2   "American Power and Global Change." Made before the annual convention of the International Platform Association in Washington, D.C.

APPENDIX C

Sep 17   "Vision of Peace." Made before the World Jewish Congress in New York.

Oct 10   Remarks before the annual assembly of the Atlantic Treaty Organization.

Oct 11   Remarks at the Pulaski Memorial Dinner in Savannah, Georgia.

1980

Feb 21   Remarks to the Women's National Democratic Club in Washington, D.C.

May 9   "The Twin Strands of American Foreign Policy." Made before the Baltimore Council on Foreign Affairs in Baltimore.

Oct 25   "The Quest for Global Security: The Third Phase." Made before the Council on Foreign Relations in Denver, Colo.

APPENDIX D | *Major Foreign Policy Actions*

1977

Jan 18   Defense Department authorizes the development of two versions of the cruise missile.

Jan 19   Defense Department plans to sell military arms and equipment to Israel, Greece, South Korea, Thailand, Sweden, Spain, and the Netherlands.

Jan 23   Vice President Mondale takes ten-day diplomatic mission to five European capitals and Tokyo.

Jan 26   Mondale reaffirms U.S. commitment to Berlin's security and freedom.

Jan 26   State Department charges Czechoslovakia violation of 1975 Helsinki agreement on human rights (first public accusation concerning Helsinki accords).

Jan 27   State Department accuses Soviet Union of attempt to "intimidate" dissident physicist Andrei Sakharov.

Jan 30   President Carter says that the State Department statement was not cleared by him or Secretary of State Vance

Jan 31   Vice President Mondale agrees with Japanese Premier Kukuda on broad program for economic recovery (of the capitalist countries).

Feb 2   Oman agrees to allow the United States to have navy and air force base facilities.

APPENDIX D

Feb 2	The Securities and Exchange Commission charges Indonesia's Pertamina Oil Company with coercion of U.S. and foreign companies to invest in a New York City restaurant.
Feb 5	State Department expels Tass correspondent.
Feb 5	President Carter sends letter to Sakharov asserting U.S. commitment to human rights.
Feb 7	State Department informed the Soviet Union that it is "watching with concern" the case of Alexander I. Ginzberg.
Feb 8	Commerce Department announces that on March 1 the United States will expand its coastal fishing zone to 200 miles.
Feb 11	United States reaches fishing agreement with Japan (for Japanese fishing in U.S. waters).
Feb 15	United States signs a fishing agreement with the European Common Market (accepting the new U.S. 200-mile zone).
Feb 18	Carter cancels weapons sale (CBU–72 antipersonnel concussion bombs) to Israel.
Feb 18	Carter stops CIA payments to King Hussein of Jordan (after a twenty-year period).
Feb 24	United States plans to reduce foreign aid to Argentina, Uruguay, and Ethiopia because of human rights violations (the first time an administration has reduced foreign aid on human rights grounds).
Mar 1	Carter meets Soviet dissident Vladimir Bukovsky.
Mar 2	United States agrees to prisoner transfer with Canada.
Mar 3	Administration relaxes trade embargo with Vietnam (permitting foreign ships and planes to refuel in the United States).
Mar 15	United States signs agreement with Canada to exchange bribe data (concerning Boeing).
Mar 15	United States sends emergency airlift of military and medical supplies to Zaire (to help repel the Katangan invasion).
Mar 16	Leonard Woodcock leads official White House mission to Vietnam (to determine fate of MIAs).
Mar 18	United States repeals Byrd amendment (which permitted the importation of chrome from Rhodesia).
Mar 24	United States holds talks with Cuba on fishing rights and maritime boundaries (first time since relations suspended).
Mar 25	Treasury Department lifts ban on spending of dollars by U.S. visitors in Cuba.
Mar 31	Vance leaves Moscow after disappointing three-day SALT discussions.

APPENDIX D

Apr 7	Carter announces plutonium policy (will delay the development of plutonium-based fast breeder nuclear reactor and will refrain from reprocessing plutonium for export).
Apr 9	United States seizes Soviet trawler (for violating 200-mile fishing zone).
Apr 12	United States sends ''nonlethal'' military equipment to Zaire.
Apr 23	United States closes five diplomatic offices in Ethiopia (demanded by Ethiopia following closer U.S. relations with Sudan).
Apr 26	United States approves $1.66 billion arms sale to Middle East.
Apr 28	United States reaches agreement with Cuba on fishing rights.
May 2	State Department outlines U.S. guidelines on reprocessing spent fuel rods before the International Atomic Energy Agency (will give its fuel customers permission for reprocessing abroad only on a case-by-case basis, based upon a country's storage capacity).
May 7	United States resumes supplying enriched uranium to Western Europe (after suspended for several months).
May 8	United States participates in two-day economic summit with seven major industrial democracies.
May 19	Carter recalls Major General Singlaub from Korea (for opposing withdrawal policy).
May 19	Carter announces six-point program to restrict arms sales abroad (including a cut in arms sales after 1977, a ban on developing advanced weapon systems intended only for export, and ending production agreements with other countries for significant weapons).
May 26	Ambassador to the U.N. Young two-week trip to South Africa and Great Britain stirs controversy.
May 26	Carter signs Treaty of Tlatelolco (prohibiting possession, use, and fabrication of nuclear arms in Latin America).
May 27	United States resumes supply of enriched uranium to India (cut off in 1974 after India's explosion of nuclear device).
May 30	United States and Cuba each agree to open an ''interest'' section.
Jun 1	Carter orders MK–12A warhead to be mounted on ICBMs.
Jun 3	United States agrees to exchange middle-rank diplomats with Cuba (first time in sixteen years).
Jun 7	United States plans to renew diplomatic relations with the Republic of the Congo.
Jun 12	Rosalynn Carter takes twelve-day trip to Jamaica, Costa Rica, Ecuador, Peru, Brazil, Colombia, and Venezuela.

APPENDIX D

June 15	United States recalls Lieutenant General Starry (for speech saying Sino-Soviet war likely in the future).
Jun 17	United States decides against selling 250 F–181 jets to Iran.
Jun 22	Carter signs legislation prohibiting U.S. firms from complying with the Arab trade boycott against Israel.
Jun 24	Carter requests Congress to appropriate money for the development of the neutron bomb.
Jun 28	United States temporarily blocks economic loans to Chile (first time economic aid held up for humanitarian reasons).
Jun 30	United States formally ends membership in SEATO (after twenty-three years).
Jun 30	Carter cancels B–1 production.
Jul 14	U.S. Army helicopter shot down over North Korean territory.
Jul 14	Carter says helicopter crew made mistake.
Jul 16	United States agrees to supply enriched uranium to South Korea.
Jul 17	United States holds up sale of police weapons to Argentina, Uruguay, El Salvador, and other countries (for suppressing human rights).
Aug 10	United States agrees to basic elements of Panama Canal treaties.
Aug 25	Vance ends four-day visit to China.
Sep 7	Carter signs Panama Canal treaties.
Sep 8	Carter signs pipeline agreement with Canada.
Sep 9	State Department allows Soviet trade unionists to visit United States.
Oct 1	United States and the USSR jointly issue Mideast Peace guidelines.
Oct 3	Treasury Department cites Japan for dumping steel.
Oct 13	United States agrees to expand military ties to Yugoslavia.
Oct 19	United States announces official inquiry into charges of Japan dumping steel (these means chosen over the imposition of quotas).
Nov 1	Carter withdraws United States from the ILO.
Nov 1	United States prohibits military and economic aid to Uganda, Cambodia, Laos, Vietnam, Mozambique, Angola, and Cuba; and military aid to Argentina, Ethiopia, Uruguay, Brazil, El Salvador, Guatemala, and the Philippines (for violating human rights).
Nov 2	United States withdraws two government officials from South Africa.
Nov 4	United States votes in U.N. Security Council for a mandatory six-month renewable arms embargo against South Africa.

APPENDIX D

Dec 2	United States signs trade agreement with Mexico (first in thirty-five years).
Dec 9	United States begins prisoner exchange with Mexico.
Dec 19	United States resumes Paris talks with Vietnam on normalization of relations.
Dec 29	Carter takes world trip to Poland (signs trade and aid agreements), Iran (agrees to sale nuclear reactors), India (agrees to supply heavy water and enriched uranium), Saudi Arabia, France, and Belgium.

1978

Jan 4	Carter makes stopover for talks with President Sadat (lays out three fundamental principles for peace in the Middle East).
Jan 6	Carter pledges more military troops for Europe to European Common Market in next eighteen months.
Jan 6	Vance formally returns Crown of St. Stephen to Hungary (acquired by the U.S. Army at end of World War II).
Jan 12	State Department warns Italy on communism.
Jan 13	United States agrees with Japan on trade relations (to equalize trade to erase Japan's surplus).
Jan 23	Carter sends to Congress proposed $115 billion defense budget (3.1% increase over 1978).
Jan 26	Federal grand jury charges three Chilean secret policemen with ordering and arranging the assasination of former Chilean foreign minister Orlando Letelier.
Feb 1	Carter sets $8.6 billion ceiling on U.S. arms sales outside NATO-Japan area.
Feb 1	United States cuts off military aid to Nicaragua (for human rights violations).
Feb 3	United States orders Vietnamese Ambassador to the U.N. to leave the country (first expulsion of U.N. mission chief).
Feb 14	United States plans to sell $4.8 billion in military hardware to Israel, Egypt, and Saudi Arabia.
Feb 21	Justice Department requests two lower-ranking Chilean military officers for questioning in Letelier case.
Mar 6	Carter receives President Tito of Yugoslavia for official three-day visit (first communist leader received by Carter).
Mar 9	Carter and President Tito issue joint statement declaring support for Yugoslavia's unity (the furthest a U.S. administration has gone in backing Yugoslav national security).

APPENDIX D

Mar 13	United States and West Germany announce joint measures to stabilize the dollar and coordinate their economic policies.
Mar 16	Congress approves Panama Canal treaties.
Mar 20	Treasury Department plans to sell gold monthly to support the dollar.
Apr 1	Carter visits Nigeria (first U.S. president since 1943).
Apr 7	Carter defers production of neutron weapons.
Apr 21	Carter orders slowdown in planned withdrawal of U.S. ground troops in South Korea.
Apr 28	United States grants $38 million loan to Chile (first in two years).
May 1	Japanese Premier Fukuda begins three-day official visit.
May 19	White House sends eighteen Air Force C–141 transports to Zaire to assist Franco-Belgium airlift.
May 20	National Security Advisor Brzezinski begins three-day official visit to China.
May 25	Carter accuses Cuba of training and equipping the rebels who invaded Zaire.
May 28	Brzezinski accuses Soviets of worldwide activities that are incompatible with detente.
May 31	United States protests Soviet spying of U.S. embassy in Moscow (after finding secret underground tunnel).
Jun 9	United States agrees to sell airborne geological survey equipment to China (denied to Soviets because of potential military use).
Jun 16	Carter visits Panama and exchanges the instruments of ratification on the Canal treaties.
Jun 23	State Department recalls U.S. Ambassador to Chile Landau for consultation (for their failure to cooperate with the Letelier investigation).
Jun 26	United States agrees to swap two Soviet spies for U.S. businessman Francis J. Crawford.
Jun 30	State Department calls in three Soviet correspondents to review their accreditation (in response to Soviet slander charges against two U.S. reporters).
Jul 3	State Department announces that "mutual cooperation" with Chile has been established on the Letelier case.
Jul 8	Vance cancels two planned government missions to Moscow (to protest scheduled trials of Soviet dissidents Shcharansky and Ginzburg).
Jul 18	Carter adds new controls on U.S. oil technology sales and cancels Sperry Univac computer sale to the Soviet Union.

APPENDIX D

Aug 1   House of Representatives approves easing of arms embargo against Turkey.

Aug 16   United States turns down Iranian request for thirty-one F4G fighters (offers instead the F4E).

Aug 16   United States releases $26 million in food and security support to Zaire (as sign of approval for recently improved Zaire-Angola relations).

Aug 17   Carter vetoes $37 billion weapons authorization bill because of inclusion of nuclear aircraft carrier (other defense items more necessary).

Sep 5   Carter begins thirteen-day summit with Egyptian President Sadat and Israel Premier Begin.

Sep 17   United States, Egypt, and Israel agree to Camp David accords.

Sep 20   United States requests extradition of three Chilean secret police agents.

Sep 24   Vance concludes Mideast tour to Syria, Jordan, and Saudi Arabia to discuss Camp David accords.

Oct 3   Carter signs into law the Diplomatic Relations Act (sharply limiting the protection from legal prosecution of foreign diplomats; brings U.S. policy into line with most other countries).

Oct 23   United States ends eighth round of SALT II talks (some issues still unresolved).

Oct 27   United States will begin to monitor exports to communist countries (Poland and Romania more favorable treatment; Hungary favorable discrimination; evenhanded toward China and the Soviet Union on technological transfers).

Oct 30   Federal Judge sentences two Soviet U.N. employees convicted of espionage to fifty years in prison.

Nov 1   United States acts to support the falling exchange rate of the dollar.

Nov 7   United States reduces military personnel by half in Taiwan (to 750).

Nov 11   United States agrees to no longer block Western European arms sales to China.

Nov 16   United States approves sale of X-ray inspection devices and metal detectors to Soviet Union (first time).

Nov 28   United States admits more Indochinese refugees (beyond the 25,000 yearly limit), plus those from Cuba and Lebanon.

APPENDIX D

Nov 29	Carter announces $8.43 billion ceiling on arms sales for FY 1979 to those not allied with United States (8% cut from previous ceiling).
Dec 5	United States announces "serious concern" over new Soviet-Vietnamese friendship treaty and over escalation of Vietnamese-Cambodian fighting.
Dec 8	Treasurer Secretary Blumenthal meets with Romanian President Ceausescu (gives support for its independent foreign policy).
Dec 13	United States begins withdrawing U.S. combat troops from South Korea.
Dec 15	United States agrees to establish formal diplomatic relations with China effective January 1.
Dec 17	United States appeals oil price increase to OPEC.
Dec 23	Vance says most SALT II issues resolved.

1979

Jan 4	Carter meets with government leaders from France, Great Britain, and West Germany for an informal two-day summit at Guadeloupe.
Jan 4	United States and Taiwan continue to disagree over the form their relations will take in the future.
Jan 7	State Department calls for the speedy withdrawal of Vietnamese forces from Cambodia and the avoidance of direct Soviet and Chinese involvement in the conflict.
Jan 8	United States advises Shah of Iran to leave the country temporarily.
Jan 23	United States advanced F–15 fighters temporarily fly to Saudi Arabia.
Jan 28	Carter receives First Deputy Premier Teng Hsiao-ping for three-day summit (first official visit by a top-level Chinese leader).
Jan 29	Carter sends to Congress fiscal 1980 defense budget for $122.7 billion (up 9.7%).
Jan 30	United States orders nonessential personnel evacuated from Iran.
Feb 14	Carter arrives in Mexico City for two-day offical visit with President Jose Portillo.
Feb 15	United States recommends that all Americans leave Iran.
Feb 19	United States protests slaying of U.S. Ambassor in Afghanistan.
Mar 1	Carter accepts Chinese Ambassador to the United States.
Mar 2	United States and China agree to outstanding claims settlement.

APPENDIX D

Mar 2	United States agrees before the International Energy Agency to cut its oil consumption by 5%.
Mar 6	Carter orders U.S. naval forces to the Arabian Sea (in response to the fighting between South Yemen and North Yemen).
Mar 7	Carter leaves for Mideast trip to Egypt and Israel (to resolve final differences).
Mar 8	United States decides to send two AWACs "flying radar" planes to Saudi Arabia.
Mar 9	Carter invokes national security powers to speed delivery of $390 million in arms for Yemen.
Mar 13	Congress approves legislation enabling United States to maintain unofficial relations with Taiwan while officially recognizing China.
Mar 13	Carter announces that Egypt and Israel are near agreement.
Mar 14	Carter says that peace treaty between Egypt and Israel will require the giving of U.S. aid.
Mar 18	Brzezinski holds talks with Jordan and Saudi Arabia (concerning Mideast settlement).
Mar 22	United States agrees to continue for three years aerial surveillance over the Sinai.
Apr 3	United States plans to fly modified U–2s near the southern border of the Soviet Union (to compensate for the loss of Iranian monitoring bases).
Apr 5	United States decides to reduce aid to Pakistan (following their purchase of equipment that could enable them to make an atomic bomb; military sales not affected).
Apr 9	United States raises embargo on the sale of a computer to the Soviet news agency Tass (to be used for the Olympic games).
Apr 13	U.S. orders two South African military attaches to leave the United States (in retaliation for the explusion of three U.S. embassy officials).
Apr 16	United States normalizes relations with Uganda (cut in 1973 for human rights violations).
Apr 27	United States releases two Soviet U.N. officials convicted of espionage in return for Soviet freeing of five dissidents (first time such an agreement has been negotiated directly between the United States and the Soviet Union).
May 14	United States agrees to establish normal trade relations with China.

APPENDIX D

May 15	United States recalls U.S. Ambassador to Chile for consultations (in response to Chilean refusal to extradite three army officials for murder in the Letelier case).
May 15	Senate adopts Case-Javits amendment (allowing Carter to lift sanctions against Rhodesia after the installation of a black majority government).
Jun 4	United States rejects Iranian request to name someone other than William Cutler as Ambassador to Iran.
Jun 7	Carter fails to lift the economic sanctions against Rhodesia, concluding that the mid-April elections were neither free nor fair.
Jun 8	Carter approves full-scale development of MX missile system, but defers decision on deployment.
Jun 12	Senate rejects Carter Administration-backed amendment to extend sanctions against Rhodesia until December 1.
Jun 12	United States evacuates sixty Americans from Nicaragua (in response to growing civil disorder).
Jun 15	United States embargoes all arms shipments to Nicaragua and calls on other nations to do likewise.
Jun 16	Carter begins summit conference in Vienna with Soviet President Brezhnev.
Jun 18	Carter and Brezhnev sign SALT II.
Jun 21	Vance calls for replacement of the Somoza government with a "transitional government of national reconciliation" and for OAS peacekeeping forces to restore order and democracy.
Jun 21	House of Representatives approves implementing legislation for the Panama Canal treaties.
Jun 21	United States plans rapid deployment force for the Middle East and the Third World.
Jun 23	United States votes in the OAS for the "immediate and definite replacement" of President Somoza's government.
Jun 28	Carter announces that United States will double its intake of Indochina refugees.
Jun 29	Carter agrees at Tokyo summit conference of the seven Western industrialized nations to limit oil imports (through 1985).
Jun 29	Carter arrives for official visit to South Korea.
Jul 1	Carter and South Korean President Park announce that they have jointly invited North Korea to attend a three-way meeting on reducing tensions in the Korean peninsula.
Jul 11	Carter meets with Rhodesian Prime Minister Muzorewa (refuses to lift sanctions).

APPENDIX D

Jul 15   Carter outlines a six-point program to deal with energy and the problem of the U.S. dollar.

Jul 17   United States recalls its ambassador and most of the embassy staff from Managua (in protest over interim President Urcuyo's decision to continue the civil war).

Jul 23   United States says Vietnam will allow U.S. consular officers to visit Vietnam to process people wishing to come to America.

Jul 24   State Department announces that Nicaraguan Foreign Minister d'Escoto and the U.S. embassy in Managua have exchanged notes expressing the desire to maintain relations.

Jul 29   United States evacuates U.S. families of U.S. embassy in Afghanistan (because of growing disorder).

Aug 2   United States agrees to sell an additional ten million metric tons of wheat to the USSR during next fourteen months.

Aug 8   Congressional delegation visits Vietnam for talks on refugees.

Aug 17   Carter orders halt in most cutbacks of U.S. troops in South Korea.

Aug 21   United States agrees on a set of Middle East policy recommendations (including the dropping of plans to sponsor a U.N. resolution on Palestinian rights).

Aug 24   United States holds up at Kennedy International Airport an Aeroflot plane (to determine if the recently defected Aleksandr Godunov's wife is returning to Moscow of her own free will).

Aug 25   Mondale arrives in Peking for official visit (highest U.S. official to visit since normalization).

Aug 27   Mondale says that United States is ready to give China $2 billion in trade credits over the next five years.

Sep 4   United States bans the import of tuna products from Canada (in retaliation for their seizure of U.S. tuna boats in waters off British Columbia).

Sep 7   Carter approves plans to deploy 200 MX–missiles.

Sep 7   Carter says that the alleged presence of a Soviet brigade in Cuba is "a very serious matter" and that "this status quo is not acceptable."

Sep 11   Carter asks for $130.6 billion in military spending for fiscal 1979–80 (an increase of almost $5 billion over his original January request).

Sep 19   Secretary of Defense Brown says that the Defense Department is giving "high priority" to a 100,000 RDF for use outside NATO.

Sep 21   United States agrees on the sale of Mexican natural gas to the United States (ending two-year conflict over the price).

Sep 25	Carter says that if the status quo in Cuba does not change "certain steps" will be taken.
Sep 27	Carter signs into law the bill to implement the Panama Canal treaties.
Oct 1	Carter announces a series of political and military measures designed to offset the presence of Soviet combat troops in Cuba.
Oct 1	Carter meets with Pope John Paul II (the first Pope to visit the White House).
Oct 5	United States orders Ambassador to South Korea home for consultation (to protest the expulsion of opposition leader Kim Young Sam from the National Assembly).
Oct 9	Carter rebuffs Brezhnev's proposal for military reductions in Europe.
Oct 16	Brown visits South Korea and Japan.
Oct 17	United States says that they are "surprised and disappointed" at the conviction of the dissident leader Wei Jingsheng (the first public rebuke of China since normalization).
Oct 17	U.S. Ambassador Thomas Watson arrives in Moscow to assume the senior U.S. post.
Oct 22	Carter asks Congress to approve the sale of armed reconnaissance planes and helicopter gunships to Morocco.
Oct 26	State Department warns that the United States will "react strongly" to any external attempt to take advantage of the crisis in South Korea (following the assassination of President Park).
Oct 26	Defense Department orders U.S. forces in South Korea into "Defense Readiness Condition 3" (a moderate state of alert several steps short of emergency readiness).
Oct 28	Brown announces that a U.S. aircraft carrier and radar warning plane are being positioned near South Korea (to deter outside interference during the current crisis).
Oct 31	Vance says that the Soviet Union during the last month has taken steps which have eased U.S. concern (regarding the nature of its troop presence in Cuba).
Nov 5	United States rejects Iranian demands for Shah's extradition (following seizure of U.S. Embassy in Teheran).
Nov 7	Rosalynn Carter leaves for Thailand to demonstrate the "deep concern" of the United States over the tragic plight of Cambodian refugees.
Nov 10	Carter orders the Justice Department to begin deportation proceedings against Iranian students who are in the country illegally.

APPENDIX D

Nov 12   Carter orders an immediate suspension of oil imports from Iran.

Nov 14   Carter orders all official Iranian assets in U.S. banks frozen.

Nov 15   Carter denounces the holding of the hostages as ''an act of terrorism totally outside the bounds of international law''.

Nov 19   Senate Foreign Relationas Committee publishes report on SALT II in which the majority recommend approval.

Nov 20   Carter orders more naval forces to the Arabian Sea.

Nov 22   United States orders the evacuation of more than 300 dependents of U.S. personnel in Pakistan (following Pakistani attacks against U.S. diplomatic and cultural centers).

Nov 29   United States asks International Court of Justice to order Iran to release hostages.

Nov 29   United States decides to cut back on diplomatic, military, and economic relations with Chile (in retaliation for refusal to extradite officials in Letelier case).

Dec 4   United States votes for resolution in U.N. Security Council calling for Iran to release U.S. hostages.

Dec 9   United States agrees in International Energy Agency ministers meeting to impose on themselves individual targets for oil consumption, backed up by a monitoring system.

Dec 10   Vance arrives in London on the first leg of a trip designed to gain allied support for economic sanctions against Iran.

Dec 12   State Department announces that it has ordered the Iranian Embassy in Washington to cut back its staff.

Dec 12   Carter announces he will seek five-year increase in the military budget (amounting to 4.5% a year, with $157 billion in appropriations for fiscal 1981).

Dec 13   Sol Linowitz (the new special envoy on Mideast affairs) ends first round of Cairo-Jerusalem shuttle diplomacy.

Dec 15   Carter announces he has ordered an end to twelve-year-old trade sanctions against Rhodesia.

Dec 17   Carter meets with Prime Minister Thatcher (her first official visit since the Conservative Party victory).

Dec 21   Carter announces that United States will ask U.N. Security Council to impose economic sanctions against Iran.

Dec 22   United States warns Soviet Union that any Soviet effort to block the U.N. Security Council from imposing sanctions will be looked upon as an unfriendly act.

Dec 28   Carter says that the Soviet military intervention in Afghanistan is a ''grave threat to peace.''

Dec 29   Carter discloses that he sent a message to Soviet President Brezhnev warning of "serious consequences" if the Soviet Union did not withdraw its forces from Afghanistan.

Dec 30   Brzezinski reaffirms the United States 1959 defense commitment to Pakistan in case of external aggression.

1980

Jan 2   Carter orders U.S. Ambassador to the Soviet Union home for consultation.

Jan 3   Carter asks the Senate to delay its consideration of SALT II (because of the Soviet invasion).

Jan 4   Carter announces a series of punitive measures against the Soviet Union (cut in grain shipments, halt in the sale of high technology items, curb on Soviet fishing in U.S. waters, delay in opening new consular facilities, deferral of most cultural and economic exchanges, and readiness to supply military equipment, food, and other aid to Pakistan).

Jan 5   Brown arrives in Peking for an eight-day visit.

Jan 6   Brown appeals to China to join the United States in finding "complementary actions" to counter Soviet expansionism (a departure in Carter's evenhanded policy).

Jan 8   Brown announces United States ready to sell China a ground station to receive information from the Landsat Earth Resources Satellite.

Jan 8   State Department orders the expulsion of seventeen Soviet consular officials in New York.

Jan 8   United States and Egypt undertake joint military air exercises (involving the most advanced U.S. electronic surveillance planes).

Jan 8   Civil Aeronautics Board cuts from three to two per week the number of flights by Soviet airline Aeroflot to the United States.

Jan 9   Brown says that China and the United States have laid the groundwork for greater cooperation in defense matters.

Jan 11   Commerce Secretary Klutznick says United States has denied eight applications for the export of $1 billion worth of good and services to the Soviet Union.

Jan 12   United States gets support from four major grain exporters that they will not directly or indirectly replace a 17-million-ton U.S. grain sale cancellation to the Soviet Union.

APPENDIX D

Jan 20	Carter proposes that the 1980 Moscow Olympics be moved to another country, or be postponed or canceled (if the Soviet Union does not withdraw its troops from Afghanistan within one month).
Jan 28	Carter sends Congress defense budget calling for $142.7 billion ($15 billion more than in 1980).
Feb 1	Brzezinski and Deputy Secretary of State Christopher arrive in Islamabad for talks with Pakistani officials.
Feb 4	Brzezinski and Christopher hold talks in Riyadh with Saudi Arabian officials on the Soviet invasion of Afghanistan (wants them to at least match the $400 million the Americans have pledged to Pakistan in economic and military aid).
Feb 5	United States sends former boxing champion Muhammad Ali to tour Africa in an effort to gain support for the U.S. Olympic boycott.
Feb 11	United States agrees with Oman, Kenya, and Somalia to give U.S. forces access to military facilities in their countries in return for military aid.
Feb 12	Carter orders an amphibious assault force into the Arabian Sea to demonstrate U.S. ability to project ground forces in to the Persian Gulf region.
Feb 13	Carter sends Congress a draft registration plan.
Feb 15	White House officials disclose that the United States began a CIA operation in mid-January to supply the Afghan rebels with light infantry weapons of Soviet design.
Feb 18	United States formally resumes membership in the ILO.
Feb 20	United States announces that American teams will not participate in the 1980 Olympics.
Feb 22	United States has frozen the official Soviet diplomatic presence in the United States at existing levels (the first time a ceiling has been imposed on the number of Soviet diplomatic personnel).
Feb 23	State Department officials say United States has threatened to cut off $50 million in economic and $10 million in military aid to El Salvador if the civilian-military junta is overthrown by rightists.
Feb 25	State Department announces that the United States will allow Egypt to buy F–15 and F–16 fighters (giving them symbolic equality with Israel).
Feb 25	Carter orders an embargo on shipments of phosphate fertilizer to the Soviet Union (the biggest noncrop U.S. item exported to the Soviet Union).

APPENDIX D

Feb 25	National Academy of Sciences suspends all scientific exchanges for six months.
Feb 29	FBI official says that in the last year the United States quietly expelled five Soviet-bloc diplomats for alleged involvement in espionage activities.
Mar 1	United States votes in U.N. Security Council for resolution calling on the Israeli government to dismantle its existing settlements in occupied Arab territories, including Jerusalem.
Mar 3	Carter says that U.S. vote in the U.N. Security Council was cast in error (all references to Jerusalem were to have been deleted).
Mar 5	United States offers $400 million in military and economic aid over the next two years to Pakistan (rejected).
Mar 5	Carter holds talks with West German Chancellor Schmidt in Washington on the crisis in Afghanistan.
Mar 8	Carter says that he will not agree to Iran's demand that the United States apologize for past actions, but he is willing to express concern over the situation that developed.
Mar 12	State Department issues statement condemning Israel's seizure of 1,000 acres of largely Arab-owned land on the outskirts of Jerusalem (could set back the "delicate negotiations" on Palestinian self-rule).
Mar 18	State Department says United States has received "disturbing indications" that the city of Sverdlovsk may have been contaminated a year ago by a "lethal biological agent" and, thus raises questions if the Soviet Union has violated the 1975 convention banning the development, production, or stockpiling of biological agents or toxins.
Mar 18	A twelve-nation meeting attended by the United States announces (in Geneva) plans for an international sports festival to be held after the Olympic Games.
Mar 18	Commerce Department announces new, tighter controls effective immediately.
Mar 21	United States suspends the trigger price mechanism on steel imports.
Mar 25	Brzezinski says that since the Shah of Iran has gone to Egypt from Panama against U.S. advice, the United States has no further obligations to him.
Mar 28	Carter imposes a mandatory ban on exports to the Soviet Union of sporting goods and other products related to the Olympic Games in Moscow.

APPENDIX D

Mar 29	United States agrees with Turkey to allow the United States to continue to use military base and intelligence-gathering and communications stations (in return for an undisclosed amount of assistance).
Mar 30	Administration officials acknowledge that Carter sent two written messages to Iran (but deny that any conciliatory communication had been transmitted to the Ayatollah Khomeini).
Apr 2	Undersecretary of Defense Komer confirms that United States will station Americans in Oman, Kenya, and Somalia as part of its military buildup.
Apr 7	Carter announces that the United States plans to break diplomatic relations with Iran and impose a formal embargo on exports to that country.
Apr 8	State Department says that Carter Administration has sent messages to its allies urging them to follow the U.S. lead against Iran.
Apr 10	State Department says that the United States expects ''more than rhetoric'' from its allies (in enlisting support for sanctions against Iran).
Apr 16	U.S. officials say that Egypt and Israel have pledged maximum effort for the autonomy talks.
Apr 18	United States opens embassy in Zimbabwe and agrees to provide medical assistance.
Apr 24	United States agrees with Iran to allow third countries to represent their diplomatic and consular interests in the other's capital (Algeria will represent Iran in the United States, Switzerland represents the United States in Iran).
Apr 25	White House Press Secretary Powell announces that U.S. military effort to rescue American hostages was aborted in the Iranian desert.
May 1	Carter signs five-year agreement with Japan for collaboration in scientific research.
May 2	United States expels four Libyan diplomats and recalls the last U.S. diplomats from Libya.
May 4	Carter says that the United States will do ''what it must'' to provide support for Yugoslav independence (following President Tito's death).
May 5	Carter says that United States will ''provide an open heart and open arms'' for the refugees flowing from Cuba.

APPENDIX D

May 8	Mondale and Lillian Carter represent the United States at Tito's funeral.
May 8	United States abstains on U.N. Security Council vote approving a resolution expressing "deep concern" over Israel's expulsion of three West Bank leaders.
May 16	Secretary of State Muskie meets for talks with Soviet Foreign Minister Gromyko (in Vienna) to discuss major differences in Soviet-U.S. relations.
May 17	Coast Guard begins setting up a 200-mile-long patrol zone to prevent the flow of Cuban refugees to the United States.
May 20	Muskie says France's failure to consult with its allies about a meeting between Soviet President Brezhnev and French President Giscard d'Estaing was shortsighted.
May 20	State Department criticizes Great Britain for deciding not to enact sanctions against Iran agreed to by the European Community.
May 29	Brown announces that the United States will allow China to buy air-defense radar helicopters and transport planes, and will authorize U.S. companies to build electronics and helicopter factories.
Jun 9	State Department says that Egypt and Israel will resume negotiations on Palestinian self-rule (have been suspended for a month).
Jun 12	Defense Department says that United States will send twelve F–4 fighters to Egypt for ninety days (first step in a long-range plan to establish land-based air power in the Persian Gulf region).
Jun 13	Muskie praises EC leaders concerning Palestinian issue.
Jun 17	Carter holds talks with King Hussein of Jordan (concerning Camp David accords).
Jun 19	United States agrees to sell 100 M–160 tanks to Jordan.
Jun 20	Carter warns allies against the "false belief" about detente while Soviet military forces remain in Afghanistan.
Jun 20	Administration officials say that the Cuban and Haitian refugees can temporarily remain in the United States and could become permanent residents (if Congress agrees).
Jun 21	Carter agrees with Chancellor Schmidt on plans to modernize NATO's nuclear forces in Europe.
Jun 22	United States demands Soviet troop withdrawal and denounces taking of hostages along with six other major noncommunist countries.
Jun 24	Carter assures Yugoslav leadership of continued support for their policy of nonalignment and calls for same policy in Afghanistan.

Jun 25	United States and Yugoslavia issue communique expressing great concern over deteriorating international situation.
Jun 25	Carter arrives in Madrid and says Spain should join NATO and the EC.
Jun 25	Congress approves draft registration (first time since 1975).
Jun 27	Muskie meets with ASEAN (Association of Southeast Asian Nations) foreign ministers (tells Thailand the United States will speed delivery of tanks and other battlefield equipment).
Jul 3	Carter cancels import quotas for Japanese television sets (on the recommendation of the International Trade Commission).
Jul 11	United States embargoes Mexican tuna products (following seizure of two U.S. tuna boats).
Jul 16	Carter orders new assault force of marines and warships into Indian Ocean.
Jul 22	Brzezinski asked Billy Carter to set up Libyan meeting for their assistance to free hostages.
Jul 25	Muskie announces United States is halting all economic assistance, except food and humanitarian programs, to Bolivia and will reduce diplomatic staff and withdraw military advisors (to demonstrate the "depth of our concern" over the coup).
Jul 31	United States agrees with West Germany and Japan to finance coal conversion project.
Aug 5	Carter signs PD-59 on U.S. strategic nuclear strategy.
Aug 8	Brown sends diplomatic note to NATO defense ministers (to reassure them that PD–59 is evolutionary).
Aug 13	United States cancels all cooperation with Bolivia on the control of drug traffic.
Aug 20	Defense Department has developed and flown an experimental aircraft—Stealth—that is virtually invisible to Soviet radar.
Aug 20	United States abstains in U.N. Security Council on a unanimous resolution that "censures in the strongest terms" Israel's formal annexation of the eastern, Arab sector of Jerusalem.
Aug 22	United States agrees with Somalia for U.S. forces to have access to airfields and port facilities in return for assistance (over two years).
Aug 27	Carter meets with Prime Minister Mugabe of Zimbabwe.
Sep 5	Defense Department announces that 7,000 noncommissioned officers will be shifted from Europe and South Korea to the United States to improve combat readiness.
Sep 12	Carter approves $670 million in credit guarantees for Poland.

APPENDIX D

Sep 17	United States signs major agreement with China on textile trade, consular services, and shipping.
Sep 21	United States orders 2,000 Iranian students to leave the country.
Sep 24	Senate approves (48 to 46) sale of enriched uranium fuel to India.
Sep 30	United States dispatches four AWACs and support personnel to Saudi Arabia.
Oct 1	United States sends message to Iran asserting the dispatch of AWACs to Saudi Arabia is consistent with U.S. neutrality in the Iran-Iraq conflict.
Oct 5	Brown says United States is sending additional radar and communications equipment and military personnel to Saudi Arabia.
Oct 7	Christopher says United States is willing to supply similar AWACs planes to other Persian Gulf nations if they stay out of the Iran-Iraq conflict.
Oct 11	Defense Department says cruiser and two tanker planes will be sent to Saudi Arabia.
Oct 17	Carter meets with Nigerian president and pledges U.S. effort to bring about majority rule in Southwest Africa.
Oct 17	United States signs fourteen-year agreement with Israel to guarantee to supply them with oil in case of emergency.
Oct 22	U.S. Ambassador Woodcock signs grain agreement with China.
Oct 27	Justice Department charters airline to fly home thirty Americans released from Cuba.
Nov 3	State Department embargoes tuna imports from Ecuador (in retaliation for seizure of U.S. fishing boats off coast of Ecuador).
Nov 10	The International Trade Commission votes that auto imports from Japan are not causing domestic injury.
Nov 11	U.S. Rapid Deployment Force conducts joint exercises with Egyptian troops.
Nov 14	Treasury Department bans the import of certain steel products from France (on grounds that they contain nickel from Cuba).
Dec 2	Powell says that intervention by outside forces in the Polish crisis would have serious repercussions.
Dec 3	Carter says that United States is watching Soviets closely (over their military buildup along the Polish border).
Dec 5	United States suspends $25 million in economic and military aid to El Salvador (following the killing of U.S. nuns).
Dec 9	Muskie flies to Brussels to seek allied agreement on moves that would be taken against the Soviet Union if its military forces intervened in Poland.

APPENDIX D

Dec 10	Brown threatens Western military buildup if Soviet Union intervenes in Poland.
Dec 17	United States resumes economic, but not military, aid to El Salvador's recently reorganized civilian-military government.
Dec 18	United States accepts Israel proposal to settle claims from Israel 1968 attack on U.S. naval vessel.
Dec 21	Muskie says $24 billion "guarantee" figure to Iran in exchange for the hostages is unreasonable.

1981

Jan 7	United States allows public travel to China (after thirty-two-year hiatus).
Jan 14	United States resumes military aid to El Salvador (saying that the leftist guerillas pose a threat to the government).
Jan 16	Carter orders gold in Great Britain for transfer to Iran in exchange for hostages (also orders sale of Iranian-owned treasury securities so the money can be transferred to Iran).

Bibliography

Abelson, R. P., and M. J. Rosenberg. Symbolic, Psycho-logic: A Model of Attitudinal Cognition. *Behavioral Science* 3 (1958), 1–13.

Abelson, R. P. Computers, Polls, and Public Opinion—Some Puzzles and Paradoxes. *Transaction* 5 (1968), 20–27.

Adelman, K. L. The Runner Stumbles: Carter's Foreign Policy in the Year One. *Policy Review* 3 (1978), 89–116.

Adorno, T. W., E. Frenkel-Brunswick, D. J. Levinson, and R. N. Sanford. *The Authoritarian Personality.* New York: Harper, 1950.

Ajemian, R. Vance Nearly Quit over Strauss. *Washington Star* (August 27, 1979), 1.

Ajzen, I. and M. Fishbein. *Understanding Attitudes and Predicting Social Behavior.* Englewood Cliffs, N.J.: Prentice-Hall; 1980.

Allen, G., with L. Abraham. *None Dare Call It Conspiracy.* Rossmoor, Calif.: Concord Press, 1971.

Allison, G. T. Conceptual Models and the Cuban Missile Crisis. *American Political Science Review* 63 (1969), 689–718.

Allison, G. T. *Essence of Decision.* Boston: Little, Brown, 1971.

Allison, G. T. Adequacy of Current Organization: Defense and Arms Control. *Commission on the Organization of the Government for the Conduct of Foreign Policy* (vol. 4, appendix K). Washington, D.C.: Government Printing Office, 1975.

Allison, G. T., and M. H. Halperin. Bureaucratic Politics: A Paradigm and Some Policy Implications. *World Politics* 24 (1972), 40–79.

Allport, G. W. What Is a Trait of Personality? *Journal of Abnormal and Social Psychology* 25 (1931), 368–372.

Almond, G. A. *The American People and Foreign Policy.* New York: Praeger, 1960.

Anderson, J. Brzezinski Tactic on Cuba Irks Vance. *Washington Post* (December 13, 1979).

226

BIBLIOGRAPHY

Andriole, S. J., J. Wilkenfeld, and G. W. Hopple. A Framework for the Comparative Analysis of Foreign Policy Behavior. *International Studies Quarterly* 19 (1975), 160–198.

Art, R. Bureaucratic Politics and American Foreign Policy: A Critique. *Policy Sciences* 4 (1973), 467–490.

Asch, S. E. Effects of Group Pressure upon the Modification and Distortion of Judgement. In H. Guetzkow (ed.), *Groups, Leadership and Men*. Pittsburgh: Carnegie, 1951, 177–190.

Azar, E. E., S. Cohen, T. Jukam, and J. McCormick. The Problem of Source Coverage in the Use of International Events Data. *International Studies Quarterly* 16 (1972), 373–388.

Barner-Barry, C., and R. Rosenwein. *Psychological Perspectives on Politics*. Englewood Cliffs, N.J.: Prentice-Hall, 1985.

Barnet, R. J. Carter's Patchwork Doctrine. *Harper's* (August 1977), 27–30, 32–34.

Barnet, R. J. *The Alliance: America, Europe, Japan—Makers of the Postwar World*. New York: Simon & Schuster, 1985.

Baron, R. A., and D. Byrne. *Social Psychology: Understanding Human Interaction*. Boston: Allyn & Bacon, 1981.

Bem, D. J. Self-perception: An Alternate Interpretation of Cognitive Phenomena. *Psychological Review* 74 (1967), 183–200.

Bem, D. J. *Beliefs, Attitudes, and Human Affairs*. Belmont, Calif.: Brooks/Cole, 1970.

Bem, D. J. Self-perception Theory. In L. Berkowitz (ed.), *Advances in Experimental Social Psychology* (vol. 6). New York: Academic Press, 1972.

Ben-Zvi, A. Misperceiving the Role of Perception: A Critique. *Jerusalem Journal of International Relations* 11 (1976–77), 74–93.

Ben-Zvi, A. The Outbreak and Termination of the Pacific War: A Juxtaposition of American Preconceptions. *Journal of Peace Research* 15 (1978), 33–49.

Bennett, W. L. *The Political Mind and the Political Environment*. Lexington, Mass.: Heath, 1975.

Bennett, W. L. *Public Opinion in American Politics*. New York: Harcourt Brace Jovanovich, 1980.

Berkowitz, M., P. G. Bock, and V. J. Fuccilo. *The Politics of American Foreign Policy: The Social Context of Decisions*. Englewood Cliffs, N.J.: Prentice-Hall, 1977.

Bernstein, C. Arms for Afghanistan. *New Republic* (July 18, 1981), 8–10.

Bluhm, W. T. *Theories of the Political System*. Englewood Cliffs, N.J.: Prentice-Hall, 1971.

Bobrow, D. B., S. Chan, and J. A. Kringen. Understanding How Others Treat Crises: A Multimethod Approach. *International Studies Quarterly* 21 (1977), 199–223.

Bobrow, D. B., S. Chan, and J. A. Kringen. *Understanding Foreign Policy Decisions: The Chinese Case*. New York: Free Press, 1979.

228

BIBLIOGRAPHY

Bonafede, D. Brzezinski—Stepping Out of His Backstage Role. *National Journal* (Oct. 15, 1977), 1596–1601.

Bonafede, D. How the White House Helps Carter Make Up His Mind. *National Journal* (April 15, 1978), 584–588.

Bonham, G. M. The October War: Changes in Cognitive Orientation Toward the Middle East Conflict. *International Studies Quarterly* 23 (1979), 3–44.

Bonham, G. M., and M. J. Shapiro. A Cognitive Process Approach to Collective Decision Making. In C. Jonsson (ed.), *Cognitive Dynamics and International Politics*. New York: St. Martin's Press, 1982, 19–36.

Boulding, K. E. National Images and International Systems. In J. Rosenau (ed.), *International Politics and Foreign Policy*. New York: Free Press, 1969, 422–431.

Braestrup, P. *Big Story: How the American Press and Television Reported and Interpreted the Crisis of Tet 1968 in Vietnam and Washington*. Boulder, Colo.: Westview Press, 1977.

Brim, O. G., Jr., and J. Kagan, eds. *Constancy and Change in Human Development*. Cambridge, Mass.: Harvard University Press, 1980.

Brecher, M. Toward a Theory of International Crisis Behavior: A Preliminary Report. *International Studies Quarterly* 21 (1977), 39–74.

Brecher, M., B. Steinberg, and J. Stein. A Framework for Research on Foreign Policy Behavior. *Journal of Conflict Resolution* 13 (1969), 75–101.

Brodin, K. Belief Systems, Doctrines, and Foreign Policy. *Cooperation and Conflict* 7 (1972), 97–112.

Brown, S. *The Faces of Power: Constancy and Change from Truman to Reagan*. New York: Columbia University, 1983.

Brzezinski, Z. *Between Two Ages: America's Role in the Technetronic Era*. New York: Penguin, 1970.

Brzezinski, Z. America in a Hostile World. *Foreign Policy* 23 (1976), 65–96.

Brzezinski, Z. *Power and Principle: Memoirs of the National Security Adviser, 1977–1981*. New York: Farrar, Straus & Giroux, 1983.

Brzezinski, Z., and C. J. Friedrich. *Totalitarian Dictatorship and Autocracy*. New York: Praeger, 1956.

Brzezinski, Z., and S. P. Huntington. *Political Power: USA/USSR*. New York: Viking, 1963.

Budd, R. W., R. K. Thorp, and L. Donohew. *Content Analysis of Communications*. New York: Macmillan, 1967.

Burgess, P. M., and R. W. Lawton. *Indicators of International Behavior: An Assessment of Events Data Research*. Beverly Hills: Sage, 1972.

Burgess, P. M., and R. W. Lawton. Evaluating Events Data: Problems of Conception, Reliability, and Validity. In C. W. Kegley, Jr., G. A. Raymond, R. M. Rood, and R. A. Skinner (eds.), *International Events and the Comparative Analysis of Foreign Policy*. Columbia, S.C.,: University of South Carolina Press, 1975, 106–119.

BIBLIOGRAPHY

Burrows, R. Mirror, Mirror on the Wall . . . : A Comparison of Event Data Sources. In J. Rosenau (ed.), *Comparing Foreign Policy*. New York: John Wiley, 1974, 383–406.

Burt, R. Zbig Makes It Big. *New York Times Magazine* (July 30, 1978), 8–10, 18, 20, 28, 30.

Burt, R. Carter, Under Pressure of Crises, Tests New Foreign Policy Goals. *New York Times* (January 9, 1980), A1, A8.

Burton, J. *Deviance, Terrorism, and War: The Process of Solving Unsolved Social and Political Problems*. Oxford, England: Martin Robertson, 1979.

Byers, R. B., and D. Leyton-Brown. Canadian Elite Images of the International System. *International Journal* 32 (1977), 608–639.

Calder, B. J., and M. Ross. *Attitudes and Behavior*. Morristown, N.J.: General Learning Press, 1973.

Campbell, A., P. E. Converse, W. E. Miller, and D. E. Stokes. *The American Voter*. New York: Wiley, 1960.

Campbell, D. T. Social Attitudes and Other Acquired Behavioral Dispositions. In S. Koch (ed.), *Psychology: A Study of Science* (Vol. 6.). New York: McGraw-Hill, 1963, 94–172.

Carr, E. H. *The Twenty Years' Crisis, 1919–1939*. New York: Harper & Row, 1964.

Carter, J. *Why Not the Best?* New York: Bantam, 1975.

Carter, J. E. Making Foreign and Defense Policy: Openness, Coherence, and Efficiency. *National Journal* (October 23, 1976), 1528–1529.

Carter, J. *Keeping Faith*. Toronto: Bantam Books, 1982.

Claude, I. L., Jr., *Power and International Relations*. New York: Random House, 1964.

Cohen, B. C. *The Press and Foreign Policy*. Princeton, N.J.: Princeton University Press, 1963.

Converse, P. E. The Nature of Belief Systems in Mass Publics. In D. Apter (ed.), *Ideology and Discontent*. New York: Free Press, 1964, 206–261.

Converse, P. E. Attitudes and Non-attitudes: Continuation of a Dialogue. In E. D. Tufte (ed.), *The Quantitative Analysis of Social Problems*. Reading, Mass.: Addison-Wesley, 1970, 168–189.

Cook, T. D., and C. S. Reichardt, eds. *Qualitative and Quantitative Methods in Evaluation Research*. Beverly Hills, Calif.: Sage, 1979.

Coplin, W. D., and C. E. Kegley, Jr., eds. *Analyzing International Relations: A Multimethod Introduction*. New York: Praeger, 1975.

Cottam, R. W. *Foreign Policy Motivation: A General Theory and a Case Study*. Pittsburgh: University of Pittsburgh Press, 1977.

Couloumbis, T. A., and M. D. Moore. The Influence of Academicians Upon Foreign Service Officers. *World Affairs* 134 (1971), 257–260.

Crawford, A. *Thunder on the Right*. New York: Pantheon, 1980.

Crespi, I. What Kinds of Attitude Measures Are Predictive of Behavior. *Public Opinion Quarterly* 35 (1971), 327–334.

BIBLIOGRAPHY

Cronin, T. E. *The State of the Presidency*. Boston: Little, Brown, & Co., 1975.

Dean, P. D., Jr., and J. A. Vasquez. From Power Politics to Issue Politics: Bipolarity and Multipolarity in Light of a New Paradigm. *Western Political Quarterly* 29 (1976), 7–28.

DeRivera, J. *The Psychological Dimension of Foreign Policy*. Columbus, Ohio: Charles E. Merrill, 1968.

Destler, I. M., L. H. Gelb, and A. Lake. *Our Own Worst Enemy: The Unmaking of American Foreign Policy*. New York: Simon & Schuster, 1984.

Destler, I. M. *Presidents and Bureaucrats: Organizing the Government for Foreign Policy*. Princeton, N.J.: Princeton University Press, 1972.

Destler, I. M. National Security Management: What Presidents Have Wrought. *Political Science Quarterly* 95 (1980–81), 573–599.

Deutsch, K. W., and R. I. Merritt. Effects of Events on National and International Images. In H. C. Kelman (ed.), *International Behavior*. New York: Holt, Rineholt, & Winston, 1965, 132–187.

Deutscher, I. *What We Say/What We Do: Sentiments and Acts*. Glenview, Ill.: Scott, Foresman, 1973.

Dillehay, R. C. On the Irrelevance of the Classical Negative Evidence concerning the Effect of Attitudes on Behavior. *American Psychologist* 28 (1973), 887–891.

Drew, E. Brzezinski. *New Yorker* (May 1, 1978), 95–118, 121–130.

Drew, E. *Portrait of an Election*. New York: Simon & Schuster, 1981.

East, M. A., S. A. Salmore, and C. F. Hermann. *Why Nations Act: Theoretical Perspectives for Comparative Foreign Policy Studies*. Beverly Hills, Calif.: Sage, 1978.

Ehrlich, H. S. Attitudes, Behavior, and the Intervening Variables. *American Sociologist* 4 (1969), 29–34.

Elowitz, L., and J. Spanier. Korea and Vietnam: United States and the American Political System. *Orbis* 18 (1974), 510–534.

Epstein, E. J. *News from Nowhere: Television and the News*. New York: Random House, 1973.

Erikson, E. H. *Childhood and Society*. New York: W. W. Norton, 1950.

Eskine, H. G. The Polls: The Informed Public. *Public Opinion Quarterly* 26 (1962), 669–677.

Falk, R. A. *A Study of Future Worlds*. New York: Free Press, 1975.

Falkowski, L. S. Introduction: Evaluating Psychological Models. In L. S. Falkowski (ed.), *Psychological Models in International Politics*. Boulder, Colo.: Westview, 1979, 1–14.

Fallows, J. The Passionless Presidency. *Atlantic Monthly* (May 1979), 33–46, 48.

Felton, J. Muskie Seen Helping Quiet Hill Foreign Policy Discontent. *Congressional Quarterly Weekly Report* (May 3, 1980), 1155–1163.

Fenno, R. F., Jr. *Home Style: House Members in Their District*. Boston: Little, Brown, 1978.

Festinger, L. *A Theory of Cognitive Dissonance*. Evanston, Ill.: Row-Peterson, 1957.

231

BIBLIOGRAPHY

Fishbein, M. Attitude and the Prediction of Behavior. In M. Fishbein (ed.), *Readings in Attitude Theory and Measurement.* New York: John Wiley, 1967, 447–492.

Fishbein, M., and I. Ajzen. Attitudes and Opinions. *Annual Review of Psychology* 23 (1972), 487–544.

Fishbein, M., and I. Ajzen. *Belief, Attitude, Intention and Behavior: An Introduction to Theory and Research.* London: Addison-Wesley, 1975.

Fishbein, M., and F. S. Coombs. Basis for Decision: An Attitudinal Analysis of Voting Behavior. *Journal of Applied Social Psychology* 4 (1974), 95–124.

Fox, W. T. R. Isolationism, Internationalism, and World Politics: My Middle Western Roots. *International Studies Notes* 12 (1986), 34–37.

Freud, S. *Civilization and Its Discontents.* London: Hogarth Press, 1930.

Fromm, E. *Escape from Freedom.* New York: Holt, Rinehart, 1941.

Gaddis, John Lewis. *Strategies of Containment: A Critical Appraisal of Postwar American National Security Policy.* Oxford: Oxford University Press, 1982.

Galtung, J. *The True Worlds: A Transnational Perspective.* New York: Free Press, 1980.

Gelb, L. H. Beyond the Carter Doctrine. *New York Times Magazine* (February 10, 1980a), 18–19, 24–26, 28, 31, 40, 42.

Gelb, L. H. The Struggle over Foreign Policy: Muskie and Brzezinski. *New York Times Magazine* (July 20, 1980b), 26–28, 34–35, 38–40.

Gelb, L. H. The Vance Legacy. *New Republic* (May 10, 1980c), 13–15.

Gelb, L. H., with R. K. Betts. *The Irony of Vietnam: The System Worked.* Washington, D.C.: Brookings, 1979.

George, A. L. Quantitative and Qualitative Approaches to Content Analysis. In I. S. Pool (ed.), *Trends in Content Analysis.* Urbana, Ill.: University of Illinois Press, 1959, 7–32.

George, A. L. The "Operational Code": A Neglected Approach to the Study of Political Leaders and Decision Making. *International Studies Quarterly* 13 (1969), 190–222.

George, A. L. The Causal Nexus Between Cognitive Beliefs and Decision-making Behavior: The "Operational Code" Belief System. In L. S. Falkowski (ed.), *Psychological Models in International Politics.* Boulder, Colo.: Westview, 1979, 95–124.

George, A. L. *Presidential Decisionmaking in Foreign Policy: The Effective Use of Information and Advice.* Boulder, Colo.: Westview, 1980.

George, A. L., and J. L. George. *Woodrow Wilson and Colonel House.* New York: Dover Publications, 1956.

George, A. L., and R. O. Keohane. The Concept of National Interests: Uses and Limitations. In A. L. George, *Presidential Decisionmaking in Foreign Policy: The Effective Use of Information and Advice.* Boulder, Colo.: Westview, 1980, 217–238.

George, A. L., and R. Smoke. Theory for Policy in International Relations. *Policy Sciences* 4 (1973), 387–414.

BIBLIOGRAPHY

Geyelin, P. *Lyndon B. Johnson and the World*. New York: Praeger, 1966.

Gilbert, J. D. John Foster Dulles' Perceptions of the People's Republic of China: An Assessment of Accuracy. Paper Presented at the Annual Meeting of the Southwestern Political Science Association, San Antonio, Texas, 1975.

Gilpin, R. *War and Change in World Politics*. New York: Cambridge University Press, 1981.

Glad, B. *Jimmy Carter: In Search of the Great White House*. New York: W. W. Norton, 1980.

Goldmann, K. Change and Stability in Foreign Policy: Detente as a Problem of Stabilization. *World Politics* 34 (1982), 230–266.

Graber, D. A. *Mass Media and American Politics*. Washington, D.C.: Congressional Quarterly Press, 1984.

Greenfield, J. *The Real Campaign*. New York: Summit, 1982.

Greenstein, F. I. *Personality and Politics: Problems of Evidence, Inference, and Conceptualization*. New York: W. W. Norton, 1975.

Gwertzman, B. Cyrus Vance Plays It Cool. *New York Times Magazine* (March 18, 1979), 32–35, 100, 102–104.

Gwertzman, B. Vance, Looking Back, Lauds Pact on Arms and Retorts to Brzezinski. *New York Times* (December 3, 1980), A1.

Haas, E. The Balance of Power: Presumption, Concept, or Propaganda. *World Politics* 5 (1953), 442–477.

Hah, C., and F. C. Bartol. Political Leadership as a Causative Phenomenon: Some Recent Analyses. *World Politics* 36 (1983), 100–120.

Halperin, M. H. *Bureaucratic Politics and Foreign Policy*. Washington, D.C.: Brookings, 1974.

Harris, S. A. Issue Politicization and Policy Change: The United States and China, 1949–1972. Paper presented to the International Studies Association, St. Louis, Mo., 1977.

Hart, T. G. The Cognitive Dynamics of Swedish Security Elites: Beliefs about Swedish National Security and How They Change. *Cooperation and Conflict* 11 (1976), 201–219.

Heradstveit, D. *The Arab-Israeli Conflict: Psychological Obstacles to Peace*. Oslo: Universitites Forlaget, 1979.

Herberlein, T. A., and J. S. Black. Attitudinal Specificity and the Prediction of Behavior in a Field Setting. *Journal of Personality and Social Psychology* 33 (1976), 474–479.

Hermann, C. F., ed. *International Crisis: Insights from Behavioral Research*. New York: Free Press, 1972.

Hermann, C. F. Foreign Policy Behavior: That Which Is to Be Explained. In M. A. East, S. A. Salmore, and C. F. Hermann (eds.), *Why Nations Act*. Beverly Hills: Sage, 1978, 25–47.

BIBLIOGRAPHY

Hermann, C. F., M. A. East, M. A. Hermann, B. G. Salmore, and S. A. Salmore. *CREON: A Foreign Events Data Set* (Sage Professional Papers in International Studies). Beverly Hills: Sage, 1974.

Hermann, M. G. Effects of Personal Characteristics of Political Leaders in Foreign Policy. In M. A. East, S. A. Salmore, and C. F. Hermann (eds.), *Why Nations Act.* Beverly Hills: Sage, 1978, 49–68.

Hermann, R. K. *Perceptions and Behavior in Soviet Foreign Policy.* Pittsburgh, Pa.: University of Pittsburgh Press, 1985.

Hicks, S. M., T. A. Couloumbis, and E. M. Forgette. Influencing the Prince: A Role for Academicians? *Polity* 15 (1982), 279–294.

Higbee, N. L. Fifteen Years of Fear Arousal: Research on Threat Appeals: 1952–1968. *Psychological Bulletin* 72 (1969), 426–444.

Hilsman, R. The Foreign Policy Consensus: An Interim Research Report. *Journal of Conflict Resolution* 3 (1959), 361–382.

Hodgson, G. The Establishment. *Foreign Policy* 10 (1973), 3–40.

Hodgson, G. *America in Our Time: From World War II to Nixon, What Happened and Why.* New York: Vintage, 1976.

Hoffmann, S. The Hell of Good Intentions. *Foreign Policy* 29 (1977–78), 3–26.

Hoffmann, S. Carter's Soviet Problem. *New Republic* (July 29, 1978a), 20–23.

Hoffman, S. A View at Home: The Perils of Incoherence. *Foreign Affairs* 54 (1978b), 463–491.

Hoffman, S. *Dead Ends: American Foreign Policy in the Cold War.* Cambridge, Mass.: Ballinger, 1983.

Hoggard, G. Differential Source Coverage in Foreign Policy Analysis. In J. N. Rosenau (ed.), *Comparing Foreign Policies.* New York: John Wiley, 1974, 353–382.

Hollick, A. *U.S. Foreign Policy and the Law of the Sea.* Princeton, N.J.: Princeton University Press, 1981.

Holmes, J. *The Mood Interest Theory of American Foreign Policy.* Lexington, Ky.: University Press of Kentucky, 1985.

Holsti, O. R. The Belief System and National Images: A Case Study. *Journal of Conflict Resolution* 6 (1962), 244–251.

Holsti, O. R. Cognitive Dynamics and Images of the Enemy: Dulles and Russia. In D. J. Finlay, O. R. Holsti, and R. R. Fagen (eds.), *Enemies in Politics.* Chicago: Rand McNally, 1967, 25–97.

Holsti, O. R. *Content Analysis for the Social Sciences and Humanities.* Reading, Mass.: Addison-Wesley, 1969.

Holsti, O. R. The Study of International Politics Makes Strange Bedfellows: Themes of the Radical Right and Radical Left. *American Political Science Review* 68 (1974), 217–241.

Holsti, O. R. Foreign Policy Decision-makers Viewed Psychologically: Cognitive Processes Approaches. In G. M. Bonham and M. J. Shapiro (eds.), *Thought and Action in Foreign Policy.* Basek and Stuttgart: Birkhauser Verlag, 1977, 10–74.

BIBLIOGRAPHY

Holsti, O. R., and J. N. Rosenau. Vietnam, Consensus, and the Belief Systems of American Leaders. *World Politics* 32 (1979), 1–56.

Holsti, O. R., and J. N. Rosenau. End of the 'Vietnam Syndrome?': Continuity and Change in American Leadership Beliefs, 1976–1980. Prepared for the 22nd World Congress of the International Political Science Association, Rio de Janeiro, Brazil, August 1982.

Holsti, O. R. and J. N. Rosenau. *American Leadership in World Affairs: Vietnam and the Breakdown of Consensus*. Boston: Allen & Unwin, 1984.

Hoopes, T. *The Limits of Intervention: An Inside Account of How the Johnson Policy of Escalation in Vietnam was Reversed*. New York: McKay, 1969.

Horelick, A. L., A. R. Johnson, and J. D. Steinbruner. *The Study of Soviet Foreign Policy: A Review of Decision-theory-related Approaches* (R–1334). Santa Monica, Calif.: RAND, 1973.

Howell, L. A Comparative Study of the WEISS and COPDAB Data Sets. *International Studies Quarterly* 27 (1983), 149–159.

Hyman, H. H., and P. B. Sheatsley. Some Reasons Why Information Campaigns Fail. *Public Opinion Quarterly* 11 (1947), 412–423.

Inglehart, R. The Silent Revolution in Europe: Intergenerational Change in Post-Industrial Societies. *American Political Science Review* 65 (1971), 991–1017.

Isaak, R. A. The Individual in International Politics: Solving the Level-of-analysis Problem. *Polity* 7 (1974), 264–276.

James, D. B. *The Contemporary Presidency*. Indianapolis: Bobbs-Merrill, 1974.

Janis, I. L. The Problem of Validating Content Analysis. In H. D. Casswell and others (eds.), *Language of Politics*. Cambridge, Mass.: Massachusetts Institute of Technology Press, 1965, 55–82.

Janis, I. L. *Groupthink*. Boston: Houghton Mifflin, 1982.

Jensen, L. American Foreign Policy Elites and the Prediction of International Events. *Peace Research Society (International) Papers* 5 (1966), 199–209.

Jervis, R. The Costs of the Quantitative Study of International Relations. In K. Knorr and J. N. Rosenau (eds.), *Contending Approaches to International Politics*. Princeton, N.J.: Princeton University Press, 1969, 177–217.

Jervis, R. *Perception and Misperception in International Politics*. Princeton, N.J.: Princeton University Press, 1976.

Johnson, H. *In the Absence of Power: Governing America*. New York: Viking, 1980.

Johnson, L. K. Operational Codes and the Prediction of Leadership Behavior: Senator Frank Church at Midcareer. In M. G. Hermann (ed.), *A Psychological Examination of Political Leaders*. New York: Free Press, 1977, 82–119.

Jones, E. E. Major Developments in Social Psychology During the Past Five Decades. In Gardner, C., and E. Aronson (eds.) *The Handbook of Social Psychology* (vol. 1, 3rd ed.). New York: Random House, 1985.

Jordan, H. *Crisis: The Last Year of the Carter Presidency*. New York: G. P. Putnam's Sons, 1982.

BIBLIOGRAPHY

Kahle, L. R., and J. J. Berman. Attitudes Cause Behaviors: A Cross-legged Panel Analysis. *Journal of Personality and Social Psychology* 37 (1979), 315–321.

Kaiser, R. G., and D. Oberdorfer. Concern Over Soviets, Cubans Transforms U.S. Africa Policy. *Washington Post* (June 4, 1978), A1.

Karpel, C. S. Cartergate II: The Real President. *Penthouse* (December 1977), 89–90, 94, 160, 166–167.

Katz, D. The Functional Approach to the Study of Attitudes. *Public Opinion Quarterly* 24 (1960), 163–204.

Kegley, C. W., Jr. Introduction: The Generation and Use of Events Data. In C. W. Kegley, G. A. Raymond, R. M. Rood, & R. A. Skinner (eds.), *International Events and the Comparative Analysis of Foreign Policy*. Columbia, S.C.: University of South Carolina Press, 1975, 91–105.

Kegley, C. W., Jr., and E. R. Wittkopf. *American Foreign Policy: Patterns and Process*. New York: St. Martin's Press, 1979.

Kegley, C. W., Jr. Assumptions and Dilemmas in the Study of Americans' Foreign Policy Beliefs: A Caveat. *International Studies Quarterly* 30 (1986), 447–471.

Kelman, H. C. Compliance, Identification and Internationalization: Three Processes of Attitude Change. *Journal of Conflict Resolution* 2 (1958), 51–60.

Kelman, H. C. Social-psychological Approaches to the Study of International Relations: Definition of Scope. In H. C. Kelman (ed.), *International Behavior: A Social-psychological Analysis*. New York: Holt, Rinehart & Winston, 1965a, 3–39.

Kelman, H. C. Social-psychological Approaches to the Study of International Relations: The Question of Relevance. In H. C. Kelman (ed.), *International Behavior: A Social-psychological Analysis*. New York: Holt, Rinehart & Winston, 1965b, 565–607.

Kelman, H. C., and A. H. Bloom. Assumptive Frameworks in International Politics. In J. N. Knutson (ed.), *Handbook of Political Psychology*. San Francisco: Josey-Bass, 1973, 261–295.

Kennan, G. F. *American Diplomacy: 1900–1950*. New York: Mentor, 1951.

Key, V. O., Jr., with M. C. Cummings, Jr. *The Responsible Electorate: Rationality in Presidential Voting*. Cambridge, Mass.: Harvard University Press, 1965.

Kinder, D. R. and D. O. Sears. Public Opinion and Political Action. In Gardner, C., and E. Aronson (eds.), *The Handbook of Social Psychology* (vol. 2, 3rd ed.). New York: Random House, 1985, 659–741.

Kingdon, J. W. *Congressman's Voting Decisions*. New York: Harper & Row, 1973.

Kirschten, R. Beyond the Vance-Brzezinski Debate Lurks an NSC under Fire. *National Journal* (May 17, 1980), 814–818.

Klineberg, O. *Tensions Affecting International Understanding*. New York: Social Science Research Council, 1950.

Klingberg, F. L. The Historical Alteration of Moods in American Foreign Policy. *World Politics* 4 (1952), 239–273.

Klingberg, F. L. Cyclical Trends in American Foreign Policy Moods and Their Policy Implications. In C. W. Kegley, Jr., and P. J. McGowan (eds.), *Challenges to*

BIBLIOGRAPHY

America: U.S. Foreign Policy in the 1980s (Sage International Yearbook of Foreign Policy Studies, vol. 4). Beverly Hills, Calif.: Sage, 1979.

Korb, L. J. National Security Organization and Process in the Carter Administration. In S. Sarkesian (ed.), *Defense Policy and the Presidency*. Boulder, Colo.: Westview Press, 1979, 111–137.

Kraar, L. Yes the Administration Does Have a Defense Policy (of Sorts). *Fortune* (June 1978), 97, 128, 130, 132, 136–139.

Krasner, S. D. *Defending the National Interest*. Princeton, N.J.: Princeton University Press, 1978.

Krippendorff, K. *Content Analysis: An Introduction to Its Methodology*. Beverly Hills, Calif.: Sage, 1980.

Kutner, B., C. Wilkins, and P. R. Yarrow. Verbal Attitudes and Voting Behavior Involving Racial Prejudice. *Journal of Abnormal and Social Psychology* 47 (1952), 649–652.

LaFeber, W. From Confusion to Cold War: The Memoirs of the Carter Administration. *Diplomatic History* 8 (1984), 1–12.

Lane, R. E. *Political Ideology: Why the American Common Man Believes What He Does*. New York: Free Press, 1962.

Lane, R. E., and D. O. Sears. *Public Opinion*. Englewood Cliffs, N.J.: Prentice-Hall, 1964.

Lanouette, W. J. Carter Moves to Center Stage as Middle East Peacemaker. *National Journal* (1978a) 1968–1972.

Lanouette, W. J. Trilateral Conspiracy Theories. *National Journal* (February 11, 1978b), 235.

LaPiere, R. T. Attitudes versus Actions. *Social Forces* 13 (1934), 230–237.

Larson, D. W. *Origins of Containment: A Psychological Explanation*. Princeton, N.J.: Princeton University Press, 1985.

Lasswell, H. D. *Psychopathology and Politics*. Chicago: University of Chicago Press, 1930.

Lebow, R. N. *Between Peace and War: The Nature of International Crisis*. Baltimore: John Hopkins University Press, 1981.

Lee, J. R. Rallying Around the Flag: Foreign Policy Events and Presidential Popularity. *Presidential Studies Quarterly* 7 (1977), 252–256.

Leites, N. *The Operational Code of the Politburo*. New York: McGraw-Hill, 1951.

Leventhal, H. Findings and Theory in the Study of Fear Communications. In L. Berkowitz (ed.), *Advances in Experimental Social Psychology* (vol. 5). New York: Academic Press, 1970, 119–186.

Lin, N. *Foundations of Social Research*. New York: McGraw-Hill, 1976.

Lijphart, A. Comparative Politics and the Comparative Method. *American Political Science Review* 65 (1971), 682–693.

Luttberg, N. E. The Structure of Beliefs among Leaders and the Public. *Public Opinion Quarterly* 32 (1968), 398–409.

BIBLIOGRAPHY

Mansbach, R. W., and J. A. Vasquez. *In Search of Theory: A New Paradigm of Global Politics*. New York: Columbia University Press, 1981.

Marder, M. Behind Carter's Annapolis Speech. *Washington Post* (June 11, 1978), 1.

Markus, H., and R. B. Zajonc. The Cognitive Perspective in Social Psychology. In Gardner, C. and E. Aronson (eds.), *The Handbook of Social Psychology* (vol. 2, 3rd ed.). New York: Random House, 1985, 139–230.

Maslow, A. *Motivation and Personality*. New York: Harper & Row, 1954.

Mayhew, D. R. *Congress: The Electoral Connection*. New Haven, Conn.: Yale University Press, 1974.

Mazlish, B., and E. Diamond. *Jimmy Carter: A Character Portrait*. New York: Simon & Schuster, 1979.

McArdle, J. B. "Positive and Negative Communications and Subsequent Attitude and Behavior Change in Alcoholics." Unpublished doctoral dissertation, University of Illinois, 1972.

McClelland, C. A. *Theory and the International System*. New York: Macmillan, 1968.

McClelland, C. A. Let the User Beware. *International Studies Quarterly* 27 (1983), 169–177.

McClelland, C. A. and G. D. Hoggard. Conflict Patterns in the Interaction among Nations. In J. N. Rosenau (ed.), *International Politics and Foreign Policy*. New York: Free Press, 1969, 711–723.

McCombs, M. E., and D. L. Shaw. The Agenda-setting Function of Mass Media. *Public Opinion Quarterly* 36 (1972), 176–185.

McCormick, J. M. International Crises: A Note on Definition. *Western Political Quarterly* 31 (1978), 352–358.

McGeehan, R. Carter's Crises: Iran, Afghanistan, and Presidential Politics. *World Today* 36 (1980), 163–171.

McGuire, W. J. Personality and Susceptibility to Social Influence. In E. F. Borgatta & W. W. Lambert (eds.), *Handbook of Personality Theory and Research*. Chicago: Rand McNally, 1968, 1130–1187.

McGuire, W. J. The Nature of Attitudes and Attitude Change. In G. Lindzey and E. Aronson (eds.), *The Handbook of Social Psychology* (vol. 3, 2nd ed.). Reading, Mass.: Addison-Wesley, 1969, 136–314.

McGuire, W. J. Attitudes and Attitude Change. In Gardner, C. and E. Aronson (eds.), *The Handbook of Social Psychology* (vol. 2, 3rd ed.). New York: Random House, 1985, 233–346.

McLellan, D. S. *Cyrus Vance*. Totowa, N.J.: Rowman & Allenheld, 1985.

McLeod, J. M., L. B. Becker, and J. E. Byrnes. Another Look at the Agenda-setting Function of the Press. *Communications Research* 1 (1974), 131–166.

Mennis, B. *American Foreign Policy Officials: Who They Are and What They Believe Regarding International Politics*. Columbus, Ohio: Ohio State University Press, 1971.

Merritt, R. L. Foreign Policy Studies. *Policy Studies Journal* 3 (1974), 124–128.

BIBLIOGRAPHY

Minard, R. D. Race Relationships in the Pocahontas Coalfield. *Journal of Social Issues* 8 (1952), 29–44.

Modelski, G. *Principles of World Politics*. New York: Free Press, 1972.

Moore, J., ed. *The Campaign for President: 1980 in Retrospect*. Cambridge, Mass.: Ballinger, 1981.

Morgenthau, H. J. *Scientific Man Vs. Power Politics*. Chicago: University of Chicago Press, 1946.

Mueller, J. E. Trends in Popular Support for the Wars in Korea and Vietnam. *American Political Science Review* 65 (1971), 358–375.

Mueller, J. E. *War, Presidents, and Public Opinion*. New York: Wiley, 1973.

Nash, G. H. *The Conservative Intellectual Movement in America*. New York: Basic Books, 1979.

Nathan, J. A., and J. K. Oliver. *United States Foreign Policy and World Order*. Boston: Little, Brown, 1981.

Nathan, J. A., and J. K. Oliver. *Foreign Policy Making and the American Political System*. Boston: Little, Brown, 1983.

National Security Policy Integration (President's Reorganization Project). Washington, D.C.: September 1979.

Nelson, K. L., and S. C. Olin, Jr. *Why War? Ideology, Theory, and History*. Berkeley: University of California Press, 1979.

Neustadt, R. E. *Presidential Power: The Politics of Leadership*. New York: John Wiley & Sons, 1960.

Newcomb, T. M., K. E. Koenig, R. Flacks, and D. P. Warwick. *Persistence and Change: Bennington College and Its Students after 25 Years*. New York: Wiley, 1967.

Nie, N. H., with K. Anderson. Mass Belief Systems Revisited: Political Change and Attitude Structure. *Journal of Politics* 36 (1974), 540–587.

Nie, N. H., S. Verba, and J. R. Petrocik. *The Changing American Voter*. Cambridge, Mass.: Harvard University Press, 1976.

Niebuhr, R. *The Children of Light and the Children of Darkness*. New York: Charles Scribner's Sons, 1944.

Nisbett, R. E., and L. Ross. *Human Inference: Strategies and Shortcomings in Social Judgement*. Englewood Cliffs, N.J.: Prentice-Hall, 1980.

Oberdorfer, D. *Tet!* New York: Doubleday, 1971.

Oberdorfer, D. U.S. Receives Plan, Extended Version Arms to Somalia. *Washington Post* (June 2, 1978), Al.

Osgood, C. E., G. J. Suzi, and P. H. Tannebaum. *The Measurement of Meaning*. Urbana, Ill.: University of Illinois Press, 1957.

Osgood, C. E. The Representational Model and Relevant Research Methods. In I. S. Pool (ed.), *Trends in Content Analysis*. Urbana, Ill.: University of Illinois Press, 1959, 33–88.

239

BIBLIOGRAPHY

Osgood, R. E. *Ideals and Self-Interest in America's Foreign Relations: The Great Transformation of the Twentieth Century.* Chicago: University of Chicago Press; 1953.

Osgood, R. E. Carter Policy in Perspective. *SAIS Review* (1981), 11–22.

Oskamp, S. *Attitudes and Opinions.* Englewood Cliffs, N.J.: Prentice-Hall, 1977.

Page, B. I., and R. A. Brody. Policy Voting and the Electoral Process: The Vietnam War Issue. *American Political Science Review* 66 (1972), 979–995.

Pear, T. H. *Psychological Factors of War and Peace.* London: Hutchinson, 1950.

Perlmutter, A. The Presidential Political Center and Foreign Policy: A Critique. *World Politics* 27 (1974), 87–106.

Petras, J. U.S. Foreign Policy: The Revival of Inverventionism. *Monthly Review* 9 (1980), 15–27.

Piaget, J. *The Moral Judgement of the Child.* New York: Free Press, 1932.

Pious, R. M. *The American Presidency.* New York: Basic Books, 1979.

Pomper, G. M. The Impact of "The American Voter" on Political Science. *Political Science Quarterly* 93 (1978–79), 617–628.

Pool, I. S. *Trends in Content Analysis.* Urbana, Ill.: University of Illinois Press, 1959.

Presidential Directive/NSC–1. January 20, 1977a.

Presidential Directive/NSC–2. January 20, 1977b.

Quinn, S. Courting the White House and Sniping at State. *Washington Post* (December 20, 1979a).

Quinn, S. The Politics of the Power Grab: Nine Rules of Notoriety. *Washington Post* (December 19, 1979b).

Quinn, S. Zbigniew Brzezinski: Insights, Infights, Kissinger and Competition. *Washington Post* (December 21, 1979c).

Raphael, A. Media Coverage of the Hostage Negotiations—From Fact to Fiction. *Executive Seminars in National and International Affairs.* (U.S. Department of State, Foreign Service Institute). 24th Session (1981–82).

Riesman, D., with N. Glazer and R. Denney. *The Lonely Crowd: A Study of the Changing American Character.* New York: Doubleday, 1953.

Ripley, R. B. *Congress: Process and Policy.* New York: W. W. Norton, 1983.

Robinson, J. A. Crisis: An Appraisal of Concepts and Theories. In C. Hermann (ed.), *International Crises: Insights from Behavioral Research.* New York: Free Press, 1972, 20–35.

Rokeach, M. *The Open and Closed Mind.* New York: Basic Books, 1960.

Rokeach, M. Attitude Change and Behavioral Change. *Public Opinion Quarterly* 30 (1966), 529–550.

Rokeach, M. *Beliefs, Attitudes, and Values.* San Francisco: Josey-Bass, 1968.

Rokeach, M. *The Nature of Human Values.* New York: Free Press, 1973.

Rosati, J. A. Developing a Systematic Decision-Making Framework: Bureaucratic Politics in Perspective. *World Politics* 33 (1981), 234–252.

Rosati, J. A., and J. Creed. "Perceptual Dissensus: National Elite Perspectives on American Foreign Policy." Paper Presented at the Tenth Annual Scientific Meeting of the International Society of Political Psychology, San Francisco, July 4–July 7, 1987.

Rosecrance, R. N. *Action and Reaction in World Politics: International Systems in Perspective*. Boston: Little, Brown, 1963.

Rosenau, J. N. *Public Opinion and Foreign Policy*. New York: Random House, 1961.

Rosenau, J. N. Pre-theories and Theories of Foreign Policy. In R. B. Farrell (ed.), *Approaches to Comparative and International Politics*. Evanston, Ill.: Northwestern University Press, 1966, 29–62.

Rosenberg, M. J. An Analysis of Affective-Cognitive Consistency. In M. J. Rosenberg, C. I. Houland, W. J. McGuire, R. P. Abelson, and J. W. Berlin (eds.), *Attitude Organization and Change: An Analysis of Consistency among Attitude Components*. New Haven, Conn.: Yale University Press, 1960, 15–64.

Rosenberg, M. J. Attitude Change and Foreign Policy in the Cold War Era. In J. N. Rosenau (ed.), *Domestic Sources of Foreign Policy*. New York: Free Press, 1967, 111–159.

Roskin, M. From Pearl Harbor to Vietnam: Shifting Generational Paradigms and Foreign Policy. *Political Science Quarterly* 89 (1974), 563–588.

Rossi, P. H. Trends in Voting Behavior Research: 1933–1963. In E.C. Dreyer and W. A. Rosenbaum (eds.), *Political and Electoral Behavior*. Wadsworth, 1966, 67–78.

Rostow, E. V. The Giant Still Sleeps. *Orbis* 24 (1980), 311–321.

Rourke, F. The Domestic Scene. In R. Osgood, et al. (eds.), *America and the World*. Baltimore: John Hopkins Press, 1970.

Russett, B., and D. R. DeLuca. Don't Tread on Me: Public Opinion and Foreign Policy in the Eighties. *Political Science Quarterly* 96 (1981), 381–400.

Sanders, J. W. *Peddlers of Crisis: The Committee on the Present Danger and the Politics of Containment*. Boston: South End Press, 1983.

Sarnoff, I., and D. Katz. The Motivational Bases of Attitude Change. *Journal of Abnormal and Social Psychology* 49 (1954), 115–124.

Schelling, T. C. *Micromotives and Macrobehavior*. New York: W. W. Norton, 1978.

Schlesinger, A., Jr. The Great Carter Mystery. *New Republic* (April 12, 1980), 18–21.

Schneider, W. Conservatism, Not Interventionism: Trends in Foreign Policy Opinion, 1974–1982. In K. A. Oye, R. J. Lieber, and D. Rothchild (eds.), *Eagle Defiant: United States Foreign Policy in the 1980s*. Boston: Little, Brown, 1983, 33–64.

Schram, M. The Ascendency of Cyrus Vance: Dominant Voice Is His. *Washington Post* (August 6, 1978), A1.

Schuman, H. Attitudes vs. Actions Versus Attitude vs. Attitudes. *Public Opinion Quarterly* 36 (1972), 347–354.

Schwartz, S. H. Temporal Instability as a Moderator of the Attitude-behavior Relationship. *Journal of Personality and Social Psychology* 36 (1978), 715–724.

Sears, D. O., and R. E. Whitney. *Political Persuasion*. Morristown, N.J.: General Learning Press, 1973.

BIBLIOGRAPHY

Semmel, A. K. Evolving Patterns of U.S. Security Assistance, 1950–1980. In C. W. Kegley and E. R. Wittkopf (eds.), *Perspective on American Foreign Policy*. New York: St. Martin's, 1983, 79–95.

Serfaty, S. Brzezinski: Play It Again, Zbig. *Foreign Policy* 32 (1978), 3–21.

Serfaty, S. *American Foreign Policy in a Hostile World: Dangerous Years*. New York: Praeger, 1984.

Shaw, M. E. *Group Decisions: The Psychology of Small Group Behavior*. New York: McGraw-Hill, 1976.

Sick, G. *All Fall Down: America's Tragic Encounter with Iran*. New York: Random House, 1985.

Singer, J. D. Man and World Politics: The Psycho-cultural Interface. *Journal of Social Issues* 24 (1968), 127–156.

Sites, P. *Control: The Basis of Social Order*. New York: Dunellen, 1973.

Smith, G. *Morality, Reason and Power: American Diplomacy in the Carter Years*. New York: Hill & Wang, 1986.

Smith, M. B. Opinions, Personality, and Political Behavior. *American Political Science Review* 52 (1958), 1–17.

Smith, M. B. A Map for the Analysis of Personality and Politics. *Journal of Social Issues* 24 (1966), 15–28.

Smith, M. B., J. S. Bruner, and R. W. White. *Opinions and Personality*. New York: Wiley, 1956.

Snyder, G., and P. Diesing. *Conflict Among Nations*. Princeton, N.J.: Princeton University Press, 1977.

Snyder, R. C. A Decision-making Approach to the Study of Political Phenomena. In R. Young (ed.), *Approaches to the Study of Politics*. Evanston. Ill.: Northwestern University Press, 1958, 3–37.

Snyder, R. C., H. W. Bruck, and B. Sapin. *Foreign Policy Decision Making*. New York: Free Press, 1962.

Spanier, J. *Games Nations Play: Analyzing International Politics* (2nd ed.). New York: Praeger, 1975.

Spanier, J. *American Foreign Policy Since World War II*. New York: Holt, Rinehart & Winston, 1983.

Sprout, H., and M. Sprout. *The Ecological Perspective on Human Affairs*. Princeton, N.J.: Princeton University Press, 1965.

Stang, A. It's Time to Expose the Conspiracy. *American Opinion* 23 (1980) 25–30, 75–78.

Starr, H. The Kissinger Years: Studying Individuals and Foreign Policy. *International Studies Quarterly* 24 (1980), 465–496.

Starr, H. *Henry Kissinger: Perception of International Politics*. Lexington, Ky.: University Press of Kentucky, 1984.

Steinbruner, J. D. *The Cybernetic Theory of Decision*. Princeton. N.J.: Princeton University Press, 1974.

Steinfels, P. *The Neoconservatives*. New York: Simon & Schuster, 1979.

BIBLIOGRAPHY

Stuart, D., and H. Starr. The "Inherent Bad Faith Model" Reconsidered: Dulles, Kennedy, and Kissinger. *Political Psychology* 3 (1981–82), 1–33.

Stupak, R. J. Dean Rusk on International Relations: An Analysis of His Philosophical Perceptions. *Australian Outlook* 25 (1971), 13–28.

Sullivan, M. P. *International Relations: Theories and Evidence.* Englewood Cliffs, N.J.: Prentice-Hall, 1976.

Sullivan, M. P. Foreign Policy Articulations and U.S. Conflict Behavior. In J. D. Singer and M. D. Wallace (eds.), *To Augur Well: Early Warning Indicators in World Politics.* Beverly Hills: Sage, 1979, 215–235.

Sullivan, M. P. *The Vietnam War: A Study in the Making of American Policy.* Lexington, Ky.: University Press of Kentucky, 1985.

Sullivan, W. H. Dateline Iran: The Road Not Taken. *Foreign Policy* 40 (1980), 175–186.

Szulc, T. The New Brinksmanship. *New Republic* (November 8, 1980), 18–21.

Taubman, P., and R. Burt. U.S., in '79, Said to Have Weighed Backing Iranian Military in a Coup. *New York Times* (April 20, 1980), 1, 14.

Thistlethwaite, D. L. Impact of Disruptive External Events on Student Attitudes. *Journal of Personality and Social Psychology* 30 (1974), 228–242.

Tucker, R. W. America in Decline: The Foreign Policy of Maturity. *Foreign Affairs* 58 (1979), 449–484.

Tucker, R. W. Reagan Without Tears: His 'Simple' World View Is Truer Than Carter's 'Complex' One. *New Republic* (May 17, 1980), 22–25.

Tucker, R. W. *The Purposes of American Power: An Essay on National Security.* New York: Praeger, 1981.

Tweraser, K. Changing Patterns of Political Beliefs: The Foreign Policy Operational Codes of J. William Fulbright, 1943–1967. *Sage Professional Papers in American Politics* (Series No. 04–016). Beverly Hills, Calif.: Sage, 1974.

U.S., Congress, House Committee on International Relations. *Congress and Foreign Policy—1977* (Committee Print). Washington, D.C.: U.S. Government Printing Office, 1978.

U.S., Council on Environmental Quality. *The Global 2000 Report to the President.* Washington, D.C.: Government Printing Office, 1980.

U.S., Department of State. *Secretariat Handbook.* 1979.

U.S., NSC Assistant, Brzezinski, Z. Interview with *U.S. News and World Report* on May 30, 1977. *DOD Selected Statements* (June 1, 1977a).

U.S., NSC Assistant, Brzezinski, Z. Interview with the *Washington Post* on October 9, 1977. *DOD Selected Statements* (November 1, 1977b).

U.S., NSC Assistant, Brzezinski, Z. American Policy and Global Change (address made before the Trilateral Commission in Bonn, Germany, on October 25, 1977). *Congressional Record* (November 1, 1977c), H11999–H12002.

U.S., NSC Assistant, Brzezinski, Z. Interview on *Face the Nation* on October 30, 1977. *State Department Bulletin* (December 5, 1977d), 800–805.

BIBLIOGRAPHY

U.S., NSC Assistant, Brzezinski, Z. Address made to the American Foreign Service Association in Washington, D.C., on December 9, 1977. *DOD Selected Statements* (March 1, 1978a).

U.S., NSC Assistant, Brzezinski, Z. Interview on *Look Up and Live* (CBS), on May 7, 1978. *DOD Selected Statements* (June 1, 1978b).

U.S., NSC Assistant, Brzezinski, Z. Interview on *Meet the Press*, on May 28, 1978. *State Department Bulletin* (July 1978c), 26–28.

U.S., NSC Assistant, Brzezinski, Z. Remarks to the Foreign Policy Association in Washington, D.C., on December 20, 1978. *White House Press Release* (1978d).

U.S., NSC Assistant, Brzezinski, Z. The Wider Meaning of National Security (remarks at the annual convention of the American Society of Newspaper Editors in New York, on May 1, 1979). *White House Press Release* (May 1, 1979a).

U.S., NSC Assistant, Brzezinski, Z. American Power and Global Change (remarks at the annual convention of the International Platform Association in Washington, D.C., on August 2, 1978). *White House Release* (August 2, 1979b).

U.S., NSC Assistant, Brzezinski, Z. Remarks at the anniversary assembly of the Atlantic Treaty Organization in Washington, D.C., on October 10, 1979. *White House Press Release* (October 10, 1979c).

U.S., NSC Assistant, Brzezinski, Z. Interview on ABC's *Issues and Answers*. *DOD Selected Statements* (November 1, 1979d).

U.S., NSC Assistant, Brzezinski, Z. Interview with James Reston of the *New York Times*, on December 31, 1978. *DOD Selected Statements* (January 1, 1979e).

U.S., NSC Assistant, Brzezinski, Z. Interview on *MacNeil/Lehrer Report*, on October 15, 1980. *DOD Selected Statements* (November 1, 1980a).

U.S., NSC Assistant, Brzezinski, Z. Interview with *Wall Street Journal*, on January 15, 1980. *Wall Street Journal* (January 15, 1980b).

U.S., NSC Assistant, Brzezinski, Z. Remarks before the Woman's National Democratic Club in Washington, D.C., on February 21, 1980. *White House Press Release* (February 21, 1980c).

U.S., NSC Assistant, Brzezinski, Z. The Twin Strands of American Foreign Policy (address before the Baltimore Council on Foreign Relations, on May 9, 1980). *Transcript* (1980d).

U.S., NSC Assistant, Brzezinski, Z. The Quest for Global Security: The Third Phase (remarks before the Council on Foreign Relations in Denver, Colorado, on October 25, 1980). *White House Press Release* (October 25, 1980e).

U.S., Office of Management and Budget. *Budget of the United States Government: Fiscal Year 1979.* Washington, D.C.: Government Printing Office, 1979.

U.S., Office of Management and Budget. *Budget of the United States Government: Fiscal Year 1981.* Washington, D.C.: Government Printing Office, 1981.

U.S., President, Carter, J. Press conference of February 8, 1977. *State Department Bulletin* (February 28, 1977a), 157–160.

U.S., President, Carter, J. Peace, Arms Control, World Economic Progress, Human Rights: Basic Priorities of U.S. Foreign Policy (address made to representatives to the United Nations in the U.N. General Assembly Hall, on March 17, 1977). *State Department Bulletin* (April 11, 1977b), 329–334.

U.S., President, Carter, J. Press conference of March 24, 1977. *State Department Bulletin* (April 18, 1977c), 357–362.

U.S., President, Carter, J. A Foreign Policy Based on America's Essential Character (address made at the commencement exercises of Notre Dame University in South Bend, Ind., on May 22, 1977). *Department of State Bulletin* (June 13, 1977d), 621–625.

U.S., President, Carter, J. The U.S.-Soviet Relationship (remarks made before the Southern Legislative Conference at Charleston, S.C., on July 21, 1977). *State Department Bulletin* (August 15, 1977e), 193–197.

U.S., President, Carter, J. Remarks at Yazoo City, Mississippi, on July 21, 1977. *State Department Bulletin* (August 15, 1977f), 197–200.

U.S., President, Carter, J. U.S. Role in a Peaceful Global Community (address made before the 32nd U.N. General Assembly, on October 4, 1977). *State Department Bulletin* (October 24, 1977g), 547–552.

U.S., President, Carter, J. New Agenda for Democracy (remarks made before the Palais Des Congress, Paris, France, on January 4, 1978). *State Department Bulletin* (February 1978a), 12–15.

U.S., President, Carter, J. National Security Interests (address made at Wake Forest University, Winston-Salem, N.C., on March 17, 1978). *State Department Bulletin* (April 1978b), 17–19.

U.S., President, Carter, J. Question and Answer session at a Spokane Town Meeting, on May 5, 1978. *State Department Bulletin* (July 1978c), 20–22.

U.S., President, Carter, J. The United States and the Soviet Union (address made at the U.S. Naval Academy's commencement exercises in Annapolis, Md., on June 7, 1978). *State Department Bulletin* (July 1978d), 14–16.

U.S., President, Carter, J. Press Conference of June 26, 1978. *State Department Bulletin* (August 1978e), 8–10.

U.S., President, Carter, J. The United States and Its Economic Responsibilities (remarks made at the opening session of the 26th World Conference of the International Chamber of Commerce in Orlando, Fla., on October 1, 1978). *State Department Bulletin* (December 1978f), 12–14.

U.S., President, Carter, J. Interview for *Bill Moyers' Journal*, on November 13, 1978. *State Department Bulletin* (December 1978g), 14–17.

U.S., President, Carter, J. Remarks at a White House ceremony on December 6, 1978, commemorating the 30th anniversary of the adoption of the Universal Declaration of Human Rights. *State Department Bulletin* (January 1979a), 1–2.

U.S., President, Carter, J. News Conference of January 17. *State Department Bulletin* (February 1979b), 3–5.

U.S., President, Carter, J. State of the Union (address before a joint session of the Congress on January 23, 1979). *State Department Bulletin* (February 1979c), 1–2.

BIBLIOGRAPHY

U.S., President, Carter, J. State of the Union Message to the Congress on January 25, 1979 (an elaboration of the address two days earlier). *State Department Bulletin* (March 1979d), 24–30.

U.S., President, Carter, J. America's Role in a Turbulent World (address upon receiving an honorary Doctor of Engineering degree from the Georgia Institute of Technology in Atlanta, on February 20, 1979). *State Department Bulletin* (March 1979e), 21–23.

U.S., President, Carter, J. Remarks before a foreign policy conference for editors and broadcasters held at the Department of State on February 22, 1979. *State Department Bulletin* (April 1979f), 4–5.

U.S., President, Carter, J. Interview on *Meet the Press*, on January 20, 1980. *Weekly Compilation of Presidential Documents* (January 20, 1980a), 107–114.

U.S., President, Carter, J. State of the Union Message (to the Congress on January 21, 1980). *Department of State Bulletin* (February 1980b), D–P.

U.S., President, Carter, J. State of the Union (address before a joint session of the Congress, on January 23, 1980). *State Department Bulletin* (February 1980c), A–D.

U.S., President, Carter, J. U.S. Course in a Changing World (address before the American Society of Newspaper Editors in Washington, D.C., on April 10, 1980). *State Department Bulletin* (May 1980d), 3–6.

U.S., President Carter, J. Interview with Frank Reynolds of ABC-TV's *World News Tonight*, on January 19, 1980. *New York Times* (January 20, 1980e), 4.

U.S., President Carter, J. Farewell address, on January 14, 1981. *New York Times* (January 15, 1981), B10.

U.S., President, Carter, J. Message to People of Other Nations on Assuming Office, January 20, 1977. *American Foreign Policy Basic Documents, 1977–1980* (Department of State). Washington, D.C.: Government Printing Office, 1983, 1.

U.S., Secretary of State, Muskie, E. The Middle East: Outlook for Peace (address before the Washington Press Club in Washington, D.C., on June 9, 1980). *State Department Bulletin* (July 1980a, 3–5).

U.S., Secretary of State, Muskie, E. The Costs of Leadership (address before the Foreign Policy Association in New York on July 7, 1980). *State Department Bulletin* (August 1980b), 28–29.

U.S., Secretary of State, Muskie, E. Review of Discussions Abroad (statement before the House Foreign Affairs Committee on July 30, 1980). *State Department Bulletin* (September 1980c), 20–23.

U.S., Secretary of State, Muskie, E. Human Freedom: America's Vision (address before the United Steelworkers of America in Los Angeles, on August 7, 1980). *State Department Bulletin* (September 1980d), A–C.

U.S., Secretary of State, Muskie, E. Essentials of Security: Arms and More (address before the World Affairs Council in Pittsburgh, on September 18, 1980). *State Department Bulletin* (November 1980e), 27–28.

U.S., Secretary of State, Muskie, E. Dealing with the World's Realities (remarks before the Economic Club of Memphis and the Memphis in May International

BIBLIOGRAPHY

Festival, Inc., in Memphis, on October 6, 1980). *State Department Bulletin* (November 1980f), A–B.

U.S., Secretary of State, Muskie, E. The Challenge of Peace (address at Notre Dame University in South Bend, Ind., on October 11, 1980). *State Department Bulletin* (November 1980g), 35–36.

U.S., Secretary of State, Vance, C. News conference of March 4, 1977. *State Department Bulletin* (March 28, 1977a), 277–283.

U.S., Secretary of State, Vance, C. Overview of Foreign Assistance Programs (statement before the Subcommittee on Foreign Operations of the House Committee on Appropriations on March 2, 1977. *State Department Bulletin* (March 28, 1977b), 284–289.

U.S., Secretary of State, Vance, C. Human Rights and Foreign Policy (address made at the law day ceremonies of the University of Georgia School of Law in Athens, Ga., on April 30). *State Department Bulletin* (May 23, 1977c), 505–508.

U.S., Secretary of State, Vance, C. Interview on *Issues and Answers* on June 19, 1977. *State Department Bulletin* (July 18, 1977d), 78–83.

U.S., Secretary of State, Vance, C. The United States and Africa: Building Positive Relationships (address made before the annual convention of the National Association of Colored People at St. Louis, Mo., on July 1, 1977). *State Department Bulletin* (August 8, 1977e), 165–170.

U.S., Secretary of State, Vance, C. Statement made before the Senate Foreign Relations Committee on September 26, 1977. *State Department Bulletin* (November 7, 1977f), 615–618.

U.S., Secretary of State, Vance, C. Interview with *U.S. News and World Report* on November 7, 1977. *State Department Bulletin* (November 21, 1977g), 732–738.

U.S., Secretary of State, Vance, C. Foreign Policy Decisions for 1978 (address before the Los Angeles World Affairs Council on January 13, 1978). *State Department Bulletin* (February 1978a), 23–26.

U.S., Secretary of State, Vance, C. Arms Control and National Security (address before the American Society of Newspaper Editors in Washington, D.C., on April 10, 1978). *State Department Bulletin* (May 1978b), 20–22.

U.S., Secretary of State, Vance, C. Elements of U.S. Policy Toward the Soviet Union (statement before the House Committee on International Relations on June 19, 1978). *State Department Bulletin* (August 1978c), 14–16.

U.S., Secretary of State, Vance, C. U.S. Relations with Africa (address before the 58th annual meeting of the U.S. Jaycees in Atlantic City, on June 20, 1978). *State Department Bulletin* (August 1978d), 10–13.

U.S., Secretary of State, Vance, C. The U.S.-European Partnership (address before the Royal Institute of International Affairs in London, on December 9, 1978). *State Department Bulletin* (January 1979a), 12–16.

U.S., Secretary of State, Vance, C. Where We Stand with SALT II (address at the Florida Blue Key Banquet in Gainesville, Florida, on October 26, 1979). *State Department Bulletin* (December 1979b), 21–23.

BIBLIOGRAPHY

U.S., Secretary of State, Vance, C. America's Commitment to Third World Development (address before the Northwest Regional Conference on the Emerging International Order in Seattle, on March 30, 1979). *State Department Bulletin* (May 1979c), 33–37.

U.S., Secretary of State, Vance, C. Meeting the Challenges of a Changing World (address before the American Association of Community and Junior Colleges in Chicago, on May, 1979). *State Department Bulletin* (June 1979d), 16–19.

U.S., Secretary of State, Vance, C. America's Growing Relationship with the Developing World (address before the National Urban League in Chicago, on July 23, 1979). *State Department Bulletin* (September 1979e), 6–8.

U.S., Secretary of State, Vance, C. Common Needs in a Diverse World (address before the 34th session of the U.N. General Assembly in New York, on September 24, 1979f). *State Department Bulletin* (November 1979f), 1–6.

U.S., Secretary of State, Vance, C. Meeting the Challenge in Southwest Asia (statement before the Senate Appropriations Committee on February 1, 1980). *State Department Bulletin* (March 1980a), 35–37.

U.S., Secretary of State, Vance, C. Afghanistan: America's Course (address before the Council on Foreign Relations in Chicago, on March 3, 1980). *State Department Bulletin* (April 1980b), 12–14.

U.S., Secretary of State, Vance, C. U.S. Foreign Policy: Our Broader Strategy (statement before the Senate Foreign Relations Committee on March 27, 1980). *State Department Bulletin* (May 1980c), 16–24.

Vance: Man on the Move. *Time* (April 24, 1978), 12–21.

Vance, C. Address at the Commencement Exercises at Harvard University on June 5, 1980. *New York Times* (June 6, 1980), A12.

Vance, C. *Hard Choices: Four Critical Years in America's Foreign Policy.* New York: Simon & Schuster, 1983.

Wahlke, J. C. Pre-Behavioralism in Political Science. *American Political Science Review* 73 (1979), 9–31.

Walker, S. G. Cognitive Maps and International Realities: Henry A. Kissinger's Operational Code. Paper Prepared for the Annual Meeting of the American Political Science Association, San Francisco, September 1975.

Walker, S. G. The Interface Between Beliefs and Behavior: Henry Kissinger's Operational Code and the Vietnam War. *Journal of Conflict Resolution* 21 (1977), 129–168.

Waltz, K. N. *Man, the State, and War: A Theoretical Analysis.* New York: Columbia University Press, 1954.

Waltz, K. N. *Foreign Policy and Democratic Politics: The American and British Experience.* Boston: Little, Brown, 1967.

Waltz, K. *Theory of International Politics.* Reading, Mass.: Addison-Wesley, 1979.

Watts, W., and L. Free. Internationalism Comes of Age . . . Again. *Public Opinion* (April–May 1980), 49.

BIBLIOGRAPHY

Weinstein, A., and M. R. Beschloss. The Best National Security Council System: A Conversation with Zbigniew Brzezinski. *Washington Quarterly* 5 (1982), 71–82.

Weintraub, W. Personality Profiles of American Presidents as Revealed in Their Public Statements: The Presidential news conferences of Jimmy Carter and Ronald Reagan. *Political Psychology* 7 (1986), 285–295.

Whiting, A. S. The Scholar and the Policy-maker. In R. Tanter and R. H. Ullman (eds.), *Theory and Policy in International Relations*. Princeton, N.J.: Princeton University Press, 1972, 229–247.

Wicker, A. L. Attitudes versus Actions: The Relationship of Verbal and Overt Behavioral Responses to Attitude Objects. *Journal of Social Issues* 25 (1969), 41–78.

Wicker, T. A Tale of Two Silences. *New York Times* (May 4, 1980), E23.

Wilson, G. C. U.S. Steps Up Planning for Mideast Bases. *Washington Post* (August 7, 1980), A1; A7.

Winter, D. The Carter-Niebuhr Connection—The Politician as Philosopher. *National Journal* (February 4, 1978), 188–192.

Wooten, J. Here Comes Zbig. *Esquire* (November 1979).

Wray, J. H. Comments on Interpretations of Early Research into Belief Systems. *Journal of Politics* 41 (1979), 1173–1181.

Wright, Q. *The Study of International Relations*. New York: Appleton, 1955.

Yankelovich, D., and L. Kaagen. Assertive America. *Foreign Affairs* 59 (1980), 696–713.

Young, O. R. The Perils of Odysseus: On Constructing Theories of International Relations. In R. Tanter & R. H. Ullman, (eds.), *Theory and Policy in International Relations*. Princeton, N.J.: Princeton University Press, 1972, 179–203.

Index

Abelson, Robert, 37n
Adelman, Kenneth, 14n
Adorno, Theodor, 25
Afghanistan, Soviet invasion of,
  general behavior toward, 143–144
  general image of, 82, 84, 86–87, 92, 105
  importance to administration, 82, 87, 90,
    91, 105, 108–109, 112
African conflict. *See also* Ethiopia-Somalia
    conflict.
  general behavior toward, 120, 126–127,
    129, 135–136, 145
  general image of, 47–48, 58–61, 63–64, 68
  Namibia, 129, 136
  preventive diplomacy, 48, 61–62
  South Africa, 68, 120, 136
  Zaire's Katanga province, 58, 127
  Zimbabwe, 120, 129, 136, 146
Ajemian, Robert, 115n
Ajzen, Icek, 15, 30, 38n, 175, 199
Ali Muhammad, 144
Allen, Gary, 162
Allison, Graham, 20, 22, 36n
Allport, Floyd, 36n
Allport, Gordon, 168
Almond, Gabriel, 27
American foreign policy. *See also* Carter
    Administration.
  conflicting interpretations, 7, 154
  establishment, 111, 115n, 156
  historical evolution, 5, 75, 87, 154,
    156–158
  impact of Vietnam War, 28, 74, 87, 156
  importance of the Soviet Union, 52, 132
  policy of containment, 5, 28, 41, 42–43,
    54, 75, 88, 154, 156
  policy of detente, 156
  radical interpretations, 162n

resignations, 113
role of domestic forces, 27–29
American Voter, The, 37n
Amin, Idi, 134
Anderson, Jack, 150
Anderson, Kristi, 23
Andriole, Stephen, 179n
Angola, 58, 127
Arabs, 50
Argentina, 120
Arms control,
  arms sales, 47, 121, 129, 145
  general behavior toward, 121, 129, 137,
    145
  general image of, 47
  nonproliferation, 47, 121, 137, 145
  SALT (Strategic Arms Limitation Talks),
    47, 121, 129, 137, 145
Art, Robert, 18
Asch, Solomon, 29
Association for Southeast Asian Nations
    (ASEAN), 50
Australia, 121, 144
Authoritarian Personality, The, 25
Azar, Edward, 196

B-1 bomber, 122
Barner-Barry, Carol, 31, 38n
Barnet, Richard, 14n
Baron, Robert, 29
Bartol, Frederick, 106
Becker, Lee, 28
Begin, Menachem, 129, 134
Behavioralism, 36n, 165
Belgium, 127
Beliefs. *See also* Beliefs, impact on behavior;
    Belief system approaches.
  central, 22, 24–25, 115n, 175, 180n
  concept of worldview, 17, 39, 185

consensus, 19–21, 158–161
defined, 15–16
image of international system, 17, 39,
  185–188
image of the future, 187
in international relations, 16, 24, 29–30,
  161–162, 186 (*see also* International
  relations, study of)
in psychology, 15–16, 21, 23, 29, 161–162
individual and collective, 4, 17–19, 21, 35,
  158–162 (*see also* Decision-making)
non-attitudes, 32
operational, 190–192
policy relevance, 178
private, 190
public, 190–192
stability vs. change, 4, 21–30, 102–103,
  116n, 158–161, 175 (*see also* Congitive
  consistency; Communications,
  persuasive; Domestic forces; Events;
  Personality)
Beliefs, impact on behavior, 4. *See also*
  Beliefs.
as intervening variable, 168–170
causality, 34, 37n, 166–167
in international relations, 33–34, 160–162,
  172, 174–176, 186 (*see also*
  International relations, study of)
in psychology, 31–32
method of determination, 32–33, 197–198
paucity of research, 30–31, 33, 117,
  161–162
prediction, 174–176
problem of circularity, 197
problems with literature, 31–32
situational thresholds, 31, 175
Belief system approaches, 172, 186. *See also*
  Psychological approaches.
cognitive mapping, 36n
image of the opponent, 52, 198n
operational code, 33, 34, 36n, 52
Bem, Deryl, 22, 29, 37n, 192
Ben-Zvi, Abraham, 29, 170
Bennett, W. Lance, 22, 24, 29
Berkowitz, Morton, 162n
Berman, John, 32
Bernstein, Carl, 144
Beschloss, Michael, 105, 106, 198
Betts, Richard, 28
Between Two Ages, 109
Black, J. Stanley, 176
Bloom, Alfred, 165, 166
Bluhm, William, 178

Blumenthal, Michael, 114n
Bobrow, David, 37n
Bock, P. G., 162
Bolivia, 146
Bonafede, Don, 104, 182
Bonham, G. Matthew, 24, 36n
Boulding, Kenneth, 26, 117, 179
Braestrup, Peter, 29
Brazil, 120
Brecher, Michael, 16, 27, 179n
Brezhnev, Leonid, 54, 61, 68, 87, 105, 137,
  141
Brim, Orville, 21
Brodin, Katarina, 174, 191, 192, 198n
Brody, Richard, 28
Brown, Harold, 110, 114n, 145, 182, 183
Brown, Seyom, 11, 12, 154
Bruck, Howard, 179n
Bruner, Jerome, 25
Bryan, William Jennings, 115n
Brzezinski, Zbigniew,
  and the Trilateral Commission, 104, 109
  background, 109
  changes in image, 107–111
  impact of Ethiopia-Somalia conflict,
    63–64, 65, 110–111
  memoirs, 5, 107, 108
  on Administration's leadership, 106
  on American power, 56, 74, 87
  on arc of crisis, 65, 73, 87
  on China, 90
  on containment, 41, 65, 75, 88
  on détente, 64
  on foreign policy establishment, 115n
  on global change, 41, 43, 57, 64, 65,
    72–73, 82
  on global community, 42
  on global complexity, 41
  on global stability, 64–65, 73, 74, 82, 83,
    86, 94–95
  on human rights, 44–45, 67–68
  on Iranian revolution, 87, 138
  on issue agenda, 41
  on military force, 74, 89
  on 1980 election, 106
  on normalization, 46, 47
  on policymaker differences, 108, 115n
  on realism and idealism, 155
  on Soviet intervention in Africa, 63–65,
    108, 109, 110–111, 126–127
  on Soviet invasion of Afghanistan, 86–87,
    109

on Soviet Union, 55–57, 65, 74, 86, 87, 89–90, 107–108, 150
on third central strategic zone, 74, 75, 87
on Vance and the use of force, 115n
personality, 109–110
pessimism, 63, 65, 72–73, 74, 80
policy architect, 42
professional style, 111
role in foreign policy process, 19, 20, 182, 183
skepticism, 55, 56, 107–109
Budd, Richard, 188
Bulgaria, 128
Bureaucratic politics. See Decision-making.
Burgess, Philip, 196
Burrows, Robert, 196
Burt, Richard, 20, 105, 138, 183
Burton, John, 37n
Byers, R. B., 186
Byrd Amendment, 120
Bryne, Donn, 29
Byrnes, J. E., 28

Calder, Bobby, 15, 32
Cambodia, 76
Campbell, Angus, 22
Campbell, Donald, 31, 175
Canada, 50, 120, 129, 144
Carr, E. H., 155
Carter Administration. See also Events; Foreign policy process.
Carter Doctrine, 88
conflicting interpretations, 5, 7–12, 34–35, 153
evaluation of policy, 3
general behavior toward actors, 123, 130, 139–140, 142, 147
general behavior toward issues, 118, 126, 142
general belief-behavior relationship, 117, 118, 122, 125, 126, 132, 133, 134, 141, 142, 149, 152
general image of actors, 40–41, 49–50, 68, 80, 83–84, 100–102
general image of global change, 40, 43, 66, 78, 81–82
general image of international system, 39–44, 49, 57, 58–59, 65–68, 69, 78–80, 81–90, 94, 96–97, 113–114, 151–153, 157–158
general image of issues, 41, 44, 49, 66, 79, 82–83, 98–100
idealism vs. realism, 154–156, 157, 158
importance of human rights, 44, 45, 67

memoirs, 5, 107, 108
openness, 104, 192
paucity of information, 3, 5
policy of containment, 75, 81, 88–89, 144, 157–158, 163n
policy of preventive diplomacy, 48, 61–62, 94
policymaker differences, 4, 20–21, 55–57, 59, 63, 65–66, 69, 78, 79–80, 81, 90, 92, 93, 94, 107–108, 109, 110–111, 126–127, 138
problems with literature, 12, 13
radical interpretations, 13n, 114n
rejection of containment, 5, 41, 42–43, 54–55, 154, 157
Carter, Jimmy
a new foundation, 75
ambivalence, 75–78, 80
change in image, 104–107, 114
impact of Afghanistan, 82, 86, 105
impact of domestic politics, 105–107, 114
impact of Iran, 82, 106–107
leadership, 106–107
lessons of Vietnam War, 42, 61, 77
level of information, 104
memoirs, 5, 157
1980 election, 106–107, 148
on American power, 52, 63, 75, 87
on Arab-Israeli conflict, 48
on arms control, 47
on containment, 41, 42–43, 88
on defense spending, 132, 148, 149
on detente, 61
on global change, 40, 41, 43, 54–55, 63, 66, 76, 77–78, 81, 82
on global community, 40, 41–42, 83
on global complexity, 41, 52, 75
on global leadership, 43, 76
on global stability, 76, 90
on human rights, 45, 67
on idealism and realism, 157
on interdependence, 40, 88
on Iranian revolution, 77, 82, 138
on military force, 61, 66, 76–77, 88, 89
on normalization, 46, 47
on preventive diplomacy, 61, 62
on regional conflict, 76–77
on Soviet intervention in Africa, 59–60
on Soviet invasion of Afghanistan, 82, 86, 105
on Soviet Union, 52, 53, 54, 55, 60, 61, 62, 63, 68, 78, 84, 105
on third world development, 49

on world economy, 49
openness, 192
optimism, 43–44, 45, 53, 54, 56, 57, 61, 62, 68, 104, 105, 116n
personality, 104–105
presidential campaign of 1976, 7
role in foreign policy process, 19, 20–21, 159, 160, 183
Carter, Rosalynn, 118
Case studies, 3, 163n, 198n
Case-Javits amendment, 136
Central Intelligence Agency (CIA), 122, 144, 178
Chan, Stephen, 37n
Chile, 120, 129, 135
China, Peoples Republic of, 47, 50, 72, 76, 90, 119, 128, 134, 135, 145
Church, Frank, 33, 141
Claude, Inis, 162n
Cognitive consistency,
  dissonance theory, 192
  elites vs. mass public, 22–23
  impact on beliefs, 22 (see also Beliefs, stability vs. change)
  theory of self-perception, 192
Cognitive process, 26. See also Beliefs.
  rationality, 22, 26, 173
  schemas, 37n
Cohen, Bernard, 27, 28
Cohen, Stanley, 196
Commodity Credit Corporation, 136
Communications, persuasive,
  early research, 23
  fear arousal literature, 27
  impact on beliefs, 23, 27 (see also Beliefs, stability vs. change)
Conformity, impact on beliefs, 29. See also Domestic forces.
Congress, 37n, 123, 127, 128, 132, 134, 136, 137, 145, 167
Containment policy. See American foreign policy; Carter Administration.
Content analysis, 39
  coding, 193
  defined, 188
  problem of access, 190, 199n
  problem of authorship, 198n
  problem of inference, 190–192, 194–195
  reliability, 199n
  sources, 190, 192–193, 194
  two-step process, 194
Converse, Philip, 22, 32, 188
Cook, Thomas, 195

Coombs, Fred, 32
Coplin, William, 172, 177
Cottam, Richard, 20, 175, 178
Couloumbis, Theodore, 180n
Crawford, Alan, 106
Creed, John, 28, 156
Crespi, Irving, 32
Crises. See Events.
Cronin, Thomas, 20
Crown of St. Stephen, 128
Cruise missiles, 144
Cuba, 47, 76, 87, 119, 127, 129, 146
  foreign interventionism, 58, 59, 60, 61, 126–127, 150
  Soviet combat brigade, 141
Czechoslovakia, 119, 128

Datz, Daniel, 25
Dean, P. Dale, 187
Decision-making, 18. See also Beliefs, individual and collective; Foreign policy process.
  bureaucratic politics, 20, 36n, 160
  Chief executive and key advisors, 18, 19–20, 159–160
  choice propensities, 34, 174–175
  during crises, 27
  group, 17, 19, 36n, 161–162
  group leader, 159–160
  groupthink, 20, 38n
  in the study of beliefs, 18, 161–162
  United States, 18–19, 160
Defense,
  budget, 132, 141, 148–149
  CIA activities, 122, 144
  forces, 74, 76–77, 88–89, 91, 122, 129–130, 138, 144–145
  Rapid Deployment Force, 138, 144, 145
  South Korean withdrawal, 122, 130, 138
DeLuca, Donald, 106
Democracy. See Human rights.
Department of Defense, 199n
deRivera, Joseph, 187
Destler, I. M., 19, 37n, 111, 112, 114, 157, 199n
Deutsch, Karl, 26
Deutscher, Irwin, 31, 37n, 175
Development,
  general behavior toward, 122–123
  general image of, 49
Diamond, Edwin, 104
Diego Garcia, 144
Diesing, Paul, 18, 27, 171
Dillehay, Ronald, 31

Domestic forces. *See also* Elections; Media; Public Opinion.
impact on administration, 105–106, 114
impact on policymaker beliefs, 27–29, 103 *(see also* Beliefs, stability vs. change)
role in American foreign policy, 27–29
Donohew, Lewis, 188
Draft registration, 144
Drew, Elizabeth, 20, 106, 109, 111, 127, 182, 183
Dulles, John Foster, 17, 24

East Germany, 128
East, Maurice, 168, 199n
Eastern Europe, 50, 114n, 119
Economy,
general behavior toward, 120, 128, 137, 145
general image of, 49
most-favored-nation status, 128, 134
Tokyo round, 137
Egypt, 50, 121, 129, 134, 144
Ehrlich, Howard, 176
El Salvador, 120, 146–147
Elections. *See also* Domestic forces.
impact on policymaker beliefs, 28, 29
in American foreign policy, 28
1980, 106, 114
Elowitz, Larry, 28
Energy, 137
oil, 82, 89
program, 137
Epstein, Edward, 29
Erikson, Erik, 25
Eskine, Hazel, 22
Ethiopia, 58, 120
Ethiopia-Somalia conflict,
general behavior toward, 126–127
general image of, 58–62, 63–65
importance to administration, 58–59, 63, 108, 110–111, 126–127
European Economic Community, 120, 128, 144
Events, external. *See also* Vietnam War.
crises, 26–27, 29, 174
impact of Ethiopia-Somalia conflict, 58–59, 63, 108, 110–111, 126–127
impact of Iran hostage crisis, 82, 105, 106
impact of Iran revolution, 87, 109, 138
impact of Soviet invasion of Afghanistan, 82, 87, 90, 91, 105, 108–109, 112
impact on administration, 76, 103, 112

impact on beliefs, 26–27 *(see also* Beliefs, stability vs. change)
impact on decision-making, 27
impact on international system, 173
Events data, 117
analysis, 196
behavior defined, 149n, 179n, 199n
coding, 196
CREON, 199n
Deadline Data, 122–123, 196
defined, 195
media coverage, 122
problem of validity, 149n, 196
reliability, 199n
sources, 195
Export-Import Bank, 136

Falk, Richard, 198n
Falkowski, Lawrence, 174
Fallows, James, 8, 9, 104
Felton, John, 115n, 143
Fenno, Richard, 37n
Festinger, Leon, 192
Field research, 32
Fishbein, Martin, 15, 30, 32, 38n, 175, 199n
Flacks, O. R., 23
Ford Administration, 3, 121, 156, 158
Foreign policy process. *See also* Decision-making.
Carter Administration, 19, 181, 183
National Security Council (NSC) system, 181, 182, 183
Forgette, Eloise, 180n
Fox, William, 177
France, 120, 127, 129
Free, Lloyd, 106
Frenkel-Brunswik, Else, 25
Freud, Sigmund, 25
Friedrich, Carl, 109
Fromm, Eric, 25
Fuccillo, Vincent, 162n

Gaddis, John Lewis, 8, 154
Galtung, Johan, 198n
Gelb, Leslie, 11, 20–21, 28, 37n, 110, 111, 112, 114, 115n, 127, 157
General Agreement on Trade and Tariffs (GATT), 137
George, Alexander, 18, 34, 36n, 115n, 174, 177, 186, 190, 194, 197
George, Juliette, 115n
Geyelin, Philip, 28
Gilbert, J. D., 193
Gilpin, Robert, 173

Ginzburg, Alexander, 131
Glad, Betty, 104
Global 2000 Report, 149n
Godunov, Aleksandr, wife of, 135
Goldmann, Kjell, 198n
Graber, Doris, 29
Great Britain, 50, 120, 129, 136
Greece, 87
Greenfield, Jeff, 106
Greenstein, Fred, 168, 174, 197
Group Mind, The, 36n
Groups. *See* Decision-making.
Guatemala, 120
Gwertzman, Bernard, 111, 183

Hass, Ernst, 162n
Hah, Chong-do, 106
Haiti, 146
Halperin, Morton, 20, 28, 36n
Harris, S. A., 29
Hart, Thomas, 30, 180n
Hegemonic stability theory, 173
Helsinki accords, 119, 120
Heradstveit, Daniel, 167
Herberlein, Thomas, 176
Hermann, Charles, 27, 168, 199n
Hermann, Margaret, 174, 199n
Hermann, Richard, 36n
Hicks, Sallie, 180n
Hilsman, Roger, 28
Hitler, Adolf, 86
Hodgson, Godfrey, 28, 156
Hoffmann, Stanley, 14n
Hoggard, Gary, 195, 196
Hollick, Ann, 123
Holmes, Jack, 37n
Holsti, Ole, 14n, 17, 18, 21, 24, 28, 30, 33,
    38, 52, 156, 164, 174, 188, 190, 195,
    197, 198
Hoopes, Townsend, 112
Hopple, Gerald, 179n
Horelick, Arnold, 178
Howell, Llewellyn, 196
Hsiao-ping, Teng, 134
Human rights,
    Central America, 129, 136–137, 146–147
    defined, 45–46
    foreign assistance, 120, 129, 146
    general behavior toward, 118, 129,
        135–137, 146
    general image of, 44–46, 48, 67–68, 94
    refugees, 129, 135, 146
    Southern Africa, 48, 61, 68, 120, 129, 136,
        146

Soviet Union and Eastern Europe,
    119–120, 124, 129, 146
Hungary, 128
Huntington, Samuel, 109
Hussein, Saddam, 122, 146
Hyman, Herbert, 22

Idealism,
    liberal, 154, 155
    in American foreign policy, 156, 157, 158
    radical, 162n
Images. *See* Beliefs.
Indochina, 129, 135
Information processing. *See* Cognitive
    process.
Inglehart, Ronald, 37n
International Monetary Fund, 120
International relations, study of,
    importance of objective environment, 170,
        176
    importance of psychological environment,
        170
    islands of theory, 171
    levels of analysis, 171
    policy relevance, 176–178
    power of beliefs, 172–174, 175, 176 (*see
        also* Beliefs, impact on behavior)
    role of crises, 174
    role of phenomenology, 179n
    role of psychological approaches, 164–166,
        168–170, 172, 174
    social scientist vs. policy analyst, 5–6,
        176–177
    types of behavior, 172
    unit of explanation, 172
International system. *See also* Beliefs, image
    of international system.
    balance of power, 162n
    concept of, 186–187
    theory, 173–174
Iran, 86, 87, 138, 139, 142
    hostage crisis, 138, 139, 142, 143
    importance to administration, 82, 87, 105,
        106–107, 109, 138
    rescue mission, 112–113, 143
    revolution, 76, 77, 92, 138–139
Isaak, Robert, 179n
Israel, 50, 121, 129, 134, 146
James, Dorothy, 20
Janis, Irving, 20, 38n, 188
Japan, 29, 50, 120, 121, 128
Jensen, Lloyd, 187
Jervis, Robert, 16, 22, 26, 37n, 164, 174, 190

INDEX

Jingsheng, Wei, 135
Johnson, Haynes, 105
Johnson, Loch, 33
Johnson, Ross, 178
Jones, Edward, 36n
Jordan, 121, 122, 129, 146
Jordan, Hamilton, 5, 104, 114n
Jukam, Thomas, 196
Jung, Kim Dae, 138
Justice Department, 139

Kaagan, Larry, 106
Kagan, Jerome, 21
Kahle, Lynn, 32
Kaiser, Robert, 127
Karpel, Craig, 114n
Kegley, Charles, 19, 29, 36n, 37n, 154, 171,
    172, 177, 195, 196
Kelman, Herbert, 16, 29, 165, 166, 179n
Kennan, George, 155
Kenya, 144
Keohane, Robert, 186
Key, V. O., 22
Khomeini, Ayatolla, 138
Khrushchev, Nikita, 87
Kinder, Donald, 23
Kingdon, John, 37n
Kirschten, Dick, 183
Kissinger, Henry, 3, 17, 24, 33, 156,
    157–158, 181
Klineberg, Otto, 179n
Klingberg, Frank, 37n
Koenig, K. E., 23
Korb, Lawrence, 183
Kraar, Louis, 122
Krasner, Stephen, 18
Kringen, John, 37n
Krippendorff, Klaus, 188, 195
Kutner, Bernard, 31

LaFeber, Walter, 13n
Lake, Anthony, 37n, 111, 112, 114, 157
Landsat Earth Resources Satellite, 145
Lane, Robert, 22, 24
Lanouette, William, 114n, 182
Lansing, Robert, 115n
Laos, 120
LaPiere, Richard, 31
Larson, Deborah, 36n, 37n
Lasswell, Harold, 25
Latin America, 46, 50, 76, 118, 121, 128.
    See also Human rights.
Law of the Sea, 123
Lawton, Raymond, 196

Lebanon, 129
Lebow, Richard Ned, 26–27, 174
Lee, Jong, 27
Leites, Nathan, 36n
Letelier, Orlando, 129, 135
Leventhal, Howard, 27
Levinson, Daniel, 25
Leyton-Brown, David, 186
Lijphart, Arend, 163n
Lin, Nan, 167
Luttberg, Norman, 23

M-X missile, 138
McArdle, J. B., 27
MacArthur, Douglas, 122
McClelland, Charles, 180n, 195, 196
McCombs, Maxwell, 28
McCormack, James, 27
McCormick, James, 196
McDougall, William, 36n
McGeehan, Robert, 10
McGuire, William, 15, 22, 23, 27
McLellan, David, 112
McLeod, Jack, 28
McNamara, Robert, 111
Mansbach , Richard, 187
Marder, Murry, 198
Markus, Hazel, 37n
Maslow, Abraham, 25
Mayhew, David, 37n
Mazlish, Bruce, 104
Media. See also Domestic forces.
    agenda-setter, 28–29
    impact of Iran hostage coverage, 106–107
    impact on public opinion, 28–29, 107
    in American foreign policy, 27, 28, 29
    source of events data, 122
Mennis, Bernard, 188
Merritt, Richard, 26, 176, 177
Mexico, 120, 134
Middle East conflict. See also Afghanistan,
    Soviet invasion of; Iran.
    Arab-Israeli, 48
    Camp David accords, 129, 134, 146
    general behavior toward, 121, 128–129,
        134–135, 144, 146
    general image of, 47, 48, 89
    Geneva conference, 121, 128
    North vs. South Yemen, 76, 137
    preventive diplomacy, 48, 62
    regional security framework, 89
Miller, Warren, 22
Minard, Ralph, 31
Modelski, George, 179n

Mondale, Walter, 114n, 118, 134, 183
Moore, Jonathan, 106
Moore, M. David, 180n
Morgenthau, Hans, 155
Mozambique, 120
Mueller, John, 27, 28
Mugabe, Robert, 146
Muskie, Edmund,
    on global change, 93, 94
    on global complexity, 93
    on global stability, 92
    on human rights, 94
    on military force, 89, 93–94
    on preventive diplomacy, 94
    on Soviet Union, 93
    optimism, 94
    role in foreign policy process, 19, 20, 183
Namibia, 48, 61, 68, 129, 136, 145
Nash, George, 106
Nathan, James, 8, 19
National Security Council (NSC). See Foreign
    policy process.
Nelson, Keith, 162n
Neoconservatism, 106
Neustadt, Richard, 37n
Neutron bomb, 122, 129
New Zealand, 121
Newcomb, Theodore, 23–24
Nicaragua, 129, 136–137
Nie, Norman, 23
Niebuhr, Reinhold, 155, 162n
Nigeria, 128
Nisbett, R. E., 37n
Nixon Administration, 3, 156, 158, 181
Normalization,
    black Africa, 120, 128
    China, 47, 90, 119, 128, 134, 145
    Cuba, 119, 127
    general behavior toward, 118, 127–128,
        134, 145
    general image of, 46–47
    Panama Canal, 46, 118, 128, 134
    Vietnam, 119, 127
North Atlantic Treaty Organization (NATO),
    144
North Korea, 138
North Yemen, 137
Nuclear Proliferation Act of 1978, 121
Oberdorfer, Don, 112, 127
Odeen Report, 184n
Olin, Spencer, 162n
Oliver, James, 8, 19

Olympic Games, 144
Oman, 122, 144
Operational code. See Belief system
    approaches.
Organization of American States (OAS), 136
Osgood, Charles, 188, 190
Osgood, Robert, 11, 155
Oskamp, Stuart, 15, 16, 22, 23, 25, 32
Page, Benjamin, 28
Pakistan, 86, 87, 137, 144
Palestine Liberation Organization (PLO), 129
Palestinians, 50, 121, 134
Panama, 50, 118. See also Normalization,
    Panama Canal.
Park, Chung Hee, 137
Patriotic Front, 136
Pear, Tom, 179n
Perception. See Beliefs.
Perlmutter, Amos, 18
Pershing IIs, 144
Persian Gulf, 82, 87, 89, 144
Personality,
    developmental psychologists, 25
    functional approach, 25, 38n
    impact on beliefs, 24, 25, 26, 102–103,
        115n (see also Beliefs, stability vs.
        change)
    power-seeker vs. power-holder, 115n
    psychoanalytic theorists, 25
    role of human needs, 25
Petras, James, 14n
Petrocik, John, 23
Philippines, 120
Piaget, Jean, 25
Pious, Richard, 20
Podhoretz, Norman, 115n
Poland, 128, 146
Policy analysts, 5, 176–177
Policy Review Committee, 182
Pomper, Gerald, 37n
Pool, Ithiel, 190
Power and Principle, 162n
President. See Carter, Jimmy; Decision-
    making; Foreign policy process.
President Review Memorandum (PRM), 182
Presidential Directive (PD), 182
    PD 13, 121
    PD 18, 122
    PD 59, 145
Propaganda. See Communications,
    persuasive.
Psychological approaches. See also Beliefs.

in the study of international relations,
164–166, 168–170, 172, 174 (*see also*
International relations, study of)
relevance in foreign policy, 3–4, 13, 34,
35, 161–162, 178
Publc opinion. *See also* Domestic forces.
bipartisan consensus, 28
breakdown of consensus, 28
defined, 37n
during the 1970s, 105–107
elites vs. mass public, 22–23
fear of losing Vietnam, 28
impact on policymakers, 28, 29
in American foreign policy, 27, 28, 29
rise of conservatism, 106

Quinn, Sally, 109, 198

Raphael, Arnold, 115n
Rationality. *See* Cognitive process.
Realpolitik, 155, 156, 157, 158
Reichardt, Charles, 195
Reynolds, Frank, 105
Rhodesia. *See* Zimbabwe.
Riesman, David, 38n
Ripley, Randall, 37n
Robinson, James, 27
Rokeach, Milton, 15, 24, 26, 29, 32, 36n,
37n, 38n, 115n, 116n, 168, 180n, 198n
Rosati, Jerel, 18, 28, 36n, 156
Rosecrance, Richard, 180n
Rosenau, James, 27, 28, 30, 156, 171
Rosenberg, Milton, 28, 37n
Rosenwein, Robert, 31, 38n
Roskin, Michael, 26, 37n
Ross, L., 15, 32
Ross, Michael, 37n
Rossi, Peter, 23
Rostow, Eugene, 14n
Rourke, Francis, 37n
Rumania, 128
Rusk, Dean, 186
Russett, Bruce, 106

Sadat, Anwar, 129, 134
Sakharov, Andrei, 120
Salmore, Barbara, 199n
Salmore, Stephen, 168, 199n
Sam, Kim Young, 135
Sanders, Jerry, 11, 106, 114n, 115n, 157
Sandinistas, 136, 137
Sanford, R. Nevitt, 25
Sapin, Burton, 179n
Sarnoff, Irving, 25
Saudi Arabia, 137, 144

Schelling, Thomas, 180n
Schlesinger, Arthur, Jr., 9
Schneider, William, 106
Schram, Martin, 20, 110
Schuman, Howard, 175
Schwartz, Shalom, 175
Sears, David, 23, 24, 25, 37n
Semmel, Andrew, 121
Serfaty, Simon, 10, 109
Shah of Iran, 138
Shapiro, Michael, 36n
Shaw, Donald, 28
Shaw, Marvin, 19
Shcharansky, Anatoly, 131
Sheatsley, Paul, 22
Sick, Gary, 104, 106, 138, 143
Singer, J. David, 190, 197
Singlaub, John, 122
Sites, Paul, 25
Smith, Gaddis, 11, 107, 115n, 120, 162n,
192
Smith, M. Brewster, 25, 38n, 179n
Smoke, Richard, 177
Snyder, Glenn, 18, 27, 171
Snyder, Richard, 179n, 191, 192
Social scientists, 5, 176–177
Solidarity, 146
Somalia, 58, 127, 144. *See also* Ethiopia-
Somalia conflict.
Somoza, Anastasio, 136
South Africa, 48, 50, 68, 136, 145
South Korea, 122, 130, 135, 137, 138
South Yemen, 137
Southeast Treaty Organization (SEATO), 119
Soviet Union. *See also* Afghanistan, Soviet
invasion of; Ethiopia-Somalia conflict.
belief-behavior relationship, 123–124,
130–131, 140, 147–148
capabilities, 52, 63, 87
general behavior toward, 119, 121, 124,
126–127, 128, 129, 131–132, 135, 137,
140–141, 143–144, 146, 148
general image of, 50, 52–57, 58–65, 71,
72, 74, 78, 80, 82, 84–88, 89, 90, 92,
93, 102, 105, 107–108, 110–111
intentions, 36n, 53, 54, 58, 62, 84, 86, 90
international constraints, 40, 52, 68, 93
policymaker differences, 55, 56, 57, 59,
79, 80, 110, 111, 126
significance for major issues, 55, 58, 59,
66, 79, 84, 124, 131, 140, 147
Spanier, John, 10, 28, 180n
Special Coordinating Committee, 182

Sprout, Harold, 170
Sprout, Margaret, 170
Stang, Alan, 14n
Starr, Harvey, 17, 24, 52, 198
State of the Union address, 198n
Stealth bomber, 145
Stein, Janice, 16, 179n
Steinberg, Blema, 16, 179n
Steinbruner, John, 22, 178
Steinfels, Peter, 106
Stokes, Donald, 22
Strauss, Robert, 115n
Stuart, Douglas, 198
Study of International Relations, The, 165
Stupak, Ronald, 186
Sullivan, Michael, 33, 115n
Sullivan, William, 138
Suzi, George, 188
Sweden, 30, 180n
Syria, 121, 129
Szulc, Tad, 145

Taiwan, 128, 130, 134
Tannenbaum, Percy, 188
Taubman, Philip, 138
Third World, 41, 46, 49, 50, 68, 71, 118, 122
Thistlethwaite, Donald, 26
Thorp, Robert, 188
Tito, Josip, 128
Top Secret Umbra, 150n
Treaty of Tlatelolco, 121
Trilateral Commission, 104, 109
Tucker, Robert, 9–10
Turkey, 87
Tweraser, Kurt, 17, 174

Uganda, 120, 134
United Nations, 50, 120, 136, 139
Uruguay, 120

Vance, Cyrus,
    background, 112
    continuity in image, 111–113
    impact of events, 112
    lessons of Vietnam War, 111–112
    memoirs, 5
    on China, 72
    on global change, 66, 70–71, 91
    on global community, 70, 91, 113
    on global complexity, 66, 69
    on global leadership, 70, 72, 91
    on human rights, 45–46, 68
    on interdependence, 49, 69
    on Iran rescue mission, 113
    on Iranian revolution, 112, 138

    on issue agenda, 44
    on military force, 71–72, 91, 112, 113
    on normalization, 46
    on policymaker differences, 110, 112
    on preventive diplomacy, 48, 61–62, 71, 91, 112
    on regional conflict, 48, 61, 71, 72
    on Soviet intervention in Africa, 60, 61, 68, 92
    on Soviet invasion of Afghanistan, 90–91, 92, 112
    on Soviet Union, 54, 62, 63, 71, 72, 90, 91, 92
    on third world development, 49, 71
    on world economy, 49
    optimism, 56, 63, 70, 80, 92, 112
    pragmatism, 46, 54
    professional style, 111
    resignation, 92, 112–113
    role in foreign policy process, 19, 20, 182, 183
Vasquez, John, 187
Verba, Sidney, 23
Vietnam, 47, 50, 76, 119, 127
Vietnam War. *See also* Events.
    impact on American foreign policy, 28, 74, 87, 156
    impact on media, 28
    impact on public opinion, 28, 29, 30, 156
    lessons for Carter policymakers, 42, 61, 77, 111–112
    MIAs, 119
Vladivostok, 121, 137

Wahlke, John, 32n, 38n
Walker, Stephen, 17, 33
Waltz, Kenneth, 28, 155, 165, 180n, 186
Warnke, Paul, 114n
Warwick, D. P., 23
Watts, William, 106
Weinstein, Allen, 105, 106, 198
Weintraub, Walter, 192, 198n
West Germany, 128, 129, 130
Western Europe, 50, 74, 75
White, Robert, 25
Whiting, Alan, 177
Whitney, Richard, 23, 25, 37n
Wicker, Allan, 31, 32
Wicker, Tom, 143
Wilkenfeld, Jonathan, 179n
Wilkins, Carol, 31
Wilson, George, 144
Wilson, Woodrow, 115n
Winter, Don, 162

INDEX

Wittkopf, Eugene, 19, 29, 154, 171
Wooten, James, 110
World Bank, 120
Wray, J. Harry, 22
Wright, Quincy, 165, 177

Yankelovich, Daniel, 106
Yarrow, Penny, 31

Yom Kippur War, 24
Young, Andrew, 114n, 118, 183
Young, Oran, 177
Yugoslavia, 128, 145

Zaire, 127
Zajonc, R. B., 37n
Zimbabwe, 48, 50, 61, 68, 129, 136, 146